Self-Deception and Paradoxes of Rationality

CSLI LECTURE NOTES
NUMBER 69

Self-Deception and Paradoxes of Rationality
edited by Jean-Pierre Dupuy

CSLI Publications
CENTER FOR THE STUDY OF
LANGUAGE AND INFORMATION
STANFORD, CALIFORNIA

Special thanks go to Katarina Kivel for her editorial assistance and without whose hard work and dedication, this volume would not have been possible.

Library of Congress Cataloging-in-Publication Data

Self-deception and paradoxes of rationality / edited by Jean-Pierre Dupuy.
    p.   cm.–(CSLI lecture notes ; no. 69)
Includes bibliographical references and index.
ISBN 1-57586-069-4 (alk. paper). –ISBN 1-57586-068-6 (pbk. : alk. paper)
1. Self-deception.   I. Dupuy, Jean Pierre, 1941–   .   II. Series.
BD439.S47   1998
128'.3–dc21   98-3095
CIP

∞ The acid-free paper used in this book meets the minimum requirements of the American National Standard for Information Sciences – Permanence of Paper for Printed Library Materials, ANSI Z39.48-1984.

Detail on front cover of the paperback edition of this book is from *Le Tricheur à l'as de carreau,* circa 1635, (The Card-Sharper with the Ace of Diamonds), by Georges de la Tour, from the collection of the Louvre Museum. Full framing of painting appears on page ii. Oil on canvas: 1.46 x 1.06 m.

This book was designed and composed by Tony Gee in Adobe Garamond, a typeface drawn by Robert Slimbach and based on the work of Claude Garamond, and ITC Kabel, designed by Rudolf Koch and redrawn by the International Typeface Corporation (ITC). The book was printed and bound in the United States of America.

Contents

Contributors

Mark Rogin Anspach, anthropologist, is a researcher at the CREA, Ecole Polytechnique, Paris.

Kent Bach, educated at Harvard College and the University of California, Berkeley, is professor of philosophy at San Francisco State University. He has written extensively on philosophy of language, theory of knowledge, and philosophy of mind. His books include *Thought and Reference* (Oxford, 1987) and, with Robert Harnish, *Linguistic Communication and Speech Acts* (MIT Press, 1979).

Lawrence Beyer is completing a doctoral dissertation, on the organization of the mind and the nature of belief, in the Department of Philosophy at Stanford University.

Donald Davidson teaches at the University of California, Berkeley. He has written on the philosophy of action, ethics, epistemology, and semantics.

Jean-Pierre Dupuy is professor of social and political philosophy at the Ecole Polytechnique, Paris; Director of research at the CNRS (Philosophy); founding director of CREA (Centre de Recherche en Epistémologie Appliquée), the philosophical research group of the Ecole Polytechnique; and professor in the Departments of French and Italian and Political Science at Stanford University. He is also a CSLI researcher.

John Ferejohn is the Carolyn S. G. Munro Professor of Political Science and Senior Fellow of the Hoover Institution at Stanford University. He has written on politics and government, political philosophy, and philosophy of social sciences.

Ariela Lazar teaches in the Department of Philosophy at Northwestern University. She has written articles on irrationality, self-deception, and acting against one's better judgment.

Alfred R. Mele is Vail Professor of Philosophy at Davidson College, North Carolina. He is the author of *Irrationality* (Oxford, 1987), *Springs of Action* (Oxford, 1992), and *Autonomous Agents* (Oxford, 1995), editor of *Philosophy of Action* (Oxford, 1997), and coeditor of *Mental Causation* (Oxford, 1993).

Preface
Jean-Pierre Dupuy

Fifty-five years ago, Jean-Paul Sartre (1966) thought it appropriate to begin his voluminous treatise in transcendental phenomenology, *Being and Nothingness*, with a chapter on "Bad Faith." The reason for this unexpected opening? Sartre was convinced that the shortest path to revealing the structure of consciousness was to bring out the conditions of possibility of that strange condition he equated with lying to oneself. His goal was to answer the question, "What must be the being of man if he is to be capable of bad faith?" (96). He thought it possible to show that, in the end, bad faith shares the same structure as consciousness itself, a paradoxical structure, which, for a phenomenologist, can be described as one of self-transcendence, or transcendence within immanence.

Contemporary analytic philosophy, although expressing itself in a very different style and resorting to quite a distinct terminology, cannot but agree. As Brian P. McLaughlin and Amélie Oksenberg Rorty (1988) put it in their introduction to a kindred volume:

> Explaining, or explaining away, the phenomena of self-deception raises many of the central problems in the philosophy of mind. We have used self-deception as a microcosmic case study that bears on a range of issues dividing contemporary philosophical psychology. The discussion of the issues surrounding self-deception gives us a

red-dye tracer for tracking what is at stake in a variety of debates central to the philosophy of mind. Disagreements about the existence and analysis of self-deception express disagreements about the unity of consciousness, homuncularism in psychological explanation, the criteria for the attribution of belief, the conditions for intentionality and rationality, the primacy of cognition in psychological processes, the viability of functionalist and computational accounts of psychological states and processes, the relation between motivational and epistemic attitudes, the social formation and malformation of belief and self-deception, and moral constraints on responsible belief. (1)

Much has been written in the Anglo-American literature on the phenomenon of self-deception. If the present volume has some originality, it is not in its broad scope—a feature usually associated with the treatment of the topic—but, rather, in its focusing on two distinct, although related, issues: (1) the thorough questioning of the validity and merit of what Ariela Lazar calls here the "standard approach" to self-deception, an approach associated with Donald Davidson's work; (2) the role played by the concept of self-deception in the treatment of a series of paradoxes that jeopardize the foundations of the rationalist paradigm.

Here, this preface is intended to shed some light on the relationship between those two issues. In the general framework of Davidson's philosophy of mind, any form of irrationality appears deeply paradoxical. It is not by accident that one of Davidson's seminal papers is titled "Paradoxes of Irrationality" (1982). If one is to interpret a subject's behavior and make sense of it, it is necessary to see her as basically and globally rational, in the sense that the beliefs, desires, intentions, plans, decisions, etc., one abscribes to her are related to one another and her observable actions in consistent ways. A diagnosis of irrationality runs the risk of backfiring: it may signal the interpreter's incompetence or own lack of rationality. Against such an interpretive background, saying of someone that she is self-deceived is highly problematic, because, according to Davidson, this attributes to her two beliefs that are both contradictory in terms of their content but nevertheless causally connected. In Davidson's own terms, "the first problem about self-deception is that as a form of irrationality it undermines its own clarity of application" (1998, 7).

Davidson's celebrated account is fleshed out by himself once again here, and commented upon, amended, criticized and/or rejected by Ariela Lazar, Al Mele, Mark Anspach, Larry Beyer, and Kent Bach.[1] Moreover, each of these various authors proposes his or her own interpretation, and refers to other authors' alternative accounts. Once more, the reader will be struck by the lack of consensus in the very characterization of the phenomenon and the wide variety of approaches in the attempts at explaining it (or explaining it away), even at the most elementary or basic level. For instance, does self-deception involve the formation of an irrational belief? If most authors answer yes, Bach disagrees: according to him, the self-deceiver merely keeps away from his thinking process the rational but unpleasant belief. Among those who cannot conceive of a self-deceived subject without her having acquired a false belief, there is deep disagreement as to what drives the belief-formation process: is it the desire that a (possibly) pleasant state of affairs be the case, or is it the desire to *believe* that such a state of affairs is the case? Although Bernard Williams (1973) very forcefully brought out the importance of making that distinction some time ago, certain authors do not seem to care or else adopt the second alternative. This is a point on which Lazar takes Davidson to task, whereas Mele, in general, seems to choose the first alternative with the possible exception of the case of intentional self-deception. Furthermore, there is, of course, the widely debated issue of whether self-deception involves the simultaneous presence of contradictory beliefs, and how such a coexistence might be possible at all. Here, Mele takes exception to that standard characterization and Anspach, drawing on both Sartre's treatment of bad faith and Gregory Bateson's concept of the double bind, maintains that self-deception can imply that both beliefs, the rational and the irrational ones, are held by the subject, but that there is no need to posit a partitioning of the mind à la Davidson to make sense of it.

xi

---

1. Some of the papers collected in this volume were presented at a conference organized by Dupuy on February 26 and 27, 1993, at Stanford University. Entitled "Self-Deception: Philosophy, Psychology, Anthropology, Literature," this conference was sponsored by the Program of Interdisciplinary Research at Stanford and the CREA of the Ecole Polytechnique in Paris. Davidson, Mele, Dupuy, Ferejohn, Bach and Anspach read first drafts of their papers, along with René Girard, Robert Harrison, Arnold Davidson, Sylvia Wynter, Seth Lerer, Joss Marsh, and the late Amos Tversky. Although the present publication is narrower in scope than the conference, some of the papers (most notably Davidson's and Mele's) retain the literary flavor that they were invited to develop in the context of a confrontation with scholars for whom literature is a greater source of knowledge about self-deception, because it is the science of human desire, than any other discipline.

"It is only by showing ourselves largely rational and consistent that we show ourselves capable of irrationality and inconsistency," Davidson writes (1998, 7). The major problem with this rationalistic account may well be that there are important cases in which there exists no unassailable answer to the question, What is rational? or worse, contexts in which what is supposedly rational appears quite unreasonable. In the framework of Rational Choice Theory, the basic elements of what constitutes the social bond turn out to be irrational or even impossible: for instance, making good on one's promises when so doing runs against one's interests; trusting one's partner; forming an intention to retaliate if under attack, thereby deterring a potential attacker, etc. Rationality emerges as no less paradoxical than irrationality. Rational Choice Theory should indeed be credited with having brought out this fundamental weakness, by discovering a number of paradoxes, the elucidation of which has generated a literature no less abundant than the one on self-deception: Newcomb's Paradox, Prisoner's Dilemma, Chain-Store Paradox, Deterrence Paradox, Backwards Induction Paradox, Toxin Puzzle, etc.

Each of these paradoxes takes the form of a dilemma. One branch is deemed rational by orthodox Rational Choice theorists in spite of its sounding, as the case may be, unreasonable, unethical, absurd, self-defeating, self-stultifying or what have you. Undaunted, a few heterodox minds choose the other option, the one which *they* declare rational. In his contribution, Dupuy puts forward a general framework in which he analyzes the paradoxes in question. He submits that, indeed, a form of rationality underwrites the heterodox choice, but that some of its features are shared in common with the Davidsonian characterization of self-deception—as if the paradoxes of irrationality and those of rationality belonged to the same family. Without some kind of "bootstrapping of the self," there would be no way to deceive oneself, but there would be no autonomy in the Kantian or Rousseauian sense either: the ability to limit one's individuality by giving oneself a transcendent, fixed law or rule, and following it. Dupuy's attempt at grounding a form of Kantian rationalism in a Hobbesian view of the world where Rational Choice Theory is held to provide the best account of how agents form mental states such as beliefs, desires and intentions, and of how they reason and act, is resolutely criticized by Ferejohn and Bach. These two authors expound their own conceptions of rationality, ones in which paradoxes are avoided at the cost of settling for a much more modest ambition.

References

Davidson, D. 1982. "Paradoxes of Irrationality." In R. Wollheim and J. Hopkins, eds., *Philosophical Essays on Freud.* Cambridge: Cambridge University Press.

————. 1998. "Who Is Fooled?" Paper presented at the Symposium on Self-Deception, Stanford, California, February 1993. In J. P. Dupuy, ed., *Self-Deception and Paradoxes of Rationality.* Stanford: CSLI Publications (this volume).

McLaughlin, B. P. and A. O. Rorty, eds. 1988. *Perspectives on Self-Deception.* Berkeley: University of California Press.

Sartre, J.-P. 1966. *Being and Nothingness.* Trans. H. E. Barnes. New York: Washington Square Press (French edition first published in 1943).

Williams, B. 1973. "Deciding to Believe." *Problems of the Self.* Cambridge: Cambridge University Press.

Who Is Fooled?

Donald Davidson

According to the memoirs of former Secretary of State George Schultz, Ronald Reagan was aware that his agents were offering Iran a ransom of arms to obtain the release of hostages, and George Bush was a full participant in that decision, despite his repeated claims that he was "out of the loop." William Safire, who does not want us to forget these matters, claims that Schultz's evidence shows that "Reagan lied to himself, sticking to a script denying reality; Bush lied only to investigators and the public" (Safire 1993). Safire does not say that Reagan lied not only to himself but also to investigators and the public; the "only" in "Bush lied only to investigators and the public" suggests this, but it also hints at the idea that since Reagan lied to himself, his behavior was less cynical, less knowingly self-serving, than Bush's. This would, of course, be the case only if Reagan, in lying to himself, succeeded in persuading himself that the deal in which he had connived was not an arms-for-hostages deal.

Suppose that Reagan did persuade himself that he had not agreed to and abetted an arms-for-hostages deal; to what extent would this diminish his responsibility? Well, to the extent that no memory at all of his original knowledge—the knowledge of which his lie relieved him—remained, he would not be guilty of lying to the investigators or the public, for he would not be deliberately saying what he had come to believe to be false. His fault would be rather in the original lie to himself. In this case we

1

might think of him as the only victim of his deceit. But before we decide to hold him relatively blameless, we need to consider his motives in lying to himself, for a lie is an intentional act, and requires a motive. If the motive was to avoid either the political consequences of telling what he at first knew or the pain of perjuring himself, then the motive included all that we despise in Bush's direct lie, for Reagan's intention, when he lied to himself, could be expressed as: intending to mislead the investigators and the public by persuading someone to whom the investigators and the public would appeal (himself) to say what he then knew to be false. Reagan would have lied to the messenger (Reagan) with the expectation (or intention) that the messenger (the future Reagan) would say in good faith what he (Reagan in the present) knew to be false. It is difficult to find any degree of exculpation in behavior that can be thus described.

But how accurate is this description? This partly depends, of course, on things we do not know, for example, whether Reagan lied to himself primarily out of vanity—a wish to think well of himself, or in order to avoid the legitimate censure of others. But there are also conceptual problems. The first such problem concerns the clarity of the notion of lying to oneself. Is it possible to lie to oneself? In trying to answer this question, we must first ask what is involved in telling a lie to anyone. Telling a lie pretty clearly requires a speech act performed with the intention that someone be deceived, that is, misled with respect to the truth of some proposition.[1] In any case, the common assumption that lying involves a speech act already puts a strain on the idea of lying to oneself. Perhaps we can allow that silently addressing words to oneself is a form of speech, but the notion of action demands that this be done with an intention. We do sometimes repeat to ourselves exhortations like "No more cookies today!" or "I shall give up smoking for the next two months!" and these self-addressed remarks may be real acts, even if entirely silent. It is a question, though, whether this is what we typically have in mind when we speak of lying to oneself. We are inclined to think that if we lie to ourselves, we must be unaware that this is what we are doing. Is lying something one can do without knowing it? Maybe.

There is also a difficulty in identifying the proposition with respect to

---

1. Here the phrase "misled with respect to the truth of some proposition" must, of course, fall under the scope of the intention: the proposition the liar intends his victim to believe may, contrary to the liar's belief, be true.

which the liar wishes to mislead. In many cases it is easy to recognize the ultimate intended deception. "It's solid gold," says the seller, intending to persuade the buyer that it is solid gold though the seller knows it is not. Suppose, however, that the seller believes the buyer knows him (the seller) to be a liar, and so says, "This is a worthless plated trinket; you shouldn't buy it," hoping the buyer will then insist on the purchase. Has the seller lied? He has uttered words literally true, though with the intention of misleading the customer both with respect to his own belief and with respect to the value of the object. While this may be as bad as a lie–or worse–it is not, I think, a genuine lie. The reason it is not helps to characterize the central concept of lying. In both stories the seller can accomplish his end only by asserting what he says, and assertion requires (among other things, no doubt) that the speaker represent himself as believing what he says: thus, in saying "It's solid gold," he represents himself as believing what he does not; in saying it is a worthless trinket, he represents himself as believing what he actually believes. A liar must make an assertion, and so represent himself as believing what he does not.

3

The liar succeeds in deceiving his audience only if his intention to misrepresent what he believes is not discerned. On the other hand, there is an intention he must intend to be recognized, namely, the intention to be taken as making an assertion, for if *this* intention is not recognized, his utterance will not be taken as an assertion, and so must fail in its immediate intention. (One cannot make an assertion without intending to be taken as making, and so intending to make, an assertion.) We can now see the difficulty in taking the notion of lying to oneself too literally: it would require that one perform an act with the intention both that that intention be recognized (by oneself) and not recognized (since to recognize it would defeat its purpose).

We had better, then, take the expression "lying to oneself" as a kind of metaphor–a dead metaphor, since we use it so often; at best, then, an idiom. William Safire may be politically astute and a whiz at language, but in this case he would have done better to say Reagan was self-deceived. The reason it is more plausible to hold that Reagan deceived himself than that he lied to himself is simply that, though the aim of lying to oneself, if this were possible, would be self-deception, there are less improbable techniques for achieving this end.

A lookout on the *Pinta* was, we are told, the first to sight land–an outlying island of America, but Columbus insisted that it was he. "This insistence has been variously interpreted by some as naked, mean greed, by others as honorable self-deception, born of the arrogance of lust for fame," writes Felipe Fernández in *The London Review of Books* (Fernández 1993, 3). Let us simplify the second suggestion to this: Columbus was self-deceived, and his lust for fame helps explain his self-deception. What form can this explanation take, and what is it supposed to explain? If Columbus simply believed from the start that he was the first to sight land, he would have been wrong, but no one would have had to deceive him. We might explain his false belief as a case of wishful thinking, but wishful thinking may be as simple as a desire that something be the case begetting the belief that it is the case. Self-deception may involve wishful thinking, but it is more complicated. One complication is perhaps not important: in wishful thinking what we come to believe is also desired, while the self-deceived may come to believe what is distressing or feared. What is important is that to be self-deceived one must at some time have known the truth, or, to be more accurate, have believed something contrary to the belief engendered by the deception. To be self-deceived, Columbus must at one time have known, or at least believed, that he was not the first to sight land; Reagan at one time knew of the arms-for-hostages deal.

This original knowledge must, of course, have played a causal role in the self-deception. Columbus would not have needed to deceive himself if he had not known that it was not he who had made the fateful sighting. It was *because* he remembered the arms-for-hostages deal that Reagan "stuck to a script denying reality," to use Safire's words. We are apparently asking the belief that is to be rejected to serve as part of the motivation for the rejection. This may at first appear fairly straightforward. Someone has a belief he finds disagreeable or painful or ego-deflating. He thus has a reason to change things, to rid himself of the belief. He then acts, or thinks, in a way that causes him to reject the unwelcome thought. But to see this as straightforward is to neglect a distinction between two senses in which one can be said to have a reason for a belief. If one would be happier, prouder, more relaxed, less fraught if one had a certain belief, that is a reason, putting other considerations aside, to have the belief. But such a reason is not, in itself, a reason to suppose the desirable belief is true. It may or may not be rational for Columbus to believe he was first to sight the new land, but it would certainly not be rational for him to believe it solely on the grounds that he would like to believe it.

The explanation of self-deception remains not merely obscure, but apparently mired in contradiction. Self-deception requires that we do something with the intention of coming to believe what we do not believe; yet it provides us with no reason to hold the wished for belief true: the agent is to perform an action with the intention of coming to believe what he does not believe. Since what drives the self-deceiver to perform this action is his unwanted doubt or belief, we seem to have to say the agent both believes and disbelieves the same proposition. If disbelieving a proposition entails not believing it, then the puzzle is ours: we would have to say that the agent did and did not believe the same thing. But however wild the pattern of beliefs we are willing to attribute to the self-deceiver, we must not fall into contradiction ourselves in describing his confusion.

We can, and should, escape from this particular difficulty by refusing to accept the entailment: we should not agree that believing the contradictory or contrary of a proposition entails not believing that proposition. It is possible for a person to believe contradictory propositions, not only when the contradiction is too subtle for normal detection, but also when the contradiction is obvious (for the contradiction must be obvious if it is to move someone to self-deceit). At the same time, we should balk at attributing to anyone belief in a plain contradiction. The distinction we need here is between believing contradictory propositions and believing a contradiction, between believing that p and believing that not-p on the one hand, and believing that [p and not-p] on the other.

Still, it is hard enough to comprehend how it is possible to have beliefs that are contradictory. Why is this a problem? To see it as a problem—indeed, to see any form of irrationality as a problem—one must accept a degree of holism. If beliefs are atomic features of the brain, which can be individually added, changed, and deleted without regard to their propositional environment, as Jerry Fodor and Ernie Lepore seem to hold (Fodor and Lepore 1992), then any degree of inconsistency is possible. But if you think, as I do, that the mere possession of propositional attitudes implies a large degree of consistency, and that the identification of beliefs depends in part on their logical relations to other beliefs, then inconsistencies impose a strain on the attribution and explanation of beliefs (and, of course, other propositional attitudes). It is such considerations that make the attribution of a straightforward contradiction—a belief in an obvious contradiction—unintelligible. Of course we can say, "She thinks she is younger than she is"; but Russell showed us how to get out of this without saddling her with a contradiction. It is hard, but not impossible, to understand how someone can hold contradictory beliefs; hard, because there can scarcely be a better reason for supposing someone does not believe he is, say, stout, than that he believes he is not stout.

Even setting aside hard-line mental atomists, many philosophers have a difficult time grasping why irrationality creates a conceptual difficulty; they regard someone who emphasizes the tie between rationality and explicability, and the centrality of consistency in rationality, as an obsessed rationalist who cannot understand any form of reason not based on simple logic. I want to plead guilty, and throw myself on the mercy of my (largely rational) readers–after, of course, explaining myself.

6

Here is why I am inclined to hold that all genuine cases of irrationality–akrasia, wishful thinking, self-deception, bad reasoning–involve inconsistency. Sticking to this condition may require a degree of verbal legislation, but legislation is sometimes the best way to promote conceptual order and clarity. Thus, I do not want to call someone irrational because he has beliefs or desires that in themselves seem mad as long as the person has not arrived at these attitudes through faulty thinking, failure to take into account evidence he acknowledges, or willful disregard of contrary considerations. I have a cognitive view of evidence: it consists of beliefs, and does not include sensations. Sensations, no matter how complex or systematic, cannot be inconsistent with anything; unless they beget thoughts, they play no role in creating or constituting inconsistencies.

Let us consider possible exceptions. Is it irrational to hold oneself exempt from moral imperatives one applies to others? Not in itself, I would say, since one can easily construct a consistent rule that calls for special exemptions. But if one also believes that moral imperatives apply to everyone without exception, then one has inconsistent values. This is not a matter of conflicting values; conflict of values is not inconsistency. Is it irrational to agree that in every known case death by hemlock has been extremely messy and painful, but to fail to expect the next case to be the same? It all depends, but it is not necessarily irrational to have deviant standards of good inductive practice.

At this point someone is sure to ask who is to be the judge of rationality and consistency. The annoying answer is that this is a bad question, a question without an answer. There is no eternal, absolute standard. At the same time, we are not thrown back on your standards or mine; relativism is not the only alternative to standards independent of all thought and judgment. It is clear that in evading the question when a set of attitudes can be recognized as inconsistent, we are quickly driven back to basic logic; there comes a point at which intelligibility is so diminished by perceived inconsistency that an accusation of inconsistency loses application for lack of identifiable contents about which to be inconsistent. One must be able to think in order to be inconsistent. It is only by showing ourselves largely rational and consistent that we show ourselves capable of irrationality and inconsistency. An agent can fail in a particular case to generalize from evidence, but only because the agent, like every creature capable of thought, usually generalizes from evidence. Someone may have what I consider deviant inductive rules, but only because that person has standards of inductive reasoning that can be recognized as such.

The first problem about self-deception, then, is that as a form of irrationality it undermines its own clarity of application. The contents of propositional attitudes are determined in part by their logical relations with the contents of other attitudes; to the extent that these relations of a particular attitude are broken or confused, the identity of that attitude is rendered less precise.

The second problem concerns explanation. Our normal mode of explanation of actions and beliefs is to review the reasons an agent had in acting, or the course of reasoning that led to the belief. Such explanations rationalize the action or belief by singling out other attitudes in the light of which the action or belief is reasonable–reasonable not only to the agent himself, but reasonable also to the explainer. This does not mean that every action or belief is reasonable everything considered; its reasonableness is only as seen in the light of the reasons that explain it. But now, given this mode of explanation, how are we to explain self-deception? The trouble is that what we want to say explains it cannot rationalize it. Columbus' lust for fame may explain why he persuaded himself he was the first to sight land, but his lust for fame does not rationalize what he came to believe. There is no reason to suppose Columbus thought his lust for fame was a good reason to believe he was the first to sight land.

To take a step in the direction of resolving these problems I have made two proposals (Davidson 1981, 1985, 1986). One is to allow that there is a mongrel form of explanation which, like explanations in both the social and the natural sciences, is causal, but unlike most explanations of actions and other intensionally described phenomena, does not rationalize what it explains. Such explanation accepts the idea that there may be mental causes of mental states or events for which they are not reasons. A simple example is wishful thinking: a desire or wish that a proposition be true causes a person to believe that it is true, but is not a reason for thinking it true. Self-deception is not this simple, since it requires the intention to alter one's beliefs, but self-deception, like wishful thinking, fits the mold: the desire to change a belief does cause the change, but is not a reason for counting the new belief true or the old one false.

The second proposal is meant to explain how it is possible at the same time both to accept and to reject a proposition—how it was possible for Reagan to know he had endorsed the arms-for-hostages deal and at the same time to believe he had not. Why didn't he juxtapose these two beliefs—though of course if he had, one or the other would have evaporated? I suggested the two obviously opposed beliefs could coexist only if they were somehow kept separate, not allowed to be contemplated in a single glance. I spoke of the mind as being *partitioned*, meaning no more than that a metaphorical wall separated the beliefs which, allowed into consciousness together, would destroy at least one.

This idea obviously echoes a long tradition: Plato, Aristotle, Augustine, Butler, Freud are just a few of those who have made semiautonomous parts of the soul part of their philosophy of mind. But my echo is a feeble one. I do not assume that the divisions are fixed, or that they deserve such names as conscience, courage, intellect, or id. More important, I do not think of the boundaries, however permanent or temporary, as separating autonomous territories. The territories overlap: there is a central core of mostly ordinary truths which the territories share (much as all rational creatures necessarily share a general, and mostly correct, picture of the world). Where territories differ is in the dissonant details. While Reagan's two "minds" shared most desires and beliefs and further attitudes, one contained the memory that he had agreed to the arms-for-hostages deal while the other denied he had any part in it. Of course, this could not be the only difference: each of the contradictory beliefs needed a supporting phalanx of ideas. Producing support for the second belief was the task of self-deception.

The image I wished to invite was not, then, that of two minds each somehow able to act like an independent agent; the image is rather that of a single mind not wholly integrated; a brain suffering from a perhaps temporary self-inflicted lobotomy.

This highly abstract account of the logical structure of self-deception is not, and never was, intended as a psychologically revealing explanation of the nature or aitiology of self-deception. Its modest purpose was to remove, or at least mitigate, the features that at first make self-deception seem inconceivable. The two main proposals were, to allow a hybrid form of explanation of mental phenomena, causal, but not rationalizing; and to distinguish firmly between accepting a contradictory proposition and accepting separately each of two contradictory propositions, the latter requiring, or perhaps just expressing, the idea of thoughts held apart.

It is natural to ask whether these suggestions, unprepossessing and schematic as they are, are so wooden and formalized as to correspond to nothing we can recognize in, or abstract from, actual or convincingly fictionalized accounts of self-deception. I am by no means certain what the outcome of an extended survey of cases would reveal with respect to my partial skeleton; I am pretty sure that no one scheme will fit all examples. But it may be illuminating to examine a few samples.

First, an example of what has been claimed to be a real case of mass self-deception. Paul Driver maintains that many of us—enough to establish and maintain a flourishing reputation—deceived ourselves about the originality and value of John Cage's work (Driver 1993). I shall express no opinion about the correctness of this claim; its validity obviously depends in part on the value of Cage's work. Suppose it is true that many of us are self-deceived about the value of Cage's work. How can our delusion be explained and described? Part of the explanation, according to Driver, is that Cage took himself so seriously that others tended to go along. Cage consistently represented himself as having been a student of Schönberg's, for example, though this was apparently a "public fantasy." Perhaps Cage told this story so often even he came to believe it; this would not be an unusual experience. If it worked in something like this fashion, the memory of the truth, being less pleasing than the fantasy, gradually caused, though it did not justify, the fantasy, and it seems clear that memory and fantasy-become-belief had, during the period crucial to self-deception, to be kept on separate tracks.

How about the rest of us? Driver suggests, among other things, that we were embarrassed to admit we could not really make much of, or honestly admire, those pretentious minutes of silence, the sudden toneless bangs and twangs, the elaborately documented random noises. Maybe, we thought, this is what modern music is, or will become, and we do not want to be found out of touch with the newest thing, stuck with last week's fashions. Driver quotes Frank Kermode on how to recognize that one is in danger of deceiving oneself (Kermode is thinking of poetry, but the same is to go for music): you sense, writes Kermode, a "certain ambiguity in your own response. *The Waste Land,* and also *Hugh Selwyn Mauberly,* can strike you in certain moments as emperors without clothes… It is [with] your own proper fictive covering that you hide their nakedness and make them wise." Kermode has not exactly described self-deception, but a sign or frequent precursor: a wavering between two views, a recognition of the possibility of delusion. If you are struck by the suspicion that the emperor is without clothes, you are not yet deluded (assuming the emperor is in fact naked). The thought so far is of the threat, or lure, of being taken in. If this thought leads to your being taken in, you are self-deceived, for it is your own thought that has caused your final delusion. If you come to accept what you at first recognized as fantasy, and the recognition plays a causal role in the acceptance, you have satisfied one of my criteria for self-deception.

Dreaming, one is now told, can be bad for the heart. The most vivid dreams, the ones accompanied by REM, the dreams that come just before waking, or that wake us, produce many of the somatic changes the events we dream of would produce: rapid heart beat, secretion of adrenaline, various sexual responses. We cry out, convulse, kick, fit real sounds into our dream. (The toll such dreams take on us explains the fact, so speculation runs, that so many heart attacks occur early in the day.) If we think, with Freud and Delmore Schwartz, that we are in some sense responsible for our dreams, that they are motivated, then to the extent that we act them out we are self-deluded. But dreams aside, we can, often quite deliberately, summon up imagined scenes. At times this is a prelude to action: we imagine what the outcome of various possible courses of action will be, and act on the one that most attracts, amuses, or, in some cases, frightens us. This legitimate and useful exercise of the imagination is not altogether easy to distinguish from cases where we picture what we know to be false, or absurdly unlikely, or simply less desirable than some alternative, and act on its attraction. The compulsive gambler is an example. Akrasia is in this category.

In *Ulysses,* Joyce, through his spokesman and representative, Stephen Dedalus, advances the theory that in *Hamlet,* Shakespeare identifies himself with Hamlet's father, the deceived and dishonored ghost. There is evidence, we are told, that Shakespeare played the part of the ghost in early productions, and we know that he had a son named Hamnet. Here is

Stephen's description of Shakespeare's fantasy:

> —The play begins. A player comes on under the shadow, made up in the castoff mail of a court buck, a wellset man with a bass voice. It is the ghost, the king, a king and no king, and the player is Shakespeare who has studied *Hamlet* all the years of his life…in order to play the part of the spectre. He speaks the words to Burbage, the young player who stands before him…, calling him by a name:
>
> Hamlet, I am thy father's spirit
>
> bidding him list. To a son he speaks, the son of his soul, the prince, young Hamlet and to the son of his body, Hamlet Shakespeare, who has died in Stratford that his namesake may live for ever.
> Is it possible that that player Shakespeare, a ghost by absence…' speaking his own words to his own son's name… is it possible, I want to know, or probable that he did not foresee the logical conclusion of those premises: you are the dispossessed son: I am the murdered father: your mother is the guilty queen, Ann Shakespeare, born Hathaway? (Joyce 1937, 186, 187).

11

If Shakespeare really foresaw this conclusion, and accepted it, he was deluded, for he was not about to be murdered, nor did he have reason to think he would be. His delusion, if that is what it was, coexisted, but could not have cohabited, with his grasp of truth. In Joyce's *Ulysses* someone questions Stephen's account: might it not be, he asks, that Shakespeare merely made a mistake in marrying Ann Hathaway. "—Bosh! Stephen said rudely. A man of genius makes no mistakes. His errors are volitional and the portals of discovery." But a moment later we learn it was not his choice:

> He chose badly? He was chosen, it seems to me. If others have their will Ann hath a way. By cock, she was to blame. She put the comether on him, sweet and twentysix. The greyeyed goddess who bends over the boy Adonis, stooping to conquer, as prologue to the swelling act, is a boldfaced Stratford wench who tumbles in a cornfield a lover younger than herself. (Joyce 1937, 188, 189)

The confusion of Ann Hathaway with Athena (the "greyeyed goddess") may remind us of how Athena deceives Odysseus, quite obviously for the fun of it, when, deposited alone with an assortment of tripods and other gifts by his generous Phaeacian hosts, he ponders how to approach his wife and a palace full of hostile suitors. Athena disguises herself as a lad and enjoys the success of her deceit before she reveals herself and gives Odysseus some essential advice. The untrusting, flirtatious, affectionate relation between Athena and Odysseus is one of the more subtle subplots of the *Odyssey*. It strikes us as oddly modern, as if designed to leave us uncertain who it is that is fooled, and to what extent. Another quiet Homeric note sounds in the library scene in Joyce's *Ulysses*. Why, Stephen asks, did Shakespeare, a "lord of language," send another to woo for him? He answers:

> Belief in himself has been untimely killed. He was overborne in a cornfield first… and he will never be a victor in his own eyes after nor play victoriously the game of laugh and lie down. Assumed dongiovannism will not save him. No later undoing will undo the first undoing. The tusk of the boar has wounded him there where love lies ableeding…There is, I feel in the words, some goad of the flesh driving him into a new passion, a darker shadow of the first, darkening even his own understanding of himself. (Joyce 1937, 194)

We recall an eerie scene in Homer's *Odyssey*. Odysseus has entered his palace in disguise. His old nurse, Euryclea, is washing his foot when suddenly she recognizes him by an old scar. Erich Auerbach, in the marvelous first essay in *Mimesis*, calls our attention to the magical way in which Homer suspends the moment of recognition, without apology or comment, while we are told, in the present tense, the story of the ancient hunt and the wound inflicted by the boar (Auerbach 1953). The number of kinds and levels of disguise, of deception self- and other-imposed, of self-conscious and unsuspected cross identifications, gives some idea of the actual complexity and subtlety of self-deception in everyday life.

Who, then, is fooled? Well, first, Shakespeare, according to Stephen. Shakespeare was taken in by Ann Hathaway, as Hamlet's father was by his wife. In writing *Hamlet*, Shakespeare in part deceived himself (again if we accept Stephen's "theory"—a theory he will in a moment say he does not believe.)

But who is Stephen? No one can doubt, one is not *allowed* to doubt, that Stephen is Joyce himself. *A Portrait of the Artist as a Young Man* is frankly autobiographical; and to a greater extent than in most autobiographical works, Joyce invents as much as records his past and himself. Stephen–or Joyce–also identifies with Shakespeare, not to mention God. Stephen speaks of Hamlet *père* and Hamlet *fils*, "murdered and betrayed... Dane or Dubliner," and goes on:

> He found the world without as actual what was in his world as possible... Every life is many days, day after day. We walk through ourselves, meeting robbers, ghosts, giants, old men, wives, widows, brothers-in-love. But always meeting ourselves. The playwright who wrote the folio of this world... the lord of things as they are... would be a bawd and cuckold too but that in the economy of heaven, foretold by Hamlet, there are no more marriages. (Joyce 1937, 210)

13

Implicitly comparing Shakespeare's "exile" in London with his own (Joyce's, Stephen's) exile in Paris, Stephen says "Elizabethan London lay as far from Stratford as corrupt Paris lies from virgin Dublin." Has no-one made out Hamlet to be an Irishman, someone asks. ("No-one" [ὄυτισ] is, of course, Odysseus' alias when he wishes to deceive Polyphemus).

Does Joyce want us to see his Shakespeare, Stephen, himself, as self-deceived? Was Joyce to some extent self-deceived? Does it matter where we draw this line, or is there a line worth drawing? The extent to which at any moment we vividly imagine another life, that of a robber, ghost, giant, old man, etc., we have taken a first step toward accepting what we imagine. If we dwell on our fantasy, act out small parts of our imagined self, enjoy in our daydreams the excitements and triumphs we miss in reality, we are encouraging and motivating a degree of conviction in what, in the beginning, we know is false. The writer who, consciously or not, finds his characters writing their own plot, as in the case of Trollope, or finds his plot writing his own character, as in the case of Joyce, is doing what we all do when we fantasize or daydream, but doing it better. The author who thinks he is telling a secret truth about himself lends himself willingly to self-delusion: think of Proust, Genet, Dante, Lawrence, Byron, Philip Roth. The list is long.

–You are a delusion, said roundly John Eglinton to Stephen... Do you believe your own theory?

—No, Stephen said promptly.

But we are then allowed to overhear Stephen as he silently thinks: "I believe, O Lord, help my unbelief. That is, help me to believe or help me to unbelieve? Who helps to believe? *Egomen*. Who to unbelieve? Other chap." (Joyce 1937, 211) Who is fooled?

Madame Bovary brilliantly dissects the stages of self-deception. Whether or not we are inclined to sympathize or identify with Emma Bovary, the account of how she persuades herself to accept absurdly unrealistic opinions of herself, her situation, and her behavior is unerringly convincing. It begins when she is barely older than a child. She reads *Paul et Virginie* and dreams of herself in the little bamboo hut, with faithful servant, loving small brother, exotic far-away scenes. At thirteen she enters a convent. At first she is swept away by the routine religious metaphors of betrothal, divine love, and marriage everlasting. She might at this point, we are told, have awakened to the lyric call of Nature, but since she comes from the country she prefers the picturesque. Soon she is secretly reading romantic novels; Flaubert is endlessly—enthusiastically—willing to give us the flavor of these novels:

> They were all about love and lovers, damsels in distress swooning in lonely lodges, postilions slaughtered all along the road, horses ridden to death on every page, gloomy forests, troubles of the heart, vows, sobs, tears, kisses, rowboats in the moonlight, nightingales in the grove. (Flaubert 1965, 26)

Flaubert and Joyce make a strange pair, two sentimentalists posing as realists. There are many pages of *Ulysses* that are in the style and tone Flaubert here and throughout ironically uses to convey the content of Emma's heated imagination. Joyce more sympathetically mimics the manner of penny novels to introduce us to the thoughts (and reading) of Gerty MacDowell, a young woman Leopold Bloom notices with interest on the beach. Gertie fantasizes harmlessly about Bloom; here is the texture of her thinking:

> Here was that of which she had so often dreamed. It was he who mattered and there was joy on her face because she wanted him because she felt instinctively that he was like no-one else. The very

heart of the girlwoman went out to him, her dreamhusband, because she knew on the instant it was him.[2]

Bloom and Gerty, middle-aged man and the maiden, enjoy their unspoken mutual attraction and interaction, and part in good spirits, like Odysseus and Nausicaa. Such thoughts bring tragedy to the life of Madame Bovary. How does this happen? Gerty is in no danger—nor is Bloom—of losing touch with reality; reality only pushes Emma deeper into despair and a world of fantasy. This in itself would not be self-deception. What makes it self-deception is, first, her uninhibited longing for surroundings and experiences she imagines others to have, and that she believes are her due. Second, this longing engenders vivid imaginings of what she wishes and hopes for. Third, she more and more acts as if what she wants were the case. Finally, behaving in accord with a dream world, she gradually comes to believe it real. But since it is the actual world, which she detests, and which motivates and sustains the whole crazy construction, we must suppose—and this is how Flaubert describes it—that the two worlds, real and imagined, somehow occupy the same mind. Through the enormous energy of desire and weakness of will, the conflicting parts of the two worlds are kept from confronting, and so destroying, one another until the end.

When Emma returns to her father's farm after leaving the convent, "she regards herself as being utterly disillusioned, with nothing more to learn or feel." The appearance on the scene of Charles Bovary soon changes this: she comes to believe herself possessed at last of that wonderful passion about which she has dreamed. After playing briefly at being a happy homemaker, she awakens to the fact that her emotions do not match what she thought romantic love required. Sitting alone in a field she is suddenly overcome with regret: "O God, O God, why did I get married?" She tortures herself with what she imagines to be the exciting, fulfilled, lives of her old school friends.

In the development of her self-deception two things stand out: the steps she takes to nourish her illusions, and the psychic energy that goes into keeping truth and illusion separate. After the ball at the chateau of the Marquis d'Andervilliers, the memory gives Emma something to "do." She thinks of the Viscount with whom she danced, and imagines him in

15

---

2. *Ulysses*, 351.

Paris. She buys a guide to Paris and traces her way about the capital with the tip of her finger, walking up the boulevards, stopping at every turning, imagining the gay, impulsive life of poets in the cafes. When her hopes fade, she nurses her grief, seeking out circumstances that nourish it. Feeling sorry for herself, hating her husband, she welcomes a lover. While her husband sleeps she is awake to very different dreams. Thinking of her lover, who was in fact about to leave her, she imagines a romantic scene:

> To the gallop of four horses she was carried away for a week towards a new land, from where they would never return. They went on and on, their arms entwined, without speaking a word. Often from the top of a mountain there suddenly appeared some splendid city... (Flaubert 1965, 141)

When her lover rudely disillusions her, she is devastated, but takes solace in religion. Thinking she is going to die, she sees herself going off to heaven:

> This splendid vision dwelt in her memory as the most beautiful thing that it was possible to dream... Amid the illusions of her hope she saw a state of purity that floating above the earth... She wanted to become a saint... she fancied herself seized with the finest Catholic melancholy ever conceived by an ethereal soul. (Flaubert 1965, 154, 155)

Presently she takes another lover, Léon, a law-clerk with whom she had previously had an unconsummated flirtation. They urge each other on in inventing a romantic past, "For this is how they would have wished to be, each setting up an ideal to which they were now trying to adapt their past life."

Falling in love, she thinks, with Léon, she protects her secret life by taking better care of her dull husband. "[S]he was eaten up with desires, with rage, with hate... She was in love with Léon, and sought solitude that she might more easily delight in his image. His physical presence troubled the voluptuousness of this meditation." After her first seduction by Rodolphe, she ruminates ecstatically:

> She repeated: "I have a lover, a lover," delighting at the idea as if a

second puberty had come to her. So at last she was to know those joys of love, that fever of happiness of which she had despaired! She was entering upon a marvelous world where all would be passion, ecstasy, delirium... A blue space surrounded her and ordinary existence appeared only intermittently between these heights, dark and far away beneath her. (Flaubert 1965, 117)

When Rodolphe's ardor starts to cool, it only increases her passion. Her reaction to rejection makes one think of Leon Festinger's theory of cognitive dissonance, which was inspired in part by the discovery, or insight, that people who have made an irreversible choice tend to continue to invest in that choice if the choice seems objectively to have been a mistake, with the apparent motive of demonstrating their wisdom to themselves.

Doing and thinking things with the conscious or unconscious aim of changing our own beliefs or other attitudes is not necessarily bad, or even what we would normally call irrational. John Dewey, who along with Aristotle had a dim view of the possibility of doing much to change one's own values, wrote about how, with luck and effort, it might be done (Dewey 1922). His proposal had two parts: the first was that if you want to have a value or belief you do not have, you should act as if you already had it. The second part was to avert attention from the desired end and concentrate on the means. Don't keep repeating to yourself, "I will not smoke," but set out on an interesting expedition in a direction where no cigarettes are to be found. Dewey did not notice that his advice works better in the service of self-deception than of self-improvement. If your secret wish is to commit adultery, don't say to yourself, "I shall allow myself to be seduced"; just let him or her touch your hand.

Flaubert was a doctor's son. When he was 13 he wrote a friend that he would be disgusted with life if he were not writing a novel. Yet he was sometimes so annoyed with characters in *Madame Bovary* that he wrote whole scenes not intended for publication simply to relieve his feelings. But he was not annoyed with Emma. Though he claimed to make every possible effort to eliminate himself from this work, when he was asked who served as the model for Emma, he famously replied, "Madame Bovary, c'est moi!" Who was he fooling? Joyce injected himself into his work more strenuously, but nothing would satisfy him. At one point he asked Nora, his wife, to have an extra-marital affair so that he could write about the experience, hers–and his.

The moral I draw from these examples is brief. Self-deception comes in many grades, from ordinary dreams through half-directed daydreams to outright hallucination, from normal imagining of consequences of pondered actions to psychotic delusions, from harmless wishful thinking to elaborately self-induced error. It would be a mistake to try to draw firm lines within these continua. But as we approach the classic cases like that of Emma Bovary, the formal structure I have postulated also seems to be revealed more and more clearly. Such analytic exercises do not, as some philosophers apparently think, necessarily distort or misrepresent the real thing. They do, of course, ignore the details and omit the color that give particular cases their interest and psychological persuasiveness. But the philosopher's exercises do not have to be false because they are pale and rational. Or am I fooling myself?

18

References

Auerbach, E. 1953. "Odysseus' Scar." In Willard R. Trask, trans., *Mimesis: The Representation of Reality in Western Literature.* Princeton: Princeton University Press.

Davidson, D. 1981. "Paradoxes of Irrationality." In R. Wollheim, ed., *Freud: A Collection of Critical Essays.* Garden City, New York: Doubleday.

———. 1985. "Incoherence and Irrationality." *Dialectica* 39:345-54.

———. 1986. "Deception and Division." In J. Elster, ed., *The Multiple Self.* Cambridge: Cambridge University Press.

Dewey, J. 1922. *Human Nature and Conduct.* New York: Henry Holt.

Driver, P. 1993. *The London Review of Books* 7 (January).

Fernández, F. 1993. *The London Review of Books* 7 (January).

Flaubert, G. 1965. *Madame Bovary.* Trans. Paul de Man. New York: W.W. Norton.

Fodor, J. and E. Lepore. 1992. *Holism: A Shopper's Guide.* Oxford: Blackwell.

Joyce, J. 1937. *Ulysses.* New York: Random House.

Safire, W. 1993. *The New York Times,* February 4, Sec. A, p. 23.

Division and Deception:
Davidson on Being Self-Deceived
Ariela Lazar

The concept of self-deception is notoriously problematic. Philosophical inquiries into self-deception reveal a number of disturbing problems. Of the various problems encountered by philosophers in considering self-deception, the following is central. How is it possible, it is asked, for a competent subject to detect the irrationality of a belief that p, to form and maintain his belief that not-p against weighty or conclusive evidence to the contrary? Self-deception is especially intriguing, since it seems to point towards a causal connection between wanting, on the one hand, and believing, on the other. The self-deceiver's belief contrasts with the evidence that is available to her. In addition, the belief often represents a state of affairs that the self-deceiver desires would obtain: he wants to pass the test and believes (contrary to what is suggested by the evidence) that he will pass. It is natural to suppose that the desire to pass the test is causally linked with the irrational belief that he will pass. But how can a desire that something be the case cause someone to hold the corresponding belief? Another question raised with respect to self-deception concerns the state of mind of the self-deceived subject. When the process of self-deception has been successfully completed, must the self-deceived subject hold both the rational belief as well as the irrational, self-deceptive belief? Or does the self-deceiver rid herself of the rational belief altogether and hold only the irrational belief? Naturally, if it is claimed that both beliefs must be held by the subject, questions are raised about the possibility of their being held by one person, within one mind. Finally, it is often suggested that the mind of the self-deceived subject is divided. In what does this division consist?

Donald Davidson offers answers to all three questions posed above. Together, these answers constitute an account of self-deception, which has generated much interest–both enthusiastic as well as critical.[1] Here, I shall examine Davidson's answers, which include the following claims made by Davidson: First, he claims that self-deception is caused by an intention to form a belief. Second, Davidson maintains that, in self-deception, the subject holds both the rational as well the irrational belief. Third, Davidson contends that the mind of the self-deceived subject is divided. The three sections of this essay correspond to each of these respective claims.

1. Intending to Form a Belief

Davidson (1986) offers the following concise characterization of self-deception:

> A has evidence on the basis of which he believes that p is more apt to be true than its negation; the thought that p, or the thought that he ought rationally to believe p, motivates A to *act* in such a way as to cause himself to believe the negation of p.... All that self-deception demands of the action is that the motive originates in a belief that p is true (or recognition that the evidence makes it more likely to be true than not), and that *the action be done with the intention of producing a belief in the negation of p*. (88–89, emphasis added)

The idea is simple. A person recognizes that a belief, p, is justified by the evidence at his disposal. He wishes that p were not the case (but is perhaps unable to make it the case that not-p is true). The agent then forms a desire to *believe* that not-p is the case.[2] Consequently, the agent forms an

---

1. Examples include Pears (1984; 1986), Johnston (1988), Cavell (1993), and Talbott (1995).
2. I use the term "desire," after Davidson, to cover all kinds of positive evaluative attitudes

intention to form the belief that not-p. The formation of a belief cannot be done "at will" i.e., one cannot form a belief merely upon intending to hold that belief.[3] Therefore, Davidson contends that "the agent... [must] *do* something with the aim of changing his own views" (1986, 87). The role that the intention to form a belief plays in the phenomenon of self-deception is emphasized by Davidson:

> [I]t is not self-deception simply to do something intentionally with the consequence that one is deceived, for then a person would be self-deceived if he read and believed a false report in a newspaper. *The self-deceiver must intend the 'deception'.* (1986, 87, emphasis added)

21

Consider the following example of self-deception and its analysis (1986, 89–90). Carlos, a man most averse to failure, is convinced, after considering the evidence at his disposal, that he will fail his impending driving test. Carlos reasons that, other things being equal, he would rather avoid pain; therefore, Carlos would rather believe that he will pass. Now, it is impossible for Carlos to form the belief that he will pass the test merely upon realizing that he would be better off, all things considered, if he held it. In this way, the formation of beliefs is different than the performance of actions. So Carlos, says Davidson, must "act in such a way as to cause himself to believe" that he will pass the test (1986, 88). To this effect, Carlos may intentionally direct his attention away from the evidence, which supports his belief that he will not pass the test, or he may push the negative evidence "into the background" (1986, 89), or he may engage in other forms of self-manipulation.

Thus, Davidson's answer to the puzzle of how a belief is formed in self-deception is straightforward. The subject desires to form the belief, forms an intention to do so, and goes on to act in ways that, he believes, will bring about his holding the desired belief. This approach, which stresses the presence of an intention to form a belief, is endorsed by many philosophers who address this topic and constitutes the standard approach to self-deception.[4] The primary source of appeal of this approach is the fol-

("pro-attitudes," in Davidson's terminology) such as hoping that, wanting that, yearning that, etc. For an introduction to Davidson's views on action, see Davidson (1980).

3. For a defense of this view, see Williams (1973).

4. The list of philosophers who endorse this view includes Rorty (1988), Pears (1984, 1986), and Talbott (1995).

lowing: The self-deceived subject forms a belief against the weight of the evidence even when the evidence is overwhelming in support of the contradictory belief. At the same time, the presence of the irrational belief that is formed in self-deception often corresponds to a subject's goal (or goals). The irrational belief may result in, for example, enhanced levels of self-confidence or calm nerves, while the rational belief threatens the fulfillment of these goals of the subject. Thus, when Carlos believes irrationally that he will pass his driving test, this belief corresponds to (what we may assume are) his goals of maintaining a high level of self-confidence and avoiding anxiety, for instance. The suggestion that the irrational belief is acquired in order to attain a goal that is frustrated by the presence of the rational belief fits well with these features of self-deception. In further support of this suggestion, one should note that self-deception is never attributed merely to insufficient intellectual skills on the part of the subject.[5] On the contrary, self-deception is taken to occur in a subject who is intellectually competent to detect the irrationality of her belief. It may appear, therefore, that we must appeal to the subject's intention to form a belief in order to explain self-deception—that other options are simply not available.

The appeal to intention in explaining the formation (and preservation) of the irrational belief in self-deception presents it as a consequence of practical reasoning; it is viewed as a consequence of an attempt to fulfill a non-truth-oriented goal.[6] Indeed, some cases of self-deception may war-

---

5. It is implicit in accounts of self-deception that the generation and perseverance of the irrational belief are not explainable by the self-deceived person's intellectual inability to detect the irrationality of her belief: it is not the case that detecting the irrationality of the belief in question requires intellectual skills that exceed those of the self-deceived subject. In other words, a problem that is similar in structure, complexity, and framing, would result in a rational belief rather than its contrary. If it were Carlos' friend who was about to undergo a driving test, Carlos, equipped with the the analogous information, would arrive at the conclusion that his friend is about to fail. In addition, the phenomenon of self-deception may not be attributed to the presence of a mere cognitive bias such as the inclination to overvalue evidence that is encountered early on in the process of inquiry. A mere cognitive bias is equally exhibited whether it tips the scales towards the formation of a belief that corresponds to the subject's non-truth-oriented goals or whether it does not: it is not sensitive to themes. The literature on cognitive biases is very large. Some references include Nisbett and Ross (1980)—particularly chap. 10; Tversky and Kahneman (1973, 1974), and 1981); Quattrone and Tversky (1984).

6. Portraying self-deception as rationalized by a set of motivational reasons (belief-desire

rant such an explanation.[7] There are strong reasons for supposing, however, that most cases of self-deception, such as Carlos', are not best explained by appeal to an intention to form a belief. I will briefly present
one or two reasons to this effect.[8]

Assume that I strongly desire to pass my doctoral defense.[9] If I fail, I
will be compelled to turn down an excellent and rare offer for a position
in my field. No other careers are currently open to me. I have accrued
many debts during my years as a student and must start paying them off
immediately as well as support my family. Assume further, that I am
poorly prepared for the defense. I am not sufficiently advanced in my dissertation so as to be able to present a coherent and defensible thesis. Indeed, one of my prospective examiners has cautioned me and advised me
to postpone the defense. Due to economic considerations, as well as the
opportunity to take a coveted position, I decide to go ahead and defend
my thesis. The evidence at my disposal indicates that I will fail, yet I believe that I will pass. According to Davidson's account, the formation of
the irrational belief is due to my forming an intention to form the belief
in question. I choose to form this belief because I think that it will enhance some goals of mine—relieve anxiety, boost self-confidence, etc. The
portrayal of the self-deceptive subject as *choosing* to form the belief is an
essential element of this account. It is the presence of this element that
will be presently put into question.

Is it indeed reasonable to present the subject of self-deception in this
way? Is it likely that, under the circumstances outlined above, I would
choose to form the belief? It is true that holding the irrational belief is associated with a few advantages. At the same time, one disadvantage of
holding the belief is likely to be that of *decreasing* my chances of actually

23

---

pairs) does not imply either that engaging in self-deception constitutes a rational action
or that the belief adopted through self-deception is a rational one.

7. A case in point is that of a man who accepts Pascal's wager and follows a regimen of
church visits and other Christian activities with the intention of inducing faith. Naturally,
this will count as a case of self-deception only if the subject believes that God does not
exist (or that the evidence supports this belief) at the time in which he initiates the process
of inducing the belief in God's existence.

8. A discussion of cases that are explainable by this account may be found in my manuscript "Deceiving Oneself or Self-Deceived?"

9. Davidson's example is somewhat underdescribed if we are to get a taste of the despair
or deep anxiety that leads up to self-deception. Rather than fill in the details in Carlos's
example, I present a similar case of my own.

passing the test (I terminate the hectic schedule of intensive studying, do not seek the assistance of my peers, etc.). If, as is assumed, I want very much to pass the test (indeed, so strong is this desire that it causes self-deception), and I also choose to form the belief that I will, my choice of forming the irrational belief is crazy–it reduces my chances of satisfying this very desire. The standard approach to self-deception emphasizes the centrality and intensity of the desire that causes self-deception. This account cannot, without losing much of its appeal, view the self-deceptive subject as choosing to satisfy another desire at the cost of decreasing her chances of satisfying the initial desire which causes self-deception.

There is another problem here for Davidson's account. If the self-deceiver's choice is crazy, the apparent advantage of the offered explanation disappears. The advantage of this account is grounded in its explaining self-deception by appeal to practical reason: an instance of deviant belief formation is portrayed as a consequence of an instance of non-deviant practical reasoning. However, if the self-deceiver's choice is crazy, this strategy fails: the account ends up explaining the breakdown of theoretical reason by appeal to the breakdown of practical reason. There is no advantage in portraying self-deception as a deviant form of practical reason rather than as a deviant form of theoretical reason without being able to offer a further explanation. Rather than wonder why (and how) the irrational belief is formed, we end up wondering why (and how) the irrational decision is made. Many cases of self-deception are such that, if understood as involving an intention to form a belief, they must be viewed as involving a crazy choice. These cases may not be explained by appeal to an intention to form a belief.

An additional problem for Davidson's account concerns the difficulty in executing a project that is intended to generate a belief. Analyzing his own example, Davidson suggests that Carlos' self-deception is due to his *doing* something (e.g., concentrating on favorable evidence, avoiding inquiries that are likely to yield negative evidence) with the intention of producing the belief that he will pass the test. This suggestion is intended to explain how the formation of a belief may correspond to a non-truth-oriented goal. Such an explanation is necessary because, typically, beliefs are formed in correspondence to one's assessment of the evidence. Moreover, a subject cannot form a belief merely by intending to form it.[10] Davidson claims that, through acting, a subject may induce the forma-

---

10. See Williams (1973) for a defense of this view.

tion of beliefs in himself. Indeed, it is well established that there is a multitude of elements that affect belief formation.[11] Thus, evidence that is encountered early on (or very late) in the process of inquiry is overvalued and more effective in determining its outcome.

A person aware of these facts may no doubt attempt to make use of them in order to further the goal of generating a belief in himself. Note, however, that the intention to form a belief *in itself,* forms an obstacle towards the formation of the irrational belief. If, for example, Carlos knows why he devised his investigation (of whether he will pass his test) so that the favorable evidence is encountered first and last in the process of information gathering, while the negative evidence is to be examined in the middle, he is less likely to form the irrational belief. Even if, for a brief period, the evidence may appear to Carlos as if it supported the view that he will pass, the awareness that this is merely due to the order in which the evidence was surveyed (and that the order of surveyance was intended to cause this impression) is very likely to convince Carlos that he will not pass. In comparison, if the intention is absent while the positive evidence is encountered early on and very late in the process, the irrational belief is more likely to be formed.

It may be said, in defense of this account, that the intention to form a belief explains the presence of circumstances that allow for a biased assessment of the evidence. Thus, for example, the intention to form a belief explains why the subject surveyed the positive evidence very early on in the investigation. In response to this objection, it ought to be noted that the effect of the special circumstances will be offset by the presence of the intention to form a belief. We must conclude, therefore, that the present account of self-deception does not explain *how* the irrational belief is formed. We ought also to conclude that, everything equal, accounts of self-deception that do not appeal to an intention to form a belief will be superior to the suggested account.[12]

25

---

11. For a sample of references concerning the literature on cognitive biases, see note 5.
12. It may be claimed, in defense of Davidson, that the intention to form the irrational belief does not stand in the way of forming the belief as long as the subject is not aware of it. Similarly, it may be claimed that if the subject is not aware that she is engaged in an activity in order to bring about the formation of the desired belief, intentional self-manipulation is not problematic. This is not so. Assume that the self-deceived subject is not aware of her intention. If the intention to form a belief starts out in consciousness, the account must show how it ends up as a nonconscious state. Clearly, if the intention is *intentionally* pushed away into nonconsciousness, the problem arises again (the awareness of

This critique is bound to be incomplete without the presentation of an alternative account. It cannot aim at convincing that, most often, self-deception does not involve an intention to form a belief without suggesting a different answer to the puzzle of how the irrational belief is formed. The presentation of such an alternative account, though, is well beyond the scope of this essay. In this context, I will limit myself to making a few brief comments that are crucial in the understanding of self-deception. These points will suggest a different kind of process than suggested by Davidson.

26   Many factors greatly affect cognition and, as such, are excellent candidates for explaining many instances of self-deception. In particular, emotions exert systematic influence on cognition. Belief formation under the influence of an emotion is typically affected by selective features of the environment and is characterized by less systematic reasoning and a higher level of reliance on superficial cues. In addition, emotions have been associated with changes in the salience level of environmental features: what is more readily observable in one's environment or stands out in one's memory is highly correlated with the subject's emotional state.[13] When angry, the flaws in your behavior stand out. I am less likely to consider the numerous occasions on which you were kind to me. Even if reminded of those instances, they will appear minor and my previous judgment of your character will seem flawed. When depressed over losing a job, my fu-

---

one's pushing away one's intention will form an impediment toward forming the irrational belief). Alternatively, it may be claimed that the intention to form a belief starts out as a nonconscious state. In that case, it will be asked how it happens that this intention fails to exert its normal effect in consciousness. Nonconscious beliefs (and desires) still affect consciousness; they generate our thoughts and actions. Indeed, herein lies the justification for attributing nonconscious thoughts (or desires). If the intention does not exert its normal effect in consciousness (such as preventing the formation of the irrational belief), it will be asked how this failure comes about. For obvious reasons, it will not be adequate to explain this failure by appeal to an intention. Not only is it difficult to gain an explanatory advantage out of a nonconscious intention that fails to form its normal effect in consciousness, but this failure also undermines the very justification of attributing this state of mind to the self-deceived subject.

12. There is extensive literature on this topic. It presents a strong case for the view that emotions affect cognition in a variety of dimensions: less systematic thinking, less efficient processing skills, reliance on simplistic response strategies, lower level of reliance on direct evidence, and greater reliance on superficial cues. See S. Darke (1985) and R. C. Gur (1988). D. M. Mackie and D. L. Hamilton (1993), which include many useful references to relevant works in this area.

ture appears bleak. After a spending a few hours in merry company, the future seems much brighter. True, I don't yet have a plan of how to provide for my family. Still, I have a hunch that, in one way or another, things will somehow improve. I remember past incidents of having overcome adversity. Indeed, I am more likely to notice cases that resulted in a happy ending than cases that ended in defeat. Emotions are relevant in the explanation of self-deception in that they often affect a considerable change in belief *in the absence of change in relevant information*. Yet, emotions do not affect cognition via the mediation of an intention but rather exert their influence directly and in a way that is not subject to our control.

27

Another factor that affects cognition and often results in irrational belief is the level of attention with which we treat an issue. Interestingly, what we deem important, and hence pay close attention to, is also likely to be assessed by us as flawed. Adolescent girls, for example, tend to underrate their physical appearance and find many more flaws with it than do others. Similarly, ambitious people often rate the quality of their performance lower than their peers do. This can easily be explained by the fact that, if we pay close attention to something, may it be physical appearance or performance in a particular assignment, we are bound to find more flaws in it than observers who pay less attention to it. Both these factors, emotions as well as attention level, may bias cognition and are closely associated with motivation (we are depressed when frustrated; we pay attention when we are highly interested in the outcome). Yet, typically, these biasing effects do not operate through an intention to form a belief. One way of supporting this claim is to recognize that such factors affect cognition systematically in a direction that does not correspond to the subject's desires. A listing of biasing factors and their effects on cognition will form the base of a more realistic approach to self-deception.

The puzzle of "how it is done" – the question of how the irrational belief is formed by an intellectually competent subject – has not been properly formulated in most accounts of self-deception. Traditionally, the way in which the question is raised ignores emotional and other biasing factors most often at play in self-deception. The irrational belief is not formed by a calm subject who reasons carefully. On the contrary, it is formed by a subject less inclined to reason thoroughly but is rather more impressed with superficial cues. The cues that are more salient to the subject are those that correspond to the level of attention paid to the relevant issues as well as to her emotional state. Beliefs are affected by motivation through a number of biasing mechanisms. In some extreme cases, beliefs are so affected by desire (and less by evidence) that they appear to resemble fantasies. But the influence of desire on belief is not exhibited exclusively in cases of self-deception. It is exhibited in many instances of belief formation to varying degrees. Admittedly, self-deception is an extreme form of irrational belief formation but it does not display, in most instances, a unique process that leads to the formation of belief. We will be better off accounting for self-deception by appealing to biasing mechanisms rather than appealing to intention. The appeal to intention (to form a belief) in accounting for self-deception is deeply problematic.

28

Davidson endorses the intentionalist view of self-deception again in his contribution to this volume where he claims that all cases of self-deception are due to an intention to form a belief. Towards the end of "Who Is Fooled?" however, Davidson seems to concede that there are cases of self-deception that are not due to an intention to form a belief:

> Self-deception comes in many grades, from ordinary dreams through half-directed daydreams to outright hallucination, from normal imagining of consequences of pondered actions to psychotic delusions, from harmless wishful thinking to elaborately self-induced error. It would be a mistake to try to draw firm lines within these continua. But as we approach the classic cases like that of Emma Bovary, the formal structure I have postulated also seems to be revealed more and more clearly. (1997, 18)

But Davidson's concession here is minimal in the sense that he still holds that core cases of self-deception are due to an intention to form a belief. In contrast, I have suggested that the presence of an intention to form a belief is not a central means towards forming the irrational belief in self-deception. Rather, nonintentional psychological processes are much more effective in biasing cognition.

2. Retaining the Rational Belief

According to Davidson, self-deception begins with a belief that p is true (or is more likely to be true than its negation). This belief motivates the subject to form an intention to generate not-p in himself. The next feature of self-deception to be identified by Davidson is this:

Finally, and it is especially this that makes self-deception a problem, the state that motivates self-deception and the state it produces coexist; in the strongest case, the belief that p not only causes a belief in the negation of p, but also sustains it. [C]ore cases of self-deception demand that Carlos remain aware that his evidence favours the belief that he will fail, for it is awareness of this fact that motivates his efforts to rid himself of the fear that he will fail. (Davidson 1986, 89–90)

The requirement that the rational belief is maintained, even when self-deception is achieved, is justified by Davidson in the following way. Reality and memory both pose continuous threats to the agent's ability to continue holding the self-deceptive belief even after it is formed. After all, the subject's environment, by and large, does not support the irrational belief. Therefore, there is constant need to ward off thoughts that are threatening to the stability of the irrational belief. The motivation to ward off such thoughts is provided by the rational belief.

> …[C]ontinuing motivation is necessary to hold the happy thought in place. If this is right, then the self-deceiver cannot afford to forget the factor that above all prompted his self-deceiving behaviour: the preponderance of evidence against the induced belief. (1986, 90)

Davidson argues that once the rational belief is no longer held by the subject, the motivation to ward off thoughts disappears and self-deception fails. In a nutshell, the presence of the rational belief is said to be required in order to explain two distinct, yet related, facts: the *formation* of the irrational belief as well as its continuous presence after the initial formation. According to Davidson's account, the subject recognizes her predicament (and/or its foreseen effects) and this recognition causes the formation of the desire (as well as the corresponding intention) to form the contradictory belief. Maintaining the continuous presence of the irrational belief requires the same mental framework. The recognition of the consequences of holding the rational belief is key in this account, because it sets off a process of practical reasoning that is aimed at offsetting these consequences.

Davidson is right, therefore, in recognizing that the account of self-deception suggested by him implies that core cases of self-deception involve the presence of the rational belief both at the outset of the process of self-deception as well as its tail end (after self-deception is successfully achieved).[14] If the appeal to intention in explaining self-deception is justified, so is the requirement that the rational belief is maintained through self-deception. However, if self-deception is not to be explained by appeal to an intention to form a belief, this elaborate causal structure, which must be maintained as long as self-deception lasts, becomes obsolete. Indeed, an appeal to biasing mechanisms in the explanation of self-deception rids us of the need to postulate such a problematic structure. There is another advantage to avoiding the view that all cases of self-deception involve the presence of both the rational as well as the irrational belief. Some self-deceived subjects do not exhibit behavior that justifies such an attribution. The behavior of these subjects exhibits the presence of the irrational belief—it determines action as well as verbal expression—but the effects of the rational belief are not observable.

The final section is devoted to Davidson's contention that the mind of the self-deceived subject is divided.

3. A Divided Mind

According to Davidson, the self-deceived subject holds both the rational as well as the contradictory irrational belief. How is it, Davidson asks, that two beliefs, which contradict each other and are causally related, persevere within the same mind. His answer is that the beliefs are "kept separate"—they are never "put together." The self-deceived subject believes that he is bald. He also believes that it is not the case that he is bald. The self-deceived subject does not hold that he is both bald and not bald. "How can a person fail to put the inconsistent or incompatible beliefs together?" asks Davidson.[15] He promptly answers his own question by appealing to the notion of boundaries within one mind.

---

14. Davidson is therefore right in rejecting accounts of self-deception which, much like his account, rely on an intention to form a belief yet do not postulate the presence of the rational belief when self-deception is successfully completed (this view is held by, for example, D. Pears (1984, 1986).

15. This is by no means a problem that afflicts only Davidson's account of self-deception. It does not arise simply as a result of Davidson's postulation of the continuous presence of the rational belief through self-deception. The same problem will arise for other accounts. It will be asked how the subject fails to "put together" the evidence (which supports p overwhelmingly or even conclusively) and the irrational belief (non-p).

[P]eople can and do sometimes keep closely related but opposed beliefs apart. To this extent we must accept the idea that there can be
boundaries between parts of the mind; I postulate such a boundary
somewhere between any (obviously) conflicting beliefs. Such
boundaries are not discovered by introspection; they are conceptual
aids to the coherent description of genuine irrationalities. (1986, 92)

Davidson contends that irrationality of the kind that is exhibited in
self-deception (and akrasia) compels us to view the mind as divided.[16] In
making this argument, Davidson is hoping to resolve a conceptual difficulty that threatens the possibility of self-deception. The argument to this
effect relies heavily on Davidson's views on thought and language, most
of which cannot be examined here.[17] In what follows, I shall briefly mention a few elements in these views. These are essential for understanding
Davidson's conception of the divided mind. Davidson's views on thought
and language may seem at first unrelated to his conception of the divided
mind, but they will be shortly shown to be relevant.

According to Davidson, the identity of a belief or a desire is constituted
by its relations to events and objects in the world as well as its relations to
other beliefs and desires. It is constitutive of the belief that it will rain, to
use Davidson's example, that, together with the desire to stay dry, it causes the appropriate action (such as taking an umbrella when leaving the
house). Rationality is constitutive of the mental under this view, because
it establishes the framework within which we understand behavior that is
described in mental terms—beliefs, wants, actions, etc. Understanding an
action, therefore, consists in identifying its rationalizing reasons, and the
attribution of a belief must correspond to other beliefs attributed to the
subject. An interpretation of, for example, an utterance, turns on the interpreter's portraying the subject as intelligible. The belief that is taken to
be expressed by the utterance in question must correspond to related beliefs and desires; it must contribute to explaining the subject's actions in
the light of those beliefs and desires. Greater intelligibility of a subject's
(verbal as well as nonverbal) behavior turns on, providing a more coher-

---

16. Davidson's argument for the necessity of viewing the mind as divided in each case of
irrationality appears in Davidson (1982). Support and further context for this position may
be found in Davidson (1985).

17. Davidson's views on these matters have been exposed in numerous articles. The basics
of his theory on mind and language may be found in Davidson (1984).

ent view of the subject's thoughts and actions—a view according to which integration level is higher and inconsistencies are minimized. Precisely because of the connection between rationality and intelligibility, the failure to portray the subject as sufficiently rational often counts as failure in interpretation.

It ought to be clear by now that under this approach, all instances of internal irrationality (even mistakes that are due to the subject's intellectual limitations) are viewed as problematic. Because of Davidson's commitment to holism, severe irrationality must be seen as threatening the identity of the beliefs and desires involved. If one belief causes the formation of another belief, yet the beliefs are logically inconsistent, holism inclines us to reassess the presumed identity of the beliefs in question; these circumstances are taken to provide evidence to the effect that the beliefs in question are not incompatible, after all. In Davidson's view, belief is that which functions in well-defined ways in the explanation of action as well in that of verbal behavior. A belief, among other things, is that which is caused by other beliefs (which raise the likelihood of its being true), is given up in light of undermining beliefs, etc. Among cases of internal irrationality cases of self-deception are particularly difficult to accommodate within holism, since they most clearly undermine the nature of belief as understood by this approach. In self-deception (as understood by Davidson), a belief is causally effective in producing its contradictory.

It is quite difficult to accommodate instances of internal irrationality within Davidson's view of the mental. Indeed, this approach, in particular, Davidson's commitment to holism, provides a powerful explanation of the serious difficulties tencountered vis-à-vis attempts to explain self-deception. According to this view, self-deception undermines the very idea of belief. At the same time, Davidson wishes to recognize the possibility of self-deception. What allows him to accommodate self-deception (and other forms of extreme irrationality) within his view of the mental is a distinction between local versus global considerations of interpretation. The idea is simple. According to Davidson, the set of beliefs held by a person (at a given point in time) is that set of beliefs which best accounts for her behavior *in the long run*. This principle allows for the possibility that the best interpretation of a subject's behavior—that which views him as most rational overall—is that which views him as *locally* irrational even to the extent of being self-deceived. Consider a case in which a person believes, against the weight of the evidence, that the woman he admires reciprocates his love. This belief may be expressed verbally as well as determine nonverbal behavior (he declines an excellent job offer in a removed location; he shops for an engagement ring). This man's behavior would be significantly less intelligible if we did not acknowledge his belief that his love was being reciprocated. His behavior, on the whole, makes more sense, if we view him as self-deceived.

The distinction between local versus long-term considerations of interpretation alone is not sufficient for accommodating self-deception within Davidson's view of the mental. The problem, again, has to do with the holistic view of the mental. Davidson's holism determines that the identity of propositional attitudes is constituted by, among other things, the causal as well as logical relations they bear to each other. When an inconsistency in a subject's thought is exhibited, the doctrine of holism may compel us to re-interpret what is initially taken to be an irrational belief, as an altogether different, rational belief. Such local considerations may not tolerate extreme irrationality even if the initial interpretation (which portrays the subject as irrational) yields the most coherent picture of the subject's thoughts and actions over time. Davidson's postulation of divisions of the mind is a direct response to this concern. When the mind is conceived as divided, the identities of beliefs (and desires) are constituted holistically by their relations to other elements within their respective divisions alone. In this way, incompatible, causally related beliefs will not determine each other's identities.

33

The boundaries of the different divisions, as viewed by Davidson, correspond to the collapse of rational relations (so that inconsistent beliefs get assigned to different divisions) and great overlap between the divisions is maintained. In such a way, Davidson suggests to overcome the gap that opens up between local and long-term interpretative considerations in cases of internal irrationality: local considerations may require favoring an interpretative scheme that does away with the irrationality, while long-term considerations may require its acknowledgement. The suggested partitioning of the mind resolves this problem and does away, in a sense, with local irrationality by postulating rational parts of the mind.

Davidson provides only brief comments in justification of his idea of the presence of boundaries within the mind. His brief comments present this idea as a conceptual aid toward "a coherent description of genuine irrationalities." These boundaries are introduced by stipulation and the psychological reality of the "parts" of the mind is explicitly denied. This way of introducing the boundaries of the mind supports the interpretation of this idea as limited to resolving an intratheoretical dilemma. Most certainly, this conceptual device does not postulate two systems such that one is deceiving and the other is deceived.

Davidson's view of the divided mind is erroneously interpreted, on occasion, as a homuncularist view.[18] This may well be due to an analogy he draws between two divisions that constitute one mind, on the one hand, and two different agents, on the other.[19] It ought to be clear, however, that the analogy is drawn in order to stress the point that elements belonging to different divisions of the mind are mutually free from any holistic constraints—much like elements belonging to two different minds are not constitutive of each other's identities regardless of how they may be otherwise related. In Davidson's own words, the analogy "does not have to be carried so far as to demand that we speak of parts of the mind as independent agents" (1982, 304). Davidson's conception of the partitioning of the mind is best seen as portraying the mind as integrated to different degrees. In this way, Davidson accommodates irrationality within his theory, yet avoids the traps that await views of the divided mind that are humuncularist—views that portray the mind as consisting of more than one agency. Davidson makes room, within the space of his theory, for recognizing that the best interpretative scheme in certain circumstances will portray a person as being inconsistent, self-deceived or weak-willed. It is our pretheoretical intuition that self-deception is a real phenomenon and Davidson is defending it.

References

Cavell, M. 1993. *The Psychoanalytic Mind: From Freud to Philosophy.* Cambridge, Mass.: Harvard University Press.

Darke, S. 1985. "Anxiety and Working Memory Capacity." *Cognition and Emotion* 2:145–54.

---

18. David Pears (sympathetically, 1984) and Mark Johnston (critically, 1988) attribute this view to Davidson. Sebastian Gardner avoids a homuncularist interpretation of Davidson's view but mistakenly takes it to postulate "parts" that are *"real unities,* belonging to which is more than a matter of set membership" (1993, 61; see discussion, 59–64).
19. Davidson 1982, 303–4.

Davidson, D. 1980. "Actions, Reasons and Causes," 3–19; "How is Weakness of the Will Possible?" 21–42; "Agency," 43–61. In *Essays on Actions and Events*. Oxford: Oxford University Press.

———. 1982. "Paradoxes of Irrationality." In Hopkins and Wollheim, eds. (1982), 289–305.

———. 1984. *Inquiries into Truth and Interpretation*. Oxford: Oxford University Press.

———. 1985. "Incoherence and Irrationality." *Dialectica* 64:345–54.

———. 1986. "Deception and Division." In Elster, ed. (1986), 79–92.

———. 1998. "Who is Fooled" Paper presented at the Symposium on Self-Deception, Stanford, California, February 1993. In J. P. Dupuy, ed., *Self-Deception and Paradoxes of Rationality*. Stanford: CSLI Publications (this volume).

Elster, J., ed. 1986. *The Multiple Self*. Cambridge: Cambridge University Press.

Gardner, S. 1993. *Irrationality and the Philosophy of Psychoanalysis*. Cambridge: Cambridge University Press.

Gur, R. C., et al. 1988. "Effects of Task Difficulty on Regional Cerebral Blood Flow." *Psychological Physiology* 60:509–17.

Hopkins, J., and R. Wollheim, eds. 1982. *Philosophical Essays on Freud*. Cambridge: Cambridge University Press.

Johnston, M. 1988: "Self-Deception and the Nature of Mind." In McLaughlin and Rorty, eds. (1988), 63–91.

McLaughlin, B. P., and A. O. Rorty, eds. 1988. *Perspectives on Self-Deception*. Berkeley: University of California Press.

Mackie, D. M., and D. L. Hamilton. 1993. *Affect, Cognition and Stereotyping*. San Diego: Academic Press.

Nisbett, R., and L. Ross. 1980. *Human Inference: Strategies and Shortcomings of Social Judgment*. New Jersey: Prentice Hall.

Pears, D. 1984. *Motivated Irrationality*. Oxford: Oxford University Press.

———. 1986. "The Goals and Strategies of Self-Deception." In Elster (1986), 59–78.

Quattrone, G., and A. Tversky. 1984. "Causal Versus Diagnostic Contingencies: On Self-Deception and on the Voter's Illusion." *Journal of Personality and Social Psychology* 46: 237–48. Reprint in Elster (1986), 35–58.

Rorty, A. O. 1988: "The Deceptive Self: Liars, Layers, and Lairs." In McLaughlin and Rorty, eds. (1988), 11–28.

Talbott, W. J. 1995. "Intentional Self-Deception in a Single Coherent Self." *Philosophy and Phenomenological Research* 55:27–74.

Tversky, A., and D. Kahneman. 1973. "Availability: A Heuristic for Judging Frequency and Probability." *Cognitive Psychology* 5:207–32.

———. 1974. "Judgment under Uncertainty: Heuristics and Biases." *Science* 185:1124–30.

———. 1981. "The Framing of Decisions and the Psychology of Choice." *Science* 211:453–59.

Williams, B. 1973. "Deciding to Believe." In *Problems of the Self.* New York: Cambridge University Press. 67–94.

Two Paradoxes of Self-Deception
Alfred R. Mele

*There is nothing worse than self-deception—when the deceiver
is always at home and always with you.*
—Plato, *Cratylus*, 428d

Much philosophical work on self-deception revolves around a collection
of paradoxes. The paradoxes can be divided into two kinds, depending on
whether they focus on the mental *state* of a self-deceived person at a time
or on the *dynamics* of self-deception. We may call them, respectively, *static* and *dynamic* paradoxes. The former have received greater attention in
the literature, but the tide may be turning.[1]

From the outside, it might sometimes look as though philosophers
view the paradoxes merely as puzzles to be resolved for no other reason
than that others have tried and failed to resolve them. In fact, however,
philosophical interest in self-deception runs much deeper. A proper understanding of the phenomenon would reveal much about the human
mind. Some philosophers—for example, Donald Davidson and David
Pears—take self-deception to require one kind or another of mental parti-

---

1. For a review of philosophical work on self-deception from 1960 through the mid-
1980s, including references to numerous works discussing various relevant paradoxes, see
Mele 1987b.

tioning.[2] For reasons that I have presented elsewhere, I am skeptical about the usefulness of the partitioning hypotheses that have been offered (Mele 1987a, chaps. 6 and 10). But I hope to make it clear enough here that an investigation of self-deception, one focusing on the resolution of paradoxes, can shed considerable light on the influence of motivation on cognition.

A well-known static paradox may be formulated as follows:

> If ever a person A deceives a person B into believing that something, p, is true, A knows or truly believes that p is false while causing B to believe that p is true. So when A deceives A (i.e., himself) into believing that p is true, he knows or truly believes that p is false while causing himself to believe that p is true. Thus, A must simultaneously believe that p is false and believe that p is true. But how is this possible? (cf. Mele 1987a, 121)

This paradox has a dynamic counterpart; I call it the *strategy* paradox:

> In general, A cannot successfully employ a deceptive strategy against B if B knows A's intention and plan. This seems plausible as well when A and B are the same person. A potential self-deceiver's knowledge of his intention and strategy would seem typically to render them ineffective. On the other hand, the suggestion that self-deceivers typically successfully execute their self-deceptive strategies *without* knowing what they are up to may seem absurd; for an agent's effective execution of his plans seems generally to depend on his cognizance of them and their goals. So how, in general, can an agent deceive himself by employing a self-deceptive strategy? (Mele 1987a, 138)

My aim in this paper is to sketch resolutions to both paradoxes and to clarify thereby the nature and etiology of self-deception. I start with a brief discussion of skepticism about self-deception.

---

2. See Davidson 1985 and Pears 1984. For an earlier, systematic presentation of Davidson's view on partitioning, featuring attention to akratic action, see Davidson 1982.

1. Skepticism and Motivationally Biased Belief

Obviously, if one is to show that self-deception is impossible one must offer at least a partial account of what self-deception is. How is one to arrive at an account, or a partial account, of self-deception that will support skepticism? There is a familiar *lexical* route.[3] One does a bit of linguistic analysis to yield a definition of 'self-deception', or borrows a definition arrived at in this way by someone else, and then argues that the definition is unsatisfiable.

This is a risky route to take. Perhaps what ordinary folks mean by 'self-deception' diverges from any analysis of the term that can be gleaned solely from close attention to the meaning of 'deception' and its cognates and a simple prefixing of 'self-' to 'deception'. And, arguably, the meaning of the term 'self-deception' is largely a function of its use by ordinary folks anyway. One might argue that an account or analysis of self-deception should capture the defining features of the cases to which ordinary folks confidently apply the term 'self-deception'. From this point of view, if those cases are possible, so is self-deception.

I shall not try to skirt skepticism in this way. Dictionary-driven skepticism is defeasible partly on its own ground. It is often assumed that deceiving is, by definition, an intentional activity. This assumption drives many familiar puzzles about self-deception; and it is false. Consider a standard use of 'deceived' in the passive voice: "Unless I am deceived, I left my plane tickets in my room." Here 'deceived' means 'mistaken'. There is a corresponding use of 'deceive' in the active voice. In this use, to deceive is "to cause to believe what is false" (my authority is the *Oxford English Dictionary*). And, of course, one can intentionally or unintentionally cause someone to believe what is false. Suppose that, careless reader that I am, I misread a magazine article, taking it to report that *p*. I then tell you that *p* on the basis of my reading, intending to report something true but actually uttering something false. If you believe me, I have caused you to believe something false: I have deceived you, in the sense of the word at issue, but I have not done so intentionally.

If it were to turn out that nonintentionally causing oneself to believe something false is uncharacteristic of self-deception, the lexical point just made would not count for much against the skeptics. However, I have argued elsewhere that self-deception typically is not intentional deception,

---

3. A nonlexical route is identified and criticized in Mele 1987a, 130–31.

even though it is motivated (Mele 1983, 1987a). A partial characterization of intentional deception is provided by our static paradox: the deceiver knows or truly believes that p is false while causing the deceived to believe that p is true. Now, for the most part, people who allegedly deceive themselves into believing that p want it to be the case that p.[4] To take some stock examples, people who deceive themselves into believing that their spouses are not having extramarital flings normally want it to be true that they are not so engaged, and parents who deceive themselves into believing that their children were erroneously convicted of a crime normally want it to be the case that they are innocent of that crime. Imagine, to use one of these garden-variety examples of self-deception, that owing significantly to the influence of relevant desires, a woman falsely believes that her husband is not having an affair, in the face of strong evidence to the contrary. Is it likely that the woman first comes to believe that her husband is having an affair and then forms the intention to get herself to believe that he is not so engaged—which intention, perhaps after a bit of means/end reasoning, she successfully executes? Is it more likely that, owing partly to her desire that her husband not be having an affair, she acquires or retains a false belief that he is not having one without having come to believe that he *is* having one?

In exploring the latter option, we will want to understand, among other things, how one's desiring that p can lead one to believe that p in the absence of intentional deception. Not just any causal connection between the desire and the belief will do, of course. The route from desire to belief must be appropriate to self-deception.

Attention to some sources of *unmotivated* or "cold" biased belief will prove useful in this connection. Social psychologists have identified a number of such sources. Here are four[5]:

1. *Vividness of information.* The vividness of a datum for an individual is often a function of his interests, the concreteness of the datum, its "imagery-provoking" power, or its sensory, temporal, or spatial proximity (Nisbett and Ross 1980, 45). Vivid data are more likely to be recognized, attended to, and recalled than pallid data. As a result, vivid data tend to

---

4. For an exception, see Mele 1987a, 116–18.
5. The following descriptions are reproduced from Mele 1987a, 144–45. I have eliminated the notes from the quoted material, all of which provide references to supporting empirical work.

have a disproportional influence on the formation and retention of beliefs.[6]

2. *The availability heuristic.* When people make judgments about the frequency, likelihood, or causation of an event, "they often may be influenced by the relative availability of the objects or events, that is, their accessibility in the processes of perception, memory, or construction from
imagination" (Nisbett and Ross, 18). Thus, for example, a subject may
mistakenly believe that the number of English words beginning with 'r'
is significantly higher than the number having 'r' in the third position,
because he finds it much easier to produce words on the basis of a search
for their first letter (see Tversky and Kahnemann 1973). Similarly, attempts to locate the cause(s) of an event are significantly influenced by
manipulations that focus one's attention on a potential cause (Nisbett
and Ross, 22; Taylor and Fiske 1975, 1978). "[B]y altering actors' and observers' perspectives through video tape replays, mirrors, or other methods, one can correspondingly alter the actors' and observers' causal assess-
ments" (Nisbett and Ross, 22).

3. *The Confirmation Bias.* When testing a hypothesis people tend to
search (in memory and the world) more often for confirming than for
disconfirming instances and to recognize the former more readily (Nisbett and Ross, 181–82). This is true even when the hypothesis is only a
tentative one (as opposed, e.g., to a belief of one's that one is testing). The
implications of this tendency for the retention and formation of beliefs
are obvious.

4. *Tendency to search for causal explanations.* People tend to search for
causal explanations of events (Nisbett and Ross, 183–86). On a plausible
view of the macroscopic workings of the world, this is as it should be. But
given (1) and (2) above, the causal explanations upon which we so easily
hit in ordinary life may often be ill-founded; and given (3), one is likely to
endorse and retain one's first hypothesis much more often than one
ought. Furthermore, ill-founded causal explanations can influence future
inferences.

These sources of biased belief can function independently of motivation; but they may also be primed, as it were, by motivation in the pro-

41

---

6. This theme is developed in Mele 1987a, chap. 10, in explaining the occurrence of self-
deception. Kunda 1990 develops the same theme, paying particular attention to empirical
evidence that motivation sometimes primes the confirmation bias.

duction of particular *motivated* irrational beliefs. For example, motivation can enhance the salience of certain data. Data that count in favor of the truth of a hypothesis that one would like to be true might be rendered more vivid in virtue of one's recognition that they so count; and vivid data, given that they are more likely to be recalled, tend to be more "available" than pallid counterparts. Similarly, motivation can influence which hypotheses occur to one (including causal hypotheses) and affect the salience of available hypotheses, thereby setting the stage for an operation of the confirmation bias. When this happens, motivation issues in cognitive behavior that one's local epistemologist would frown upon. False beliefs produced or sustained by such motivated cognitive behavior in the face of weightier evidence to the contrary are, I will argue, beliefs that one is self-deceived in holding. And the self-deception in no way requires that the agent intend to deceive himself or intend to produce or sustain a certain belief in himself.

42

A host of studies have produced results that are far from surprising on the hypothesis that motivation sometimes biases beliefs. Thomas Gilovich reports:

> A survey of one million high school seniors found that 70% thought they were above average in leadership ability, and only 2% thought they were below average. In terms of ability to get along with others, *all* students thought they were above average, 60% thought they were in the top 10%, and 25% thought they were in the top 1%!... A survey of university professors found that 94% thought they were better at their jobs than their average colleague. (Gilovich 1991, 77)

Apparently, we have a tendency to believe propositions that we want to be true even when an impartial investigation of readily available data would indicate that they are likely to be false. A plausible hypothesis about that tendency is that our *wanting* something to be true sometimes exerts a biasing influence on what we believe.

Ziva Kunda, in a recent review essay, marshals empirical support for the view that motivation can influence "the generation and evaluation of hypotheses, of inference rules, and of evidence," and that motivationally "biased memory search will result in the formation of additional biased beliefs and theories that are constructed so as to justify desired conclusions" (Kunda 1990, 483). In a particularly persuasive study, undergraduate subjects (75 women and 86 men) read an article alleging that "women were endangered by caffeine and were strongly advised to avoid caffeine in any form"; that the major danger was fibrocystic disease, "associated in its advanced stages with breast cancer"; and that "caffeine induced the disease by increasing the concentration of a substance called cAMP in the breast" (Kunda 1987, 642). (Since the article did not personally threaten men, they were used as a control group.) Subjects were then asked to indicate, among other things, "how convinced they were of the connection between caffeine and fibrocystic disease and of the connection between caffeine and... cAMP on a 6-point scale" (643–44). In the female group, "heavy consumers" of caffeine were significantly less convinced of the connections than were "low consumers." The males were considerably more convinced than the female "heavy consumers", and there was a much smaller difference in conviction between "heavy" and "low" male caffeine consumers (the heavy consumers were slightly *more* convinced of the connections).

Given that all subjects were exposed to the same information and assuming that only the female "heavy consumers" were personally threatened by it, a plausible hypothesis is that their lower level of conviction is due to "motivational processes designed to preserve optimism about their future health" (Kunda 1987, 644). Indeed, in another study, in which the reported hazards of caffeine use were relatively modest, "female heavy consumers were no less convinced by the evidence than were female low consumers" (Kunda 1987, 644). Along with the lesser threat, there is less motivation for skepticism about the evidence.

How do the female heavy consumers manage to be less convinced than the others? One possibility—a testable one—is that, because they find the "connections" at issue personally threatening, these women (or some of them) are motivated to take a hyper-critical stance toward the article, looking much harder than other subjects for reasons to be skeptical about the merits of its contents (cf. Kunda 1990, 495). Another testable possibility is that, owing to the threatening nature of the article, they (or some of them) read it *less* carefully than the others do, thereby enabling themselves to be less impressed by it.[7]

In either case, however, there is no need to suppose that the women in-

---

7. For an interesting discussion of the effects of motivation on time spent reading threatening information, see Baumeister and Cairns 1992.

tend to deceive themselves, or intend to bring it about that they hold certain beliefs. Motivation can prompt cognitive behavior protective of favored beliefs without the agent's intending to protect those beliefs. And some cases of self-deception arguably are explicable along very similar lines.

2. The Static Paradox

Here are four common ways, I suggest, in which a person's desiring that p can contribute to his believing that p in a case of self-deception (Mele 1987a, 125–26).

1. *Negative Misinterpretation.* S's desiring that p may lead him to misinterpret as not counting against p (or as not counting strongly against p) data which, in the absence of the desire that p, he would, if the occasion arose, easily recognize to count (or count strongly) against p. Consider, for example, a man who has just been informed that an article of his was not accepted for publication. He hopes that it was *wrongly* rejected, and he reads through the comments offered. He decides that the reviewers misunderstood a certain crucial but complex point, that their objections consequently miss the mark, and that the paper should have been accepted. However, as it turns out, the reviewers' criticisms were entirely justified; and when, a few weeks later, he rereads his paper and the comments in a more impartial frame of mind, it is clear to him that this is so.

2. *Positive Misinterpretation.* S's desiring that p may lead S to interpret as supporting p data which count against p, and which, in the absence of this desire, S would easily recognize to count against p (if he considered the data). Suppose, for example, that Sid is very fond of Roz, a young woman with whom he often eats lunch. If he wants it to be the case that Roz loves him, he may interpret her refusing to go out on dates with him and her reminding him that she is very much in love with her steady boyfriend, Tim, as an effort on her part to "play hard to get" in order to encourage Sid to continue to pursue her.

3. *Selective Focusing/Attending.* S's desiring that p may lead him both to fail to focus his attention on evidence that counts against p and to focus instead on evidence suggestive of p. Attentional behavior may be either intentional or unintentional. S may tell himself that it is a waste of time to consider his evidence that his wife is having an affair, since she just is not the sort of person who would do such a thing, and he may intention-

ally act accordingly. Or, because of the unpleasantness of such thoughts, he may find his attention shifting whenever the issue suggests itself to him. Failure to focus on contrary evidence, like negative misinterpretation, may contribute negatively to S's acquiring the belief that p; for it may be the case, other things being equal, that if S had focused his attention on his evidence for not-p, he would not have acquired the belief that p. Selective focusing on supporting evidence may contribute positively to S's coming to believe that p.

4. *Selective Evidence-Gathering.* S's desiring that p may lead him both to overlook easily obtained evidence for not-p and to find evidence for p that is much less accessible. Consider, for example, the historian of philosophy who holds a certain philosophical position, who wants it to be the case that her favorite philosopher did so too, and who consequently scours the texts for evidence that he did while consulting commentaries that she thinks will provide support for the favored interpretation. Our historian may easily miss rather obvious evidence to the contrary, even though she succeeds in finding obscure evidence for her favored interpretation. Such one-sided evidence gathering may contribute both positively and negatively to the acquisition of the false belief that p. Consequently, one might wish to analyze selective evidence gathering as a combination of 'hypersensitivity' to evidence (and sources of evidence) for the desired state of affairs and 'blindness'–of which there are, of course, degrees–to contrary evidence (and sources thereof).

In none of the examples offered does the person hold the true belief that not-p and then intentionally bring it about that he or she believes that p. Yet, assuming that my hypothetical agents acquire relevant false beliefs in the ways described, these are garden-variety instances of what ordinary folks count as self-deception. The author of the rejected article is self-deceived in believing that it was wrongly rejected, Sid is self-deceived in believing certain things about Roz, and so on.

Elsewhere, I have offered a set of four characteristic and jointly sufficient conditions of a prominent species of "entering self-deception in acquiring the belief that p." The first three conditions are as follows:

1. The belief that p which S acquires is false.
2. S's desiring that p leads S to manipulate (i.e., to treat inappropriately) a datum or data relevant, or at least seemingly relevant, to the truth value of p.

3. This manipulation is a cause of S's acquiring the belief that p. (Mele 1987a, 125–26)

My fourth condition is a complicated one designed to handle deviant causal chains and interference by other agents. Since those issues may be set aside for my purposes here, I relegate the condition to a note.[8]

Some object to the first condition on the grounds that the truth or falsity of p has no special importance for the dynamics of self-deception. My response is that even if the grounds are accepted, the conclusion is misleading. Here, the dictionary does matter. A person is, by definition, *deceived in* believing that p only if p is *false*, and the same is true of being *self-deceived* in believing that p. This is a purely lexical point.

My brief discussion of various ways of entering self-deception serves well enough as an introduction to condition 2, and condition 3 is relatively straightforward. So we may return to the static paradox.

The paradox comprises a premise, two inferences, and a query that may be read either as a rhetorical question or as a challenge. The premise, again, is this: "If ever a person A deceives a person B into believing that... p is true, A knows or truly believes that p is false while causing B to believe that p is true." I have already argued that the premise is false and I have directly attacked the conclusions drawn—that all self-deceivers know or truly believe that p is false while causing themselves to believe that p is true, and that they simultaneously believe that p is false and believe that p is true. In many garden-variety instances of self-deception, the false belief that p is not preceded by the true belief that not-p, nor are the two beliefs held simultaneously. Rather, a desire-influenced treatment of data has the result both that the person does not acquire the true belief and that he does acquire (or retain) the false belief. One might worry that the paradox emerges at some other level, but I have addressed that worry elsewhere and I pass over it here (Mele 1987a, 129–30).

The conditions for self-deception that I have offered are conditions specifically for entering self-deception in *acquiring* a belief. However, as I

---

8. Condition 4 reads: "If, in the causal chain between desire and manipulation or in that between manipulation and belief-acquisition, there are any accidental intermediaries (links), or intermediaries intentionally introduced by another agent, these intermediaries do not make S (significantly) less responsible for acquiring the belief that p than he would otherwise have been."

have implied, one can also enter self-deception in *retaining* a belief. Here is an illustration that I offered in *Irrationality* (Mele 1987a, 131–32):

> Sam has believed for many years that his wife, Sally, would never have an affair. In the past, his evidence for this belief was quite good. Sally obviously adored him; she never displayed a sexual interest in another man…; she condemned extramarital sexual activity; she was secure, and happy with her family life; and so on. However, things recently began to change significantly. Sally is now arriving home late from work on the average of two nights a week; she frequently finds excuses to leave the house alone after dinner; and Sam has been informed by a close friend that Sally has been seen in the company of a certain Mr. Jones at a theater and a local lounge. Nevertheless, Sam continues to believe that Sally would never have an affair. Unfortunately, he is wrong. Her relationship with Jones is by no means platonic.

47

Each of the four types of data-manipulation mentioned earlier may be at work in a case of this kind. Sam may positively misinterpret data, reasoning that if Sally were having an affair she would want to hide it and that her public meetings with Jones consequently are evidence that she is *not* having an affair with him. He might negatively misinterpret the data, and even (nonintentionally) recruit Sally in so doing by asking her for an "explanation" of the data or by suggesting for her approval some acceptable hypothesis about her conduct. Selective focusing may play an obvious role. And even selective evidence-gathering has a potential place in Sam's self-deception. He may set out to conduct an impartial investigation, but, owing to his desire that Sally not be having an affair, locate less accessible evidence for the desired state of affairs while overlooking some more readily attainable support for the contrary judgment.

Here again the occurrence of a standard instance of self-deception is explicable independently of the assumption that the individual is manipulating data with the intention of deceiving himself, or with the intention of protecting a favored belief. Nor is there an explanatory need to suppose that at some point Sam is in the problematic condition of believing that p while also believing that not-p.

3. Gimpel the Fool

When Jean-Pierre Dupuy invited me to participate in this conference, he asked whether I would be willing to devote some time to the topic of self-deception in a literary context. I flirted with the idea of producing an argument that the best explanation of some contemporary literary theories of authorial intention is authorial self-deception. Fortunately, I decided against this.

One important use for literary works is as a source of detailed examples of ostensible self-deception, as opposed to the highly schematic examples that, for a variety of reasons, commonly appear in philosophical work. Once, after hearing me talk about garden-variety self-deception concerning spousal infidelity, a student asked what sort of evidence I thought would preclude self-deception in such a case. My off-the-cuff answer was catching one's spouse in the sexual act. But I immediately began piecing together a scenario in which even this might not be enough. Later, I came across a relevant story by Isaac Bashevis Singer, "Gimpel the Fool."

Gimpel is an uncommonly gullible man, but he is neither idiotic nor insane. One night, Gimpel enters his house after work and sees "a man's form" next to his wife in bed. He immediately leaves—in order to avoid creating an uproar that would wake his child, or so he says. The next day his wife, Elka, vehemently denies everything—even in front of their rabbi—implying that Gimpel must have been dreaming. The rabbi orders Gimpel to move out of the house, and Gimpel obeys. Eventually, Gimpel begins to long for his wife and child. This longing apparently motivates the following bit of reasoning, reported by Gimpel the narrator: "Since she denies it is so, maybe I was only seeing things? Hallucinations do happen. You see a figure or a mannequin or something, but when you come up closer it's nothing, there's not a thing there. And if that's so, I'm doing her an injustice." Gimpel bursts out in tears, and the next morning he tells his rabbi that he was wrong about Elka.

After much deliberation, taking nearly a year, a council of rabbis inform Gimpel that he may return to his home. He is thrilled, but wanting not to awaken his family, he walks in quietly after his evening's work. Predictably, he sees someone in bed with Elka, a certain young apprentice, and he accidentally awakens Elka. Pretending that nothing is amiss, Elka asks Gimpel why he has been allowed to visit and then sends him out to check on the goat, giving her lover a chance to escape. When Gimpel returns from the yard, he inquires about the absent lad. "'What lad?'" Elka asks. Gimpel explains, and Elka again insists that he must have been hallucinating. Gimpel is then struck a violent blow on the head by Elka's brother, masquerading as her first son, and is knocked unconscious. When he awakes in the morning, he confronts the apprentice, who stares at Gimpel in amazement and advises him to seek a cure for his hallucinations.

Gimpel apparently comes to believe that he has been mistaken yet again. He moves in with Elka and lives happily with her for twenty years, during which time she gives birth to many children. On her deathbed, Elka confesses that she has deceived Gimpel and that the children are not his. Gimpel the narrator reports: "If I had been clouted on the head with a piece of wood it couldn't have bewildered me more." "'Whose are they?'" Gimpel asks, utterly confused. "'I don't know,'" Elka replies. "'There were a lot... but they're not yours.'" Gimpel sees the light.

49

You know now why philosophers' cases of self-deception tend to be schematic. But a more interesting theme may be reinforced. First, although Gimpel's wife and others are out to deceive him, we naturally see him also as *self-deceived*. After all, he had hard evidence of Elka's infidelity, evidence that an impartial spectator would take to warrant a belief in her unfaithfulness. Second, even though there are times when Gimpel believes that Elka has slept with another man and times when he believes that she has never done this, Singer never implies that Gimpel ever simultaneously held both beliefs. Nor need we make this assumption to ground the common-sense judgment that Gimpel was self-deceived. In light of the earlier discussion of motivationally biased belief, we can understand how, owing to selective focusing and the like, a person can lose the belief that p and then acquire the belief that not-p. This seems to be what happens in Gimpel's case. First, he believes that Elka is unfaithful. Then, influenced by motivated attention to skeptical hypotheses, he abandons that belief, apparently withholding belief on the matter. Later, owing partly to further motivated treatment of data, he acquires the belief that she has always been faithful—a belief that he loses only when he comprehends the meaning of Elka's confession.

4. Intentional Self-Deception and the Static Paradox

It is worth noting that even *intentional* self-deception does not require simultaneously believing that p and believing that not-p. Imagine a man who, although he believes that there is no god, would like to believe that there is one. He thinks that the belief would enrich his life and he craves enrichment. Having read Pascal, the man hits upon a predictable strategy for inducing the desired belief in himself. He will associate with religious people, read religious literature, attend services, and the like—all with the hope that a religious attitude will rub off on him. The man does not intend to seek *evidence* for the existence of a god, for he is convinced that the evidence weighs heavily in the other direction and that any evidence of the supernatural that he might gather would come up woefully short. He is hoping, instead, for a change of attitude not grounded in evidence for the favored belief. Suppose that his strategy works; and suppose, as well, that there is no god and that at no point is our man's evidence such as to confer a greater probability on the existence of a god than on there being no god.

50

We can say that the man changed his mind about the existence of a god. But what happens differs from everyday changes of mind in being driven by motivation to acquire a certain belief and guided by a plan for acquiring it. At some point along the way to his doxastic conversion he may come to believe that his evidence for the nonexistence of supernatural beings is considerably weaker than he once thought, and his religious activities might increase the salience of data interpretable as pointing to the truth of theism. Owing to the etiology of these doxastic changes, and with my suppositions in place, we may plausibly count the man as self-deceived. But we need not suppose that there was a time at which he believed that there is no god while also believing that there is one. We may suppose instead that his atheistic belief was extinguished *before* he acquired the belief that a god exists. So, it seems, even in a case of *intentional* self-deception, an individual might never be in the peculiar doxastic condition at the heart of our static paradox—the condition of believing that p while also believing that not-p.

This last scenario has implications for the strategy paradox, as well. Our imagined agent's strategy apparently is not self-undermining. However, the paradox is more fruitfully addressed in connection with garden-variety self-deception.

5. The Strategy Paradox

The basic idea of the strategy paradox, crudely put, is that to the extent that self-deception is not guided by a plan or strategy it is unlikely to occur and that to the extent that it is so guided the project of deceiving oneself is likely to be self-defeating. The thrust is that self-deception is at most very rare, certainly much less common than folk-wisdom suggests. The central challenge calls for an explanation of the alleged occurrence of garden-variety instances of self-deception. If a prospective self-deceiver has no strategy, how can he succeed? And if he does have one, how can his project fail to be self-undermining in garden-variety cases?

It may be granted that self-deception typically is *strategic* at least in the following sense: when people deceive themselves they at least normally do so by engaging in potentially self-deceptive behavior, including cognitive behavior of the kinds catalogued in section 2. Behavior of these kinds can be counted, in a broad sense of the term, as *strategic*, and the behavioral types may be viewed as *strategies* of self-deception.

Strategies of self-deception divide into two kinds, depending on their locus of operation. *Internal-biasing* strategies are modes of manipulating data that one already has. *Input-control* strategies are ways of controlling (to some degree) which data one acquires. The latter also divide in two: strategies for data already present in the world (e.g., selective evidence-gathering); and strategies for generating data. What may be termed "acting as if" is an important strategy of the latter kind; I will comment briefly on it at the end of this section.[9]

Another set of distinctions is also useful (Mele 1987a, 144). There are significant differences among (1) the *non-intentional* employment of a strategy (e.g., non-intentionally focusing selectively on data supportive of *p*), (2) the *intentional* employment of a strategy (e.g., intentionally focusing selectively on data supportive of *p*), and (3) the intentional employment of a strategy *with the intention* of deceiving oneself (e.g., intentionally focusing on data supportive of *p* with the intention of deceiving oneself into believing that *p*).[10] Many puzzles about self-deception are

---

9. Pears identifies what I have called the internal biasing and input-control strategies and treats "acting as if something were so in order to generate the belief that it is so" as a third kind of strategy (1984, 61).

10. For discussion of the difference between (2) and (3) and of cases of self-deception in which an agent intentionally selectively focuses on data supportive of a preferred hypothesis (for example) without intending to deceive himself, see Mele 1987a, 146, 149–51. The discussion of "acting as if" later in this section also is relevant in this connection. On intention, intentional action, and connections between them, see Mele 1992.

motivated partly by the assumption that (3) is characteristic of self-deception.

My resolution of the strategy paradox is implicit in what I have already said. As I have argued, such strategies of self-deception as positive and negative misinterpretation, selective attending, and selective evidence-gathering do not depend for their effectiveness upon agents' employing them with the intention of deceiving themselves. Even cold mechanisms whose functioning one does not direct can bias one's beliefs. When, under the right conditions, such mechanisms are primed by motivation and issue in motivated false beliefs, we have self-deception. Strategies of self-deception, in *garden-variety* cases of this kind, are not "rendered ineffective" by the agent's "knowledge of his intention and strategy" (to use the language of the paradox); for he does not intend to deceive himself, strategically or otherwise. And since we can understand how causal processes that issue in garden-variety instances of self-deception succeed without the agent's intentionally orchestrating the process, we avoid the other horn of the paradox as well.

As I noted in *Irrationality,* "one might suppose that when mechanisms of 'cold' irrational belief work in conjunction with motivational elements, the doxastic agent is at the mercy of forces beyond his control" (1987a, 147–48). If we think of self-deception as something for which the self-deceived typically are significantly responsible, the image of someone as a helpless pawn of combined motivational and cognitive forces may incline us to view him not as self-deceived but as deceived by these forces. However, as I also pointed out,

> this is to take the image of combined forces too seriously. Indeed, I suspect that when motivation activates a cold mechanism, the ordinary agent is more likely to detect bias in his thinking than he would be if motivation were not involved; and detection facilitates control. The popular psychology of the industrialized Western world certainly owes a great deal more to Freud than to the attribution theorists; and for members of that world, a thought-biasing 'wish' is likely to be more salient than, for example, a 'cold' failure to attend to base-rate information. (148)

Return to Sam and Sally. I sketched a partial etiology of Sam's self-deception. We may suppose, additionally, that the confirmation bias, primed by a desire that Sally not be having an affair, was at work. Could Sam have avoided self-deception? An affirmative answer is plausible. Perhaps, recognizing that his desire that Sally not be having an affair might incline him to self-deception, he was capable of setting himself to be on his guard against motivated biasing. Perhaps it was within his power to commit himself to assessing the evidence from a variety of perspectives, including one that treats the case as a purely hypothetical matter designed to test his skills as a detective. And he might have been able actively to seek further evidence of an affair. In some versions of the case, Sam is psychologically incapable of taking such measures; the thought that Sally is having an affair might be so threatening that he simply cannot assess the data with anything approaching objectivity. But there is no reason to think that all possible versions must be like this; and in some Sam is capable of avoiding self-deception.

I turn now to the input-control strategy of "acting as if," which merits at least brief discussion here. As I observed in *Irrationality*:

> An agent's acting as if *p* were the case can generate data supportive of *p* both in a relatively direct, intrapersonal fashion and via a more circuitous social route. We often make inferences about ourselves on the basis of our observation of our own behavior; and by acting as if *p* were the case (e.g., as if one were courageous or kind) one may add to the evidential base. Moreover, by acting as if *p*, an agent may influence others' perceptions and treatment of him, thereby generating for himself social data supportive of *p*. The agent who consistently comports himself confidently in public is likely to be perceived and treated as a confident individual by others who observe his behavior, even if he is not. And their treatment of him may provide him with salient evidence that he is a confident person. (Mele 1987a, 151)

The general tendency to make inferences about ourselves on the basis of our own behavior requires no special motivational underpinning. In this respect, it is like the cold sources of biased belief that I discussed. It is also like them in being exploitable by motivation.

Examples of motivation to "act as if" are easily located. (1) Al believes that he can cultivate in himself the trait of kindness (or self-confidence, or courage) by acting as if he were already possessed of the trait. Given this belief, if he wants to become a kind person, he has a reason to act as if he were kind. (2) Betty values amiability, a trait that she believes she lacks. She is pleased by actions of hers that are associated with the trait, because she takes them to indicate that she is making progress. Betty may consequently have hedonic motivation to act as if she were amiable. (3) Cathy is dissatisfied with her marriage; but partly because she sees no way to improve her situation, she decides to act as if she were content, hoping thereby to make her situation more bearable.

In cases of this kind, agents might be taken in by their own behavior. The agents exert control over data-input by generating data for themselves. If agents acquire false beliefs about their traits or feelings on the basis of such data, even though stronger competing evidence is readily available to them, they may be self-deceived. And, of course, their processing of the generated data may itself be influenced by various internal-biasing strategies. Here again there is no need to suppose that a self-deceived agent acts with the intention of deceiving himself or simultaneously holds beliefs whose propositional contents are mutually contradictory.

6. A Putative Empirical Demonstration of "Strong" Self-Deception

What I shall call "*strong* self-deception" requires, by definition, the simultaneous holding of "conflicting" beliefs of the kind just mentioned. The present section briefly reviews an elegant and impressive empirical study purporting to establish the occurrence of strong self-deception. The study, conducted by George Quattrone and Amos Tversky (1984), offers compelling evidence that subjects required on two different occasions "to submerge their forearm into a chest of circulating cold water until they could no longer tolerate it" tried to shift their tolerance on the second trial, after being informed that increased tolerance of pain (or decreased tolerance, in another sub-group) was indicative of a healthy heart.[11] Most subjects denied having tried to do this; and Quattrone and Tversky argue that many of their subjects believed that they did not try to shift their tolerance while also believing that they did try to shift it. They argue, as well, that these subjects were unaware of holding the latter belief, the "lack of awareness" being explained by their "desire to accept the diagnosis implied by their behavior" (239).

---

11. The study is described and criticized in greater detail in Mele 1987a, 152–58.

Grant that many of the subjects did try to shift their tolerance in the second trial and that their attempts were motivated. Grant, as well, that most of the "deniers" *sincerely* denied having tried to do this. Even on the supposition that the deniers (or most of them) were aware of their motivation to shift their tolerance, does it follow that, in addition to believing that they did not "purposefully engage in the behavior to make a favorable diagnosis," these subjects also believed that they did do this, as Quattrone and Tversky claim? Does anything block the supposition that the deniers were effectively motivated to shift their tolerance without believing, at any level, that this is what they were doing?[12]

55

From the assumptions (1) that some motivation M that an agent has for doing something A results in his A-ing and (2) that the agent is aware that he has this motivation for doing A, it does not follow that the agent believes, consciously or otherwise, that he *is* A-ing (in this case, purposely shifting his tolerance).[13] Nor, *a fortiori*, does it follow that he believes, consciously or otherwise, that he is A-ing for reasons having to do with M. The agent may falsely believe that M has no influence whatever on his behavior, while not holding the contrary belief.

The following case illustrates the latter point. Ann, who is quite consciously desirous of her parents' love, believes that they would love her if she were a successful physician. Consequently, she enrolls in medical school. But Ann does not believe, at any level, that her desire for her parents' love is in any way responsible for her decision to enroll. She believes that she is enrolling solely because of an independent desire to become a physician. Admittedly, I have simply *stipulated* that Ann lacks the belief in question. But my point is that this stipulation does not render the case incoherent. My suggestion about the sincere deniers in Quattrone and Tversky's study is that, similarly, there is no explanatory need to suppose that they believe, at any level, that they are attempting to shift their tolerance for diagnostic purposes, or even believe that they are attempting to shift their tolerance at all. These subjects are motivated to generate favorable diagnostic evidence and they believe (to some degree) that their pulling their hands out of the water earlier/later on the second trial would

---

12. My use of "without believing, at any level, that [*p*]" is elliptical for "without believing that *p* while being aware of holding the belief and without believing that *p* while not being aware of holding the belief."

13. For a supporting argument, see Mele 1987a, 153–56.

constitute such evidence. But the motivation and belief can result in purposeful action independently of the subjects' believing, consciously or otherwise, that they are "purposefully engaged in the behavior," or purposefully engaged in it "to make a favorable diagnosis."

Quattrone and Tversky suspect that (many of) the sincere deniers are *self-deceived* in believing that they did not try to shift their tolerance. They adopt a certain "strong" analysis of self-deception and interpret their results accordingly. However, it is worth noting that an interpretation of their data that avoids the 'dual belief' assumption that I have just attacked allows for self-deception on the conception of the phenomenon that I have presented here. One can hold (*a*) that sincere deniers, due to a desire to live a long, healthy life, were motivated to infer that they had a healthy heart; (*b*) that this motivation (in conjunction with a belief that an upward/downward shift in tolerance would constitute evidence for the favored proposition) led them to try to shift their tolerance; and (*c*) that this motivation also led them to believe that they were not purposely shifting their tolerance (and not to believe the opposite). Their motivated false beliefs that they were not trying to alter their displayed tolerance can count as beliefs that they are self-deceived in holding without their *also* believing that they were attempting to do this.

How did the subjects' motivation lead them to hold the false belief at issue? Quattrone and Tversky offer a plausible, relevant suggestion:

> The physiological mechanism of pain may have facilitated self-deception in this experiment. Most people believe that heart responses and pain thresholds are ordinarily not under an individual's voluntary control. This widespread belief would protect the assertion that the shift could not have been on purpose, for how does one "pull the strings"? (243)

And notice that a belief that one did not try to alter the amount of time one left one's hand in the water, one based (in part) upon a belief about ordinary uncontrollability of "heart responses and pain thresholds," need not be completely cold or unmotivated. A subject's motivation might render the "uncontrollability" belief very salient, for example, while also drawing attention away from internal cues that he was trying to shift his tolerance.

7. Conclusion

Part of what I have argued, in effect, is that some theorists—philosophers and psychologists alike—have made self-deception more theoretically perplexing than it actually is by imposing upon the phenomena a problematic conception of self-deception. My argument focused on the static and dynamic paradoxes identified. The resolutions that I have sketched help us to understand self-deception by helping us to appreciate a variety of relevant ways in which motivation can bias cognition. I have not claimed that believing that *p* while also believing that not-*p* is conceptually or psychologically impossible. But I have yet to see a compelling illustration of that phenomenon in a case of self-deception. Some might suggest that illustrations may be found in the literature on multiple personality. However, that phenomenon, if it is a genuine one, raises thorny questions about the *self* in self-deception. In such alleged cases, does a person deceive herself, with the result that she believes that *p* while also believing that not-*p*? Or do we rather have interpersonal deception—or at any rate something more closely resembling that than self-deception? These are questions for another day. They take us far from garden-variety instances of self-deception.[14]

57

References

Baumeister, R. and K. Cairns. 1992. "Repression and Self-Presentation: When Audiences Interfere with Self-Deceptive Strategies." *Journal of Personality and Social Psychology* 62:851–62.

Davidson, D. 1982. "Paradoxes of Irrationality." In R. Wollheim and J. Hopkins, eds. *Philosophical Essays on Freud.* Cambridge: Cambridge University Press. 289–305.

————. 1985. "Deception and Division." In E. LePore and B. McLaughlin, eds., *Actions and Events.* Oxford: Basil Blackwell. 138–48.

Gilovich, T. 1991. *How We Know What Isn't So.* New York: Macmillan.

Kunda, Z. 1987. "Motivated Inference: Self-Serving Generation and Evaluation of Causal Theories." *Journal of Personality and Social Psychology* 53:636–47.

---

14. This essay was written during my tenure of a 1992–93 National Endowment for the Humanities Fellowship for College Teachers and a 1992–93 fellowship at the National Humanities Center. I am grateful to the NEH and the NHC for their support. Parts of this essay derive from chapter 5 of Mele 1995.

———. 1990. "The Case for Motivated Reasoning." *Psychological Bulletin* 108:480–98.

Mele, A. 1983. "Self-Deception." *Philosophical Quarterly* 33:365–77.

———. 1987a. *Irrationality: An Essay on Akrasia, Self-Deception, and Self-Control.* New York: Oxford University Press.

———. 1987b. "Recent Work on Self-Deception." *American Philosophical Quarterly* 24: 1–17.

———. 1992. *Springs of Action: Understanding Intentional Behavior.* New York: Oxford University Press.

———. 1995. *Autonomous Agents: From Self-Control to Autonomy.* New York: Oxford University Press.

Nisbett, R. and L. Ross. 1980. *Human Inference: Strategies and Shortcomings of Social Judgment.* Englewood Cliffs, New Jersey: Prentice-Hall.

Pears, D. 1984. *Motivated Irrationality.* Oxford: Oxford University Press.

Quattrone, G. and A. Tversky. 1984. "Causal Versus Diagnostic Contingencies: On Self-Deception and on the Voter's Illusion." *Journal of Personality and Social Psychology* 46:237–48.

Singer, I. 1953. *Gimpel the Fool and Other Short Stories.* New York: Noonday Press.

Taylor, S. and S. Fiske. 1975. "Point of View and Perceptions of Causality." *Journal of Personality and Social Psychology* 32:439–45.

———. 1978. "Salience, Attention and Attribution: Top of the Head Phenomena." In L. Berkowitz, ed., *Advances in Experimental Social Psychology.* Vol. 11. New York: Academic Press. 250–88.

Tversky, A. and D. Kahnemann. 1973. "Availability: A Heuristic for Judging Frequency and Probability." *Cognitive Psychology* 5:207–32.

Madness and the Divided Self: Esquirol, Sartre, Bateson

Mark Rogin Anspach

> *Presence to self… supposes that an impalpable fissure has*
> *slipped into being. If being is present to itself, it is because it is*
> *not wholly itself.*
> —Jean-Paul Sartre (124)

> *There is a crack in everything.*
> *That's how the light gets in.*
> —Leonard Cohen

The question posed by the phenomenon of self-deception is whether the beliefs in mutually exclusive propositions are themselves mutually exclusive. Can one believe something and, at the same time, believe the opposite? Donald Davidson and Alfred Mele have presented opposing points of view on this question.

Research funded by Laboratoires Delagrange/Synthélabo contributed to this article. Dr. Henri Grivois drew my attention to the curious statement by Esquirol's patient that became the point of departure for my own interpretations. My brother, William Anspach, put me on the right track with regard to Sartre. Jean-Pierre Dupuy gave me invaluable advice on how to improve the manuscript. Larry Beyer's detailed criticisms of the original version of this paper pushed me to flesh out the exposition and to sharpen and clarify the argument. I am of course solely responsible for all remaining shortcomings.

Davidson (1986) believes that self-deception requires the simultaneous presence of contradictory beliefs by definition. A self-deceived person is one whose belief in a proposition is motivated by a belief in the opposite proposition, or at least by the thought that one ought rationally to believe the opposite, so that "the state that motivates self-deception and the state it produces coexist" (88–89). And the paradox of simultaneous adhesion to incompatible beliefs is resolved by positing a partitioning of the mind that keeps the opposed beliefs apart (91).

Mele (1998) believes, on the contrary, that the hypothesis of mental partitioning may be avoided (38). He sets out to resolve the paradox by showing that in many cases of what ordinary people mean by "self-deception," it is possible to trace how motivation has influenced belief without there ever being a need to suppose that the self-deceived person "simultaneously holds beliefs whose propositional contents are mutually contradictory" (54). No coexistence of incompatible beliefs, no partitioning of the mind.

For my part, I believe Davidson is right: self-deception involves the simultaneous presence of contradictory beliefs. I also believe Mele is right: self-deception may exist without mental partitioning. My task, then, will be to show that these two propositions are not mutually exclusive. While I will devote particular attention to the problem of madness, my aim is to demonstrate an approach to self-division which I hope may have more general relevance.

1. Self-Division in Madness

After analyzing a number of garden-variety instances of self-deception that do not involve simultaneous presence of contradictory beliefs, Mele concludes his paper by noting that counterexamples might be found in the literature on multiple personality—but he implies that those would be the exceptions that prove the rule: they would involve not self-deception but deception between multiple selves (57).

Rather than addressing anything so esoteric as multiple personality disorders, I am going to talk about your average, run-of-the-mill lunatics—the sort of individuals who believe they are Jesus Christ, or Napoleon, or the victims of a conspiracy orchestrated by Freemasons from Mars. Now, it is certainly plausible that such manifestly deluded beliefs entail some form of *self*-deception. After all, even if the individuals in question tell us that their thoughts are electronically implanted into their heads by the CIA, *we* do not believe that. We consider their thoughts to be internally generated. And, no matter how much weight we might wish to attribute to genetic predisposition in the etiology of mental illness—with genetics filling in for the CIA—it seems unlikely that there could be a specific part of the brain hardwired to believe in Freemasons from Mars, although I suppose an especially determined believer in the modularity of mind might differ.

It would seem, then, that psychotic delusions may involve an extreme form of self-deception. So extreme, in fact, that one could argue that they constitute a particularly good test-case to assess whether the partitioning hypothesis is truly justified. For if mental partitioning is not necessary to allow an otherwise lucid man to maintain in the face of all evidence that he is Napoleon, why should it be necessary to permit a man to espouse the much less intrinsically improbable belief that his wife is not cheating on him? And, indeed, it is perhaps because madness seems to involve extreme self-deception that it has traditionally been associated with some notion of mental division. The idea of division or "splitting" is present, of course, in the prefix "schizo-." The phrase "divided self" also figures in the title of a well-known book by the antipsychiatrist R. D. Laing. However, I will take as my starting point not contemporary anti-psychiatrists but the founders of modern French institutional psychiatry.

The idea of a divided self is in fact central to what the philosopher Marcel Gauchet and the late psychiatrist Gladys Swain identify, in their book *La pratique de l'esprit humain*, as the emancipatory humanist impulse responsible for the birth of modern French psychiatry at the dawn of the nineteenth century. The liberatory thrust of the psychiatric movement they analyze is symbolized by the celebrated story of Doctor Philippe Pinel delivering the inmates of an asylum from their chains—a story all the more significant for being, as Swain has documented, perfectly apocryphal.[1] If this gesture is ascribed to Pinel, it is as a tribute to his role in introducing the so-called "moral treatment" of the mentally ill in France.

61

---

1. See the Annex to *Le sujet de la folie* (119–71), "Les chaînes qu'on enlève." As presented by Swain, the story of Pinel delivering patients from their chains would itself appear to provide a classic example of self-deception: "One believes in it without believing in it, so that objections hardly touch it: it adapts rather well to their proximity, sometimes to the point of coexisting on good terms with them" (119).

The quest for a "moral" or "psychological" treatment of the insane is fundamentally democratic, Gauchet and Swain argue, in that it is based on the recognition that even these archetypal outcasts are fellow human subjects; it is founded on the premise that the mad are not so radically Other that they cannot be reached through communication. According to Gladys Swain what was revolutionary in Pinel's 1801 treatise, the *Traité médico-philosophique sur l'aliénation mentale*, was its "critique of the idea of complete madness." "Mental alienation is never total: the alienated individual always maintains a distance from his alienation," writes Swain. Thus, far from being an opaque object upon which one must act from without, the patient becomes a "torn subjectivity with which a therapeutic exchange is possible" (22–23). In other words, the mad are not irredeemably mad because they are not totally so; the therapist's hope of communicating with the patient must rest on the possibility of appealing to a healthy component of the diseased self, and hence on the existence of a "*split [clivage]* in the alienated subjectivity"[2] (103).

62

The alienated display a distance from their own alienation: any Hegelian resonance one may detect in this notion is more than coincidental. In fact, Swain quotes Hegel, who credits Pinel with having "discovered that residue of reason in the alienated and in maniacs, having discovered it as containing the principle of their cure, and having directed their treatment according to this principle" (96). Swain emphasizes the extent to which Hegel's reading of Pinel, too often forgotten, foreshadows Freud's own embrace of the notion of "psychic splitting"; in the *Outline of Psychoanalysis*, Freud writes that the "problem of psychosis would be simple and clear if the ego detached itself totally from reality, but that is something that happens rarely, perhaps even never. Even in the case of states as far removed from the reality of the external world as are the confusional hallucinatory states (amentia), the sick, once cured, declare that in a remote corner of their mind, as they put it, a normal person lay in hiding, letting the whole morbid phantasmagoria unfold before him like a disinterested observer…" (quoted by Swain, 93–94).

Here we find ourselves at the heart of the question of mental partitioning in madness. What strikes me about this passage from Freud is that, while it certainly suggests the existence of a boundary within the mind, the image it conjures up seems to be a reversal of the usual one in which

---

2. Emphasis original in this and all following quotations.

the irrational unconscious is walled off and hidden from the rational self. In these extreme psychoses where the irrational has taken over, marginalizing the rational self, it is the other way around: the rational self is hidden, or walled off, from the irrational. This in itself means little insofar as the irrational is in either case impervious to the rational. What is new this time is that the rational self seems to peer out from its hiding place behind the wall and spy on the madness on the other side. It may be helpless to intervene, but it is not unaware of what is going on, even though this awareness will only be expressed later, after the patient is cured.

This passage from Freud himself would thus seem already to suggest that the boundary is less than hermetic. But I will later cite evidence that mental patients are occasionally able to give overt expression to their internal division even before a cure is effected, or at least during an intermediate stage of the cure. As we shall see, however, these expressions necessarily take a paradoxical form. And I will argue that this paradoxical form may even help explain how it is that the coexistence of incompatible beliefs is able to subsist despite the rationality of the mad.

For the most deluded lunatic can be quite rational. There is no shortage of method in madness. I spoke earlier of an "otherwise lucid" man who maintains that he is Napoleon. The madness is in the premise and not necessarily in the way the premise is defended. It is clearly possible to marshall rational argument on behalf of the most delusory premise. Proof of this can be found, if any is needed, in the curious nineteenth-century satire *Historic Doubts Relative to Napoleon Bonaparte*. The author, Richard Whately, devotes a long pamphlet to demonstrating, through careful argument, not that he is Napoleon, but that nobody ever was Napoleon— that in fact the belief in Napoleon is an historically produced delusion: a myth. And it is interesting to note that the point of the satire was to defend the author's real religious faith from the attacks of historical critics who used similar methods in their attempts to prove such religious beliefs delusory.[3]

Certainly there are schizophrenics who display extremely disordered and incoherent thinking, but this is universal only at the onset of the illness, when patients are overwhelmed by the enormity of the experience they are going through. It will be helpful to refer here to a distinction

---

3. I have elsewhere set out to develop a systematic comparison of religion and madness from a somewhat different perspective (Anspach 1995a and 1995b).

Gordon Claridge makes in *Origins of Mental Illness*: "schizophrenia really consists of two elements: temporary changes in dynamic brain processes, such as arousal, which help to precipitate and drive the person into a psychotic state; and delusional thoughts and ideas which form the permanent or relatively permanent bedrock of the schizophrenic condition" (148). Once schizophrenics get past that initial stage of temporary changes in brain processes, many of them find it possible to account for their experience in relatively ordered fashion, erecting elaborate theoretical edifices on the bedrock of delusional thoughts and ideas.

With these schizophrenics, then, it is possible to reason. Indeed, their deployment of rational argument may make it tempting for others to try to reason with them in order to bring them to see the error of their delusions. But, as one can imagine, reasoning with a patient in this way hardly proves to be a successful therapeutic technique. The problem could be the role of motivation in the patient's cognition, to borrow the language used by analytic philosophers. Pinel's disciple Etienne Esquirol wrote his thesis on "the passions considered as causes, symptoms and means of curing mental alienation." In this work, published in 1805, Esquirol writes that critics of the "moral treatment" of mental patients have misunderstood what it is about: "we have never claimed to cure them by arguing with them, that claim would be refuted by everyday experience: do the passions give way to reasoning? Are not alienation, and all its varieties, passions carried to the extreme? To treat them with dialectical formulas and syllogisms would be to show ignorance of the workings of the passions and of the clinical history of mental alienation." In fact, far from being freed of his beliefs, the patient will "adhere to them all the more, the more one strives to dissuade him" (quoted by Gauchet and Swain, 474–75). And Gladys Swain tells us that "All the authors participating in the innovative trend concurred on this point: it is as absurd as it is vain—not to say disastrous—to attack the delusionary certitude head-on... There is therefore no choice but to 'deal gently with [the patient's] sensitivities'..." (102).

The question may arise at this point as to whether the patient doth protest too much. One could ask if such impassioned defense of delusion is not a manifestation of psychologically motivated *resistance* to the truth. On the one hand, a madman is capable of "listening to reason" in the sense that he can follow rational argument, but, on the other hand, his madness is impervious to reason inasmuch as no amount of rational argument will win him over. If, indeed, a reasoned attack on his deluded beliefs actually provokes the patient to cling to them all the more strongly, one might surmise that the patient is resisting recognizing something as true out of a belief, or at least a nagging suspicion, that it *is* true. This resistance would then qualify as self-deception—or, in Sartrian terms, "bad faith."

I will not try to settle the question of whether such a patient's apparent resistance actually does manifest bad faith. Indeed, I propose for the time being to set the question of madness aside entirely and to review Sartre's analysis of bad faith as a general phenomenon affecting ordinary people. Sartre's demonstration that contradictory beliefs can coexist in the absence of mental partitioning is premised on a type of self-division quite different from that posited by Freud or Davidson. I will argue that this paradoxical type of self-division, which Sartre identifies as endemic to sane minds, is formally related to the type which Gregory Bateson associates with schizophrenia. In the concluding section, I will return to the question of what keeps the mad from being cured. The hypothesis I will present is that, even in the absence of bad-faith resistance, the mad may find themselves divided from sanity by a logic formally similar to that of Sartrean bad faith.

2. Self-Division in Sanity

Sartre's treatment of bad faith is distinguished by his insistence on the inner translucency of the mind, which leads him to reject the Freudian view of resistance. According to Freud, resistance is a phenomenon which manifests itself in the course of psychoanalytic treatment at the very moment the analyst approaches the truth. The essence of Sartre's criticism of Freud is that resistance to knowledge necessarily implies awareness of what is being resisted and hence the absence of an impermeable boundary between the contradictory beliefs. Whereas Freudian resistance rests on a division of the mind into consciousness and the unconscious, Sartre's version of self-deception as bad faith emphasizes "the unity of a *single* consciousness": "I must know in my capacity as deceiver the truth which is hidden from me in my capacity as the one deceived. Better yet I must know the truth very exactly *in order* to conceal it more carefully—and this not at two different moments, which at a pinch would allow us to re-establish a semblance of duality—but in the unitary structure of a single project" (89).

To avoid the paradoxical unity inherent in the fact of deceiving oneself, psychoanalysis "replaces the duality of the deceiver and the deceived... by that of the 'id' and the 'ego.'" By introducing this distinction, Sartre observes, "Freud has cut the psychic whole into two. I *am* the ego but I *am not* the id." I am thus encouraged to view part of myself as if it were an external reality, a thing existing "*in itself*" the way a table does (90–92). With this argument, Sartre in effect accuses psychoanalysis itself of being a sophisticated instrument of bad faith, since for Sartre a typical ploy of bad faith is precisely to try to deny one's freedom by constituting oneself as an inert reality beyond one's own reach. And yet, Sartre notes, despite the "materialistic mythology of psychoanalysis," despite "all the metaphors representing the repression as the impact of blind forces," Freud cannot get around the fact that there can be no repression without an awareness of what is to be repressed—without an awareness of it "*as to be repressed*" (93).

As a result, Freud finds himself in a bind. On the one hand, he does not want to attribute this self-aware activity of repression to the conscious ego, but, on the other hand, he cannot ascribe it to the unconscious complex itself either, for the "complex as such is rather the collaborator of the psychoanalyst since"—by smuggling clues past the repression—"it aims at expressing itself in clear consciousness" (92–93). Freud's solution is to assign the responsibility for repression to a hypothetical censor, "conceived," Sartre remarks sardonically, "as a line of demarcation with customs, passport division, currency control, *etc.*" (90). The "reflexive idea of hiding something from oneself" necessarily implies a "double activity" that tends both "to maintain and locate the thing to be concealed" and "to repress and disguise it," Sartre concludes. "By separating consciousness from the unconscious by means of the censor, psychoanalysis... has merely localized this double activity of repulsion and attraction on the level of the censor." And what is this censor if not an "hypostasized and 'reified'" version of bad faith?[4] (94–95).

---

4. Sartre goes so far as to claim that the censor in its turn must be "conscious of the drive to be repressed... *in order not to be conscious of it*," so that, in attempting to overcome bad faith, psychoanalysis has merely "established between the unconscious and consciousness an autonomous consciousness in bad faith" (94). Larry Beyer has pointed out to me that this assertion of the censor's bad faith is gratuitous. The censor's aim is to keep knowledge of what is repressed from the conscious mind, not from itself. Once we accept the existence of a reified censor, there is no need for the censor to be in bad faith.

Any theory of mental partitioning in self-deception must reckon with Sartre's argument concerning the Freudian censor. Sartre's fundamental point is that one cannot limit the scope of consciousness by positing the existence of a wall inside the mind without also positing the existence of an independent consciousness to mind the wall.[5] But if the wall cannot be effective without a homunculus to man Check-point Charlie, we will have traded in the paradoxical unity of self-deception for a merely implausible duality. Of course, the paradoxical unity will remain equally implausible until it has been better elucidated. It is clearly not enough to label it paradoxical and to leave it at that. The question remains: how is bad faith possible?

For his part, Sartre counters with an unexpected question: how is sincerity possible? Examining sincerity is an indirect route to understanding bad faith. If bad faith is hopelessly paradoxical, presumably its antithesis, sincerity, should be unproblematic. Sartre proceeds to demonstrate that this is far from being the case. Absolute sincerity with regard to oneself is, he argues, an impossible ideal. The "maxim 'one must be what one is'..." posits not merely an ideal of knowing but an ideal of *being*; it proposes for us an absolute equivalence of being with itself... In this sense it is nec-

---

However, I believe Sartre's argument stands once it is shorn of this ill-conceived crowning touch. I take Sartre's fundamental criticism to be directed at the very fact of reifying the censor as an autonomous consciousness between consciousness and the unconscious. By setting up the censor as a third party, psychoanalysis cuts the Gordian knot of *self*-deception: I am not deceived by myself at all, but by the censor who keeps me from seeing the unconscious drive. But to say that the unconscious drive is repressed by an agent of repression called the "censor" amounts to no more than putting a name on the phenomenon to be explained. The end result, Sartre comments, is "a mere verbal terminology" (94). Gregory Bateson makes the same point about the notion of unconscious drives when he defines "instinct" as an "explanatory principle" that, remaining unexplained itself, is in reality no more than a "label" (38–40).

5. Thus, while Sartre's argument is directed against Freud's theory of the unconscious, it can easily be adapted to a weaker theory of partitioning, such as that defended by Davidson, which does not posit the unconsciousness of any one of the separate territories to which the contradictory beliefs are relegated. "I see no obvious reason to suppose one of the territories must be closed to consciousness, whatever exactly that means," writes Davidson, "but it is clear that the agent cannot survey the whole without erasing the boundaries" (92). This theory would seem to call for a censor to keep the agent from surveying the whole, and if each part of the whole is open to consciousness, the censor's job would appear to be all the harder. In short, to posit the existence of boundaries—even if they are functional rather than physical—does not explain anything unless the functioning of the boundaries can be explained.

essary that we *make ourselves* what we are" (101). But that "supposes that I am not originally what I am." Rather, "I can *become* sincere; this is what my duty and my effort to achieve sincerity imply." Yet if I am not already what I am to begin with, no amount of effort will succeed in making me what I am, and "all movement toward being in itself or 'being what one is'" must be impossible. Moreover, "this impossibility is not hidden from consciousness; on the contrary, it is the very stuff of consciousness; it is the embarrassing constraint which we constantly experience; it is our very incapacity to recognize ourselves, to constitute ourselves as being what we are" (105–6).

This "embarrassing constraint" is intrinsic to consciousness. By consciously endeavoring to identify what we are, as one would identify a mere thing, an external object, we cannot avoid constituting ourselves as external to ourselves—and thus as *not* what we are.[6] In attempting to see ourselves for what we are, to observe ourselves, we inevitably find that the self doing the observing is not the self that is observed: "as soon as we posit ourselves as a certain being... then by that very positing we surpass this being..." (106). Indeed, if we do not like what we are, we can even resort to sincerity as a kind of dodge to escape being what we are: "Who can not see that the sincere man constitutes himself as a thing in order to escape the condition of a thing by the same act of sincerity?" For example, the "man who confesses that he is evil has exchanged his disturbing 'freedom for evil' for an inanimate character of evil; he *is* evil... But by the same stroke, he escapes from that *thing*, since it is he who contemplates it..." In performing the meritorious act of sincerely confessing himself to be evil, he "is not the evil man as he is evil but as he is beyond his evilness." Hence the adage, "A sin confessed is half pardoned" (108–9).

From the foregoing considerations, Sartre is able to conclude, not only that sincerity is as paradoxical as bad faith, but that "the essential structure of sincerity does not differ from that of bad faith since the sincere man constitutes himself as what he is *in order not to be it*" (109). The ideal of sincerity—to be what I am—turns out to be "a task impossible to achieve, of which the very meaning is in contradiction with the structure of my

---

6. Note that throughout this discussion Sartre is concerned "only with the sincerity which aims at itself in present immanence," and not with the "sincerity which bears on the past" (110). I can be sincere about who I was precisely because my past self is already an external object in relation to who I am.

consciousness." Whether in good faith or bad faith, I cannot get around the fact that *"consciousness is not what it is"* (105). If consciousness could be what it is, if I as a conscious being could be what I am, then bad faith would be not only paradoxical, but "forever impossible" (101). But the analysis of sincerity shows the impossibility of consciously being what I am–and therefore the possibility of consciously failing to be what I am: "Bad faith is possible only because sincerity is conscious of missing its goal inevitably, due to its very nature" (111).

"How can we believe by bad faith in the concepts which we forge expressly to persuade ourselves?" Sartre asks. In other words, how is it possible to deceive ourselves by making ourselves believe the opposite of what we already believe? Sartre's detour through the paradox of sincerity allows him to shed light on the paradox of bad faith by shifting the focus of attention from the problem of contradictory beliefs to the problematic nature of belief itself. The "essential problem of bad faith is a problem of belief," he affirms. Since the deceiver and the believer are one and the same, bad faith "can not be either a cynical lie or certainty." The only path open to it is to renounce certainty, resolving "to count itself satisfied when it is barely persuaded, to force itself in decisions to adhere to uncertain truths." While "bad faith is conscious of its structure," it is able to persuade itself that it is persuaded when it is not really persuaded because "it has taken precautions by deciding... that non-persuasion is the structure of all convictions" (112–13).

At this point the best way to appreciate Sartre's argument is to pause and compare his treatment of bad faith with Davidson's approach to self-deception. Davidsonian self-deception is in good faith. Although one belief is motivated by the desire to get away from another belief, it does not have to skulk about–a barrier protects it from running into the inimical belief. Thanks to the existence of this barrier between contradictory beliefs, self-deception can occur without there being any need to lie to oneself. Indeed, lying to oneself is quite impossible. It is impossible not because one will know the lie is not true–to believe the lie and to know the truth would in itself entail no more than the existence of contradictory beliefs–but because *one will know one is lying*. What defines a lie is not the liar's disbelief in its content, Davidson observes, but his intentional concealment of his own attitude with respect to this content. A liar must not only "intend to represent himself as believing what he does not," but also "intend to keep this intention... hidden from his hearer" (88). It is this meta-intention to hide one's intention which poses a special problem in the case of lying to oneself. Can one hide one's own mendacious intent from oneself? Davidson's answer is an unequivocal no.

Sartre's answer to the same question is, just as unequivocally, yes and no. But Davidson's admirably clear analysis will help us better understand Sartre's argument as well. Indeed, a careful reading of Sartre will reveal that he analyzes the problem of lying to oneself at the same two levels as Davidson. In the ordinary case of lying, Sartre notes, "there is no difficulty in holding that the liar must make the project of the lie in entire clarity and that he must possess a complete comprehension of the lie and of the truth which he is altering." The liar knows the truth and alters it, deceiving another person into believing an untruth. But if the person deceived is oneself, one must simultaneously believe the truth and believe the untruth. Here Sartre is addressing the first level of analysis, the level of contradictory beliefs: how can I believe the lie if I know the truth? Just as the ordinary liar must hide the truth from the other person in order to permit belief in the lie, Sartre assumes that if one is to make oneself believe a lie, one must hide the truth from oneself. I have already quoted Sartre's observation that in lying to oneself, "I must know in my capacity as deceiver the truth which is hidden from me in my capacity as the one deceived." Thus, if bad faith "is indeed a lie to oneself... what changes everything is the fact that in bad faith it is from myself that I am hiding the truth."

But the truth is not the only thing I must hide from myself. "To this difficulty is added another which is derived from the total translucency of consciousness." The ordinary liar makes the project of the lie in entire clarity: "The liar intends to deceive and he does not seek to hide this intention from himself nor to disguise the translucency of consciousness... It is sufficient that an overall opacity hide his intentions from the *Other*." Now, bad faith also entails intention: "consciousness affects itself with bad faith. There must be an original intention and a project of bad faith..." But the translucency of consciousness would seem to imply that I cannot hide my own intention to be in bad faith from myself: "That which affects itself with bad faith must be conscious (of) its bad faith..." Here Sartre is addressing the second level of analysis, the level of the intention to lie which one must intend to hide from oneself: how can I lie to myself if I know I am lying? Sartre initially acknowledges that I cannot hope to succeed "if I deliberately and cynically attempt to lie to myself" (88–89).

However, we have seen that for Sartre there is an alternative to such cynicism, and that alternative is bad faith itself. Even if I cannot cynically conceal from myself my intent to persuade myself of something in bad faith, I can always assume an attitude of bad faith with regard to this intent: "at the very moment when I was disposed to put myself in bad faith, I of necessity was in bad faith with respect to this same disposition." In other words, "the project of bad faith must be itself in bad faith." Can one hide one's intent to be in bad faith from oneself after all? Yes and no: "The decision to be in bad faith does not dare to speak its name; it believes itself and does not believe itself in bad faith; it believes itself and does not believe itself in good faith" (112–13).

A study of the architecture of this last sentence, with its carefully balanced symmetries, will allow us to grasp more clearly the way Sartre has constructed his answer to the question of how one can persuade oneself to believe something in bad faith. There are, we saw, two levels to this construction. The first level is that of the *content* of the belief: one must deceive oneself into believing something untrue even though one knows the truth. Bad faith at this level entails the coexistence of contradictory beliefs. The second level is that of the *intent* behind the belief: one must set out to deceive oneself even though one knows one is setting out to deceive oneself. In the sentence in question, Sartre is directly addressing only this second level, but he does so in a way that fully recapitulates his first-level argument. The same analysis applies to both levels since, in order to hide from oneself the true belief, one must also hide from oneself the intent to hide from oneself the true belief. The decision to be in bad faith must itself be in bad faith: it must believe itself to be in good faith even though it believes it is not. Thus, the problem of how to keep hidden from oneself one's intention to deceive likewise comes down to a problem of contradictory beliefs: one must believe one does not intend to deceive oneself even though one knows one does intend to do so.[7]

The foregoing could be summarized, in Sartre's language, by saying that the "decision to be in bad faith" believes itself in bad faith and believes itself in good faith. That indeed is what Sartre says, but he does not

71

7. It is not clear what would stop Davidson from making a parallel theoretical move within the terms of his own theory. That is, if contradictory beliefs can coexist separated by a boundary within the mind, why not posit the existence of a like boundary between the knowledge that one intends to lie to oneself and a belief that one does not so intend? There would then be no need to rule out a priori the possibility of lying to oneself.

leave it at that. The actual sentence that we just saw is considerably more complex. Not only does the "decision" believe itself in bad faith, "it believes itself and does not believe itself in bad faith," and not only does it believe itself in good faith, "it believes itself and does not believe itself in good faith." Sartre's phrasing here is far from arbitrary. It reflects the essential articulation in his argument between the coexistence of contradictory beliefs and the coexistence of belief and disbelief. The possibility of simultaneously believing contradictory propositions rests on the possibility of simultaneously believing and not believing each proposition. Because conscious belief, like conscious sincerity, is impossible, Sartre will argue, it is possible not to believe what one is conscious of believing. Because nonpersuasion is the structure of all convictions, it is possible to believe with conviction what one is conscious of not believing.

For his part, Davidson rejects out of hand the idea that a person may at once believe and not believe: how can one assert such a thing without falling into contradiction oneself? Either people believe or they don't... This objection assumes that the phenomena of consciousness can be described in the same common-sense fashion as an external object, such as a table. But one may question whether it is really common sense not to distinguish consciousness from a table. Sartre establishes such a distinction explicitly. For Sartre, the self-consciousness of consciousness, its presence to itself, paradoxically means that it can never coincide with itself.

Always one step ahead of itself, always just beyond its own grasp, consciousness "must necessarily be what it is not and not be what it is." In this sense, the principle of identity does not apply to consciousness. "Indeed it is impossible to define it as coincidence with itself. Of this table I can say only that it is purely and simply *this* table. But I can not limit myself to saying that my belief is belief; my belief is the consciousness (of) belief" (120–21). The problem is that "if I know that I believe, the belief appears to me as pure subjective determination," as in the expression "I do not know; I believe so." Hence "to know that one believes is no longer to believe" (114). Here one might retort that Sartre is playing on two meanings of the word "believe." But more than word play is involved. Sartre is asserting that a belief in the first sense cannot be known without degenerating into a belief in the second sense. The very nature of belief is transmuted by the reflexivity of consciousness.

By taking the reflexivity of consciousness as the starting point for his argument, Sartre is able to produce a theory of self-deception that is less complicated than Davidson's. More complex, perhaps, and certainly expressed in a more difficult language,[8] but less complicated in the sense of being more parsimonious, of introducing fewer complications. Davidson starts out more straightforwardly in appearance, by decreeing that beliefs are either there or they are not, with no ifs, ands, or buts. The reflexivity of consciousness is thus abstracted out of the overall picture. Yet reflexivity is rightly found to pose a problem when it comes to self-deception. Deception is easy to understand when it takes place between two different people, but not when the deceiver and the deceived are one and the same. As Sartre puts it, "How then can the lie subsist if the duality which conditions it is suppressed?" (89).

73

Davidson's solution, like Freud's, is to recreate the missing duality by introducing an artificial division within the mind. This solution is consistent with the premise that the mind is a thing like a table, susceptible to being cut into two. Sartre remarks that Freud cuts the psychic whole into two by distinguishing the ego from the id. Davidson is more parsimonious than Freud since he dispenses with the id. But he maintains the minimal complication necessary to produce the desired duality: the idea of a dividing line. The problem is that the only evidence cited for the existence of such a dividing line is the fact of contradictory beliefs. The dividing line cannot explain this fact if its own existence is deduced from the fact to be explained. That would be circular reasoning. As a rule, when a theory begins by suppressing a real circularity intrinsic to its object, that circularity comes back to haunt it in the form of circular reasoning (see Anspach 1991). The suppressed circularity in this case is the one intrinsic to consciousness as a reflexive process.

We don't know that there are dividing lines inside the mind, but we do know that consciousness is reflexive. Indeed, reflexivity is the defining feature of consciousness. In Sartre's terminology, consciousness is present to itself, and he builds his argument on the observation that "*presence to* always implies duality, at least a virtual separation" (124). By showing how the known phenomenon of reflexivity always entails a certain duality, and then relating the duality necessary to understand self-deception to this duality virtually present in all consciousness, Sartre avoids the need to invent an autonomous agent of duality not known to exist. He does not

---

8. Which I have gone out of my way to simplify as far as possible for the purposes of the present essay, even at the risk of oversimplification.

have to hew the mind in two because he has located the duality already latent in the self-reflexive unity of *one and the same* consciousness. It is a paradoxical duality, one that involves phenomenological vicious circles, but the theoretical recognition accorded these real vicious circles spares Sartre from falling into artificial vicious circles in his reasoning.

The phenomenological vicious circles described by Sartre are variants on the type of paradox to which Gregory Bateson, in a paper published the same year as the English translation of *Being and Nothingness*, would give the celebrated name "double bind." A double bind is, in essence, the pragmatic equivalent of the liar's paradox inasmuch as it involves a contradictory self-reference which confuses two different logical levels. The difference is that the liar's paradox can be deemed purely semantic and ruled out of order on the grounds that, by making the accusation of lying refer to itself as its own object, it violates the necessary logical distinction between a statement as a linguistic expression and the object to which a statement refers. The double bind, however, creates an actual pragmatic dilemma for its target by putting the person in the position of obeying a command which can neither be obeyed nor disobeyed, owing to its paradoxical form, and which cannot be ignored either, given the vital nature of the relationship between the individual giving the command and the one receiving it. Thus, where "This statement is false" is a purely semantic paradox, "Disobey this order" is a pragmatic paradox.

Although "Disobey this order" may sound improbably perverse, equivalent injunctions are not so infrequently encountered in families or couples, where one person may reproach the other for not displaying sufficient independence: "You're too submissive; don't always do what I say"; "Love me because you want to and not because I tell you to." Bateson's followers Watzlawick, Beavin, and Jackson observe that injunctions of this type boil down to "Be spontaneous!" (199–200). If one tries to be spontaneous in response, one is not being spontaneous but merely following orders. But since one is not supposed to follow orders, one is manifesting spontaneity after all—in which case one is doing exactly what one was told… One can neither obey nor disobey because obeyal leads to disobeyal and disobeyal to obeyal in a continuous oscillation.

Bateson formulated the hypothesis that pragmatic paradoxes in the communication between parent and child are a factor in the etiology of schizophrenia. In particular, he suggested that a schizophrenic's mother typically sends the child contradictory messages at different levels which keep the child trapped in an oscillation between closeness and distance: "hostile or withdrawing behavior which is aroused whenever the child approaches her" leads to "simulated loving or approaching behavior... when the child responds to her hostile and withdrawing behavior, as a way of denying that she is withdrawing." The second message is located at a second level insofar as it constitutes a comment on the first message or sequence of messages: "Yet by its nature it denies the existence of those messages which it is about, *i.e.*, the hostile withdrawal" (213).

The mother's object is to hide from the child and from herself the truth of her own hostility toward the child. This truth threatens to come to the surface whenever the child reacts to her involuntary signs of discomfort in the face of his affectionate approaches. When the child responds to the mother's withdrawal by withdrawing in turn, the mother then scolds the child in a way that reaffirms the mother's loving attitude and puts the onus for the distance between them on the child. For example, the mother of a schizophrenic patient was observed to stiffen when he threw his arm around her shoulders in greeting. When he then withdrew his arm, she asked, "Don't you love me anymore?" (217). The mother acts as an external censor in relation to the child, systematically repressing every manifestation of the child's knowledge of her hostility toward him. But this is not a simple case of the duality between deceiver and deceived. The mother reveals the truth herself before hastening to conceal it; the child is reacting to her own manifestations of hostility. Moreover, the mother's deception undercuts itself to the precise extent that it is successful: if the child responds positively to her feigned affection, she will revert to hostile withdrawal, prompting the child to withdraw once more. And a symmetrical phenomenon is observed on the child's side: any manifestation of belief in the mother's affection undercuts itself by prompting her to withdraw once more.

The self-cancelling character of both the mother's and the child's attempts to conceal the mother's hostility reflects the fact that these symmetrical attempts at deception really involve symmetrical attempts at *self-deception*. The truth of the mother's hostility is accessible to both parties at the level of involuntary communication. Bateson argues that, given the importance of the child's relationship to the mother, he will prefer to go along with her reinterpretation of the signals passing between them "rather than recognize his mother's deception. This means that he must deceive himself about his own internal state in order to support mother in her de-

75

ception." The result is that "the child must systematically distort his perception of metacommunicative signals" (214), a type of behavior which Bateson relates to the communication pathologies observed in schizophrenic patients. The child must accept at face value his mother's expressions of affection while discounting the metacommunicative signals that contradict them. Given the mother's ill-concealed hostility, her simulated affection may not be very persuasive. For the child to be persuaded, he must adopt a skewed outlook with respect to affective communication in general. To paraphrase Sartre's observation about bad faith, the child must decide that nonpersuasion is the structure of all affections.

76

The child is deceiving himself insofar as his mother's hostile withdrawal must make him conscious of the truth. At the same time, however, he is aided in the task of self-deception by his mother's periodic utterances of affectionate approach. Similarly, the mother is deceiving herself inasmuch as the child's withdrawal must make her aware of the truth, but she is helped in the task of self-deception by the child's periodic attempts at affectionate approach. The internal duality implied by each person's self-deception is able to subsist thanks to the duality manifested by the other. Just as one sometimes encounters cases of *folie à deux*, we can view this as a case of "self-deception *à deux*." The *pas de deux* of withdrawal and approach between mother and child is an outward manifestation of the "double activity of repulsion and attraction" which Sartre associates with self-deception.

We saw earlier that for Sartre, the "reflexive idea of hiding something from oneself" implies a "double activity" tending at once "to maintain and locate the thing to be concealed" and "to repress and disguise it." Sartre's analysis of self-deception enables us to discover the underlying structure of the maternal double bind described by Bateson: the physical and affective dance of withdrawal and approach derives from the double activity of repulsion and attraction involved in the parties' attempts to conceal from themselves the truth of the mother's hostility. Conversely, Bateson's analysis of the double bind allows us to better grasp the oscillatory logic of bad faith as described by Sartre. Sartre speaks of the "'evanescence' of bad faith," which "vacillates continually between good faith and cynicism" (90). The "double activity" involved in hiding something from oneself turns out to entail a kind of double bind. The difference between Sartre and Bateson is that Bateson identifies double binds in relationships between two people, while Sartre shows that there can be "a double activity in the heart of unity" (94). In Sartre, the internal duality implied by self-deception is not correlated with an external duality, as in Bateson, but with the internal duality implied by self-consciousness. The reflexivity of consciousness means that a paradoxical duality already exists in one's relationship to oneself: "The presence of being to itself implies a detachment on the part of being in relation to itself" (124). And self-deception involves a pragmatic paradox in one's relation to oneself. It is a double bind unfolding within the confines of a single mind.

Sartre does point to a pragmatic paradox in a relationship between two people when he discusses sincerity. As we have seen, the paradox of sincerity brings into play an internal duality similar to that found in bad faith. In fact, Sartre finds in both sincerity and bad faith "the same game of mirrors," "a perpetual passage from the being which is what it is to the being which is not what it is and inversely from the being which is not what it is to the being which is what it is" (110). But sincerity is more likely than bad faith to be the object of an external solicitation. So it is that Sartre comes closest to a paradoxical injunction of the type described by Watzlawick's team when he considers the case of a "champion of sincerity" who insists that the Other confess his nature: "The critic asks the man then to be what he is in order no longer to be what he is," he demands "that he constitute himself as a thing, precisely in order no longer to treat him as a thing. And this contradiction is constitutive of the demand of sincerity" (108).

The demand "Be sincere!" may sound like the equivalent of "Be spontaneous!" yet this would appear to be only half true. If saying "I am evil" can be a ploy to escape being evil, not being evil does not make one evil again. Confession of sin is, as Sartre notes, a step toward pardon, and pardon does not necessarily return the penitent to being a sinner. Despite Sartre's indications to the contrary, the paradox of sincerity does not display the oscillatory structure characteristic of bad faith. Instead, the paradox of sincerity seems to offer the hope of a one-way ticket out of being what one is. In a sense, this is the principle on which Freudian psychotherapy is founded: if I confess to the analyst what I am, I may find I am able to transcend my previous nature. Similarly, in AA's famous "12-step" approach to overcoming alcoholism—analyzed by Bateson—the "first step demands that the alcoholic agree that he is powerless over alcohol," and this "experience of defeat not only serves to convince the alcoholic that change is necessary; it *is* the first step in that change" (312–13). "Be sincere" in these cases is akin to "prescribing the symptom," a particular form of "be spontaneous" used by some of Bateson's followers to help a patient assert voluntary control over an undesirable behavioral symptom that ordinarily manifests itself independently of the patient's will—that is to say, spontaneously. Just as the ordinary double bind makes a desirable spontaneity impossible, "prescribing the symptom" operates as a "therapeutic double bind" by rendering an *un*desirable spontaneity impossible, so that a patient ordered to manifest a pathological behavior may finally succeed in controlling it (Watzlawick, Beavin and Jackson, 237). To the extent that these pragmatic paradoxes allow me to make a permanent move from *being what I am* to *no longer being what I was*, they are not true double binds. Rather than trapping me in an endless oscillation, they help me out of the trap.

We are now ready to return to the subject of madness with a new question to ask. If confessing what I am is a way of escaping what I am, why should the same tactic not work for a patient suffering from mental illness? Earlier, I raised the possibility that patients may resist recognizing the truth about themselves, and I noted that such resistance could be interpreted as a sign of bad faith. Perhaps if the patient sincerely recognized the truth, a cure could be effected… Does the paradox of sincerity offer a way out of madness?

3. Madness and Sanity: A Paradoxical Divide

The previous discussion could lead one to believe that resistance is the key obstacle to the mental patient's recovery. Whether or not one takes resistance to be in bad faith, one is liable to imagine that a stubborn refusal to accept the truth is the source of all difficulty. If only the patient would recognize he is suffering from delusions, if only the patient would acknowledge he needs help…! However, the paradox of self-division proves to be even more stubborn than resistance. For it would be a mistake to think that all psychotics vociferously resist therapy, actively defending their delusions. After observing that patients cannot be treated with dialectical formulas and syllogisms, Esquirol goes on to explain that a patient may "very well know the disorder of his intellectual faculties," follow the therapist's reasoning, and even strive to believe what he is told, and yet still "lack the force of conviction": "…I know all that, but my idea is there, and I am not cured" (quoted by Gauchet and Swain, 475).

Esquirol reports the statement of one patient in particular which suggests it is not enough for a psychotic to recognize he needs help: "'If I could believe with you that I am mad, I would soon be cured,' one of them said to me, 'but I cannot acquire this belief'"[9] (quoted by Gauchet and Swain, 477). Here we have a truly model patient: one who sincerely recognizes he is suffering from delusions, one who acknowledges he needs help. What is the obstacle here to acquiring belief? Not lack of knowledge: the patient implicitly acknowledges the validity of what he is unable to believe. He believes he *should* believe he is crazy—indeed, he believes quite literally that he is crazy not to: not to believe he is crazy is what keeps him from being cured. Now, to believe he is not yet cured is to believe that he is still crazy. So, on the one hand, he believes he is crazy, and yet, by his own testimony, he does not believe he is crazy: "I cannot acquire this belief." Note that what we have here is not the mere coexistence of contradictory beliefs, but the coexistence of belief and disbelief. Gauchet and Swain speak of a "mysterious and impalpable separation" that can prevent a patient "from receiving completely what he nevertheless succeeds quite well in understanding..." (475).

79

Let us try to get to the bottom of this mystery. What is it that separates the patient from his own belief, what is it that keeps his belief and his disbelief apart? Is there a wall between them? At this point I would like to propose an image which I think is better than that of a wall. The patient's belief and disbelief are not on opposite sides of a wall—they are on opposite sides of a Möbius strip. They are not separated, for they are inextricably linked, but they are linked in a way that forever keeps them from coming together. In other words, the connection between them is, in the true sense of the word, *paradoxical*. The best way to understand what I mean by this is to come back to the problem of lying to oneself.

Recall that for Davidson, a liar must not only "intend to represent himself as believing what he does not," but also "intend to keep this intention... hidden from his hearer" (88). I tried to show earlier that for Sartre as well as for Davidson, it is this latter intention—the meta-intention to keep one's intention hidden—which poses a special problem in the case of lying to oneself. There is nothing paradoxical in the ordinary case of lying to someone else because here the concealment of the intention to

---

9. "Si je pouvais croire avec vous que je suis fou, je serais bientôt guéri, me disait l'un d'eux, mais je ne puis acquérir cette croyance."

J

deceive is not problematic. As Sartre puts it, "The liar intends to deceive and he does not seek to hide this intention from himself... As for his flaunted intention of telling the truth ('I'd never want to deceive you! This is true! I swear it!')—all this, of course, is the object of an inner negation, but also it is not recognized by the liar as *his* intention" (88). In order to underscore that the concealment of intention is the key to lying—and not, for example, the fact of saying the opposite of what one believes— Davidson observes that "a liar who believes that his hearer is perverse may say the opposite of what he intends his hearer to believe" (88).

What if, instead, it is the liar who is perverse? What if the liar warns the hearer that what he is saying is the opposite of what the hearer should believe: "I want to deceive you! This statement is false! I swear it!" Now we have a case of lying to someone else that is just as paradoxical as lying to oneself—and, I would argue, paradoxical for the same reason. For if it is true that the concealment of the intention to deceive is ordinarily not problematic, the *disclosure* of the intention to deceive *is* problematic, even in the case of lying to someone else. To the extent that this disclosure is self-reflexive, the person on the receiving end is confronted with the liar's paradox. This is just as true if the person on the receiving end is oneself. Lying to oneself is especially susceptible to paradox because one cannot avoid disclosing one's intent to oneself. If I lie to myself, I will know that "I am lying."

Indeed, one may be tempted to conclude that lying to oneself is simply impossible: how can I lie to myself without knowing it? But the question can just as easily be turned around: how *can* I know it? For if I know I am lying, I cannot conceal from myself my intent to deceive. But if I do not conceal my intent to deceive, I am not lying—and so I cannot know that I am... And this lack of knowledge may make it easier for me to lie to myself after all. To be sure, an alternative interpretation would be that by not concealing from myself my intent to deceive, I have quite simply failed in my attempt to lie to myself. Here I would reply by citing Sartre's remark that the essence of bad faith resides in the acceptance of such failure. In fact, it will be recalled, Sartre likewise recognizes the impossibility of deliberately and cynically lying to oneself. To "the extent that I am conscious of my bad faith," he says, then it appears "that I must be in good faith." But in that case "this whole psychic system is annihilated. We must agree in fact that if I deliberately and cynically attempt to lie to myself, I completely fail in this undertaking..." (89). However, Sartre later goes on to assert that, while "it is very true that bad faith does not succeed in believing in what it wishes to believe," "it is precisely as the acceptance of not believing what it believes that it is bad faith" (115).

In other words, bad faith takes itself for good faith. And, I would add, this possibility is enhanced by the very fact that I am conscious of my bad faith, if it is precisely this fact which allows me to draw the conclusion that "I must be in good faith." Consciousness of bad faith leads to a belief in good faith, the belief in good faith makes bad faith possible, bad faith is accompanied by consciousness of bad faith, and consciousness of bad faith leads to a belief in good faith... In short, the belief in bad faith leads to a belief in good faith and the belief in good faith to a belief in bad faith. This psychic system is not annihilated, it oscillates indefinitely in the manner of the liar's paradox.

81

The oscillatory structure of the liar's paradox or its pragmatic equivalent derives from the presence of a contradictory self-reference confusing logical levels. An ordinary lie merely negates something external to itself, namely, the truth; as Sartre notes, the "negation does not bear on consciousness itself" (87). Lying to oneself is paradoxical not at the level of the consciousness of the truth, but at the level of the consciousness of consciousness. To know I am lying to myself is not to know it: the negation bears on consciousness itself. To set out to lie to oneself therefore means placing oneself in a double bind. Sincere recognition that one is lying will not put an end to the oscillation—it is responsible for it. The paradox of sincerity no longer offers a one-way ticket out of being what one is when what one confesses to being is a liar.

We are now ready to return to the case of the patient who tells the therapist he is not cured of madness because he cannot believe he is mad. In fact, the patient's statement can also be usefully compared to the liar's paradox. If Eubulides says "I am lying," is he lying? His statement is false if it is true and true if it is false. We cannot say whether it is true or false; we can only identify it as a paradoxically twisted metastatement about its own truth or falsity. In the same way, we cannot say whether the patient believes or does not believe he is mad when he says, "I cannot acquire this belief." We can only identify this as the statement of a paradoxically twisted metabelief about his own belief.

The difficulty in interpreting such a statement doubtless represents a tricky problem for the therapist. Gauchet and Swain point out that Esquirol uses the same quotation, or equivalent variants on it, in two completely opposite contexts. The first time that Esquirol quotes the patient's statement "If I could believe I am mad I would soon be cured," it is in order to show how the unexpected care the asylum gives the patient provokes a "salutary shock," a "moral contrast," which may help the patient "glimpse the possibility he is sick; and is not this result the surest token of recovery?" Later in the same book Esquirol provides a new version of the same quotation: "I comprehend very well what you are telling me… I follow quite well your reasoning, if I could understand you and if I could convince myself, I would no longer be crazy, you would have cured me."[10] This time, however, the lesson Esquirol draws is as pessimistic as it was optimistic the first time: the patient's tantalizing lucidity is not enough to accomplish the recovery it seemed to betoken (Gauchet and Swain, 477–78).

The ambivalence of the ways in which Esquirol construes the same quotation is a reflection of the intrinsic ambivalence of the quotation itself. One is tempted to accuse Esquirol of simultaneously entertaining contradictory beliefs about it, as if he were himself ensnared in the paradox. Now, if the paradox is a trap for the therapist who confronts it from the outside, how much more must it be one for the patient who struggles with it from within. The patient's statement is based on a true insight: a sure symptom of madness is that, unlike those around him, the madman does not know he is mad. Thus, when the protagonist of the Isaac Bashevis Singer story discussed by Alfred Mele, "Gimpel the Fool," lets his wife persuade him that her infidelity is only a hallucination on his part, we may take Gimpel's belief that he hallucinated as proof that he is not crazy—he is just a fool. A true madman's disbelief of the fact that he is mad is the wall that separates him from those around him. Our problem is to understand how this disbelief can coexist with knowledge in the absence of an internal wall within the patient. Esquirol's patient is no fool. He knows that if, like Gimpel, he could convince himself he is suffering from delusions, then he would no longer be mad. His knowledge can be summed up as follows: "I am crazy because I don't know I am crazy." But this paradoxical self-knowledge is of no help in moving from being crazy to not being crazy. Like Esquirol, the patient does not know what to believe about what he believes. His belief is not walled off from his disbelief,

---

10. "J'entends très bien ce que vous me dites… je suis bien vos raisonnemens, si je pouvais vous comprendre et si je pouvais me convaincre, je ne serais plus fou, vous m'auriez guéri."

it is bound to it, but the connection is as twisted as that between opposite sides of a Möbius strip, where each side leads directly to the other. As a result, he is caught up in a perpetual oscillation.

In case the reader is still not persuaded that the paradoxical form of the self-knowledge of madness constitutes the key to the problem, let us try to imagine what it would mean to escape from that paradox. I think we will find that we fall into a "catch-22" situation of the purest kind–precisely the one invented by Joseph Heller in his novel of World War II.[11] Everyone is familiar with the dilemma of Heller's anti-hero, Yossarian. Hoping to avoid flying any more combat missions, Yossarian "decides to go crazy." He consults the medic, Doc Daneeka, who fills him in on the rules. On the one hand, "There's a rule saying I have to ground anyone who's crazy," but, on the other hand, "Anyone who wants to get out of combat duty isn't really crazy." In short, "There was only one catch and that was Catch-22, which specified that a concern for one's own safety in the face of dangers that were real and immediate was the process of a rational mind" (46–47).

Now, although "Catch-22" has become a familiar symbol of the "craziness" of wartime, the "craziness" of bureaucracy, and so on, Yossarian is not really crazy, of course–he just wants to escape the "craziness" of those around him. What may be missed is that the same catch will also apply to someone who really *is* crazy and is trying to escape his own craziness. For, if instead of saying "I am crazy because I don't know I'm crazy," one cuts through that annoying paradox and goes directly to the required self-knowledge in seemingly unmediated form: "I am crazy"–one finds oneself right smack-dab back in an even purer form of the liar's paradox.[12] As

---

11. It is said that if James Watt had not invented the steam engine, someone else would have, for the idea was in the air: it was "steam-engine time." In the same way, the period during and after World War II seems to have been "double bind time." *Catch-22*–whose narrative is one long series of pragmatic paradoxes of which the one I discuss in the text is only the most famous example–appeared in 1955. Sartre's discussion of bad faith is part of *Being and Nothingness*, which was published in France during World War II and appeared in English translation in 1956. The same year saw the publication of the paper "Toward a Theory of Schizophrenia" (reprinted in *Steps to an Ecology of Mind*, 201–27) in which Gregory Bateson, Don D. Jackson, Jay Haley and John H. Weakland introduced the term "double bind." Bateson worked in psychological warfare with the Office of Strategic Services during World War II, and he later developed the double bind theory while working with patients in the Veterans Administration Hospital in Palo Alto.

12. Cp. Bateson's hypothesis "that the message 'This is play' establishes a paradoxical frame comparable to Epimenides' paradox," to the extent that the message can be re-

Doc Daneeka tells Yossarian, "you can't let crazy people decide whether you're crazy or not, can you?" (46).

By casting doubt on the judgment of crazy people, Doc Daneeka helps us see why it is so hard to judge oneself crazy. The judgment applies not to any particular deluded belief external to itself, but to the very consciousness doing the judging, and it does so in a way that negates that consciousness. The negation bears on consciousness itself. If craziness implies a lack of awareness of being crazy, then recognition of being crazy would seem to be necessary in order to stop being crazy. But the sincerest recognition that one is crazy is no better than sincere recognition that one is a liar. Like lying to oneself, recognizing one is crazy means sticking one's head in a double bind. Gregory Bateson's hypothesis is that double binds may contribute to provoking entry into psychosis. In this paper, I have considered the question from the other end. My hypothesis is that a double bind may contribute to blocking exit from psychosis. If leaving madness necessitated recognizing one is mad, the road from not recognizing one is mad to not being mad could prove impossibly twisted.

References

Anspach, M. R. 1991. "From the Double Bind to Autonomy: Epistemological Challenges in Contemporary French Theory." Ph.D. diss., Stanford University.

---

phrased "All statements within this frame are untrue" and that this statement "is itself to be taken as a premise in evaluating its own truth or untruth." Bateson anticipates an objection to this hypothesis: "It could be urged that even if the first statement is false, there remains a logical possibility that some of the other statements in the frame are untrue." Bateson's response is to note that it is "a characteristic of unconscious or 'primary-process' thinking that the thinker is unable to discriminate between 'some' and 'all', and unable to discriminate between 'not all' and 'none'. It seems that the achievement of these discriminations is performed by higher or more conscious mental processes which serve in the non-psychotic individual to correct the black-and-white thinking of the lower levels" (184–85).

I would argue that "I am crazy" should not be rephrased "All statements within this frame are untrue." The delusions of the mad can easily be limited in number rather than all-encompassing. What is at issue is less particular deluded beliefs than craziness as an overall outlook. "I am crazy" is not a statement about what is contained in the frame, but a statement about the frame itself. It should therefore be rephrased "This statement is untrue."

―――. 1995a. "Délire individuel et effervescence collective." In H. Grivois and J.-P. Dupuy, eds., *Mécanismes mentaux, mécanismes sociaux: de la psychose à la panique.* Paris: Editions La Découverte. 97–107.

―――. 1995b. "The Solitary Madman and the Madding Crowd: Symmetrical Morphogeneses of the Social Bond." *Synthesis* I: 129–45.

Bateson, G. 1972. *Steps to an Ecology of Mind.* New York: Ballantine.

Claridge, G. 1985. *Origins of Mental Illness.* Oxford and New York: Blackwell.

Davidson, D. 1986. "Deception and Division." In J. Elster, ed., *The Multiple Self.* Cambridge: Cambridge University Press. 79–92.

Gauchet, M. and G. Swain. 1980. *La pratique de l'esprit humain: l'institution asilaire et la révolution démocratique.* Paris: Gallimard. Translation forthcoming from Princeton University Press.

Heller, J. 1955; reprint, 1962. *Catch-22.* New York: Dell.

Mele, A. R. 1998. "Two Paradoxes of Self-Deception." Paper Presented at the Symposium on Self-Deception, Stanford, California, February 1993. In J. P. Dupuy, ed., *Self-Deception and Paradoxes of Rationality.* Stanford: CSLI Publications (this volume).

Sartre, J.-P. 1966. *Being and Nothingness.* Trans. H. E. Barnes. New York: Washington Square Press.

Swain, G. 1977. *Le sujet de la folie: naissance de la psychiatrie.* Toulouse: Privat.

Watzlawick, P., J. H. Beavin, and D. D. Jackson. 1967. *Pragmatics of Human Communication.* New York: Norton.

Whately, R. 1819; reprint, 1985. *Historic Doubts Relative to Napoleon Bonaparte,* ed. R. S. Pomeroy. Berkeley and London: Scholar Press.

85

Keeping Self-Deception in Perspective

Lawrence Beyer

If one accepts the suggestion that self-deception involves simultaneously held beliefs that are contradictory (that p, and that not-p) or at least inconsistent (that the evidence favors 'p,' and that not-p), then some special structure must be postulated that allows these to coexist in the same mind without either extinguishing the other. Donald Davidson sees this function served by a partitioning that bounds different, though overlapping, territories within the mind and keeps their contents from coming into contact (e.g., 1998, 8).

Mark Anspach, however, expresses Sartre-inspired misgivings about this picture. Taking psychotics (e.g., "the sort of individuals who believe they are... Napoleon" (1998, 60)) to exemplify "extreme self-deception" (61), he claims that self-deception "involves" and "requires" "the simultaneous presence of contradictory beliefs" (60),[1] produced by a *paradoxical* kind of resistance to a proposition known, believed, or suspected to be true. But Anspach says little about the central beliefs constituting the self-

---

1. In general, it is not clear whether Anspach's references to 'self-deception' and 'bad faith' ought to be taken to refer only to the contradiction form of self-deception, or whether his account can be generalized to cases involving opposed-but-not-contradictory beliefs (i.e., that the evidence argues that p, and that not-p).

deception (e.g., 'I am not Napoleon,' 'I am Napoleon'); his focus is one level removed, upon self-awareness of that condition. Such awareness is available to all self-deceivers, he suggests (73, 80–81), but only within an "oscillatory structure" shared with unawareness (77, 81). The conflicting second-order beliefs (or belief plus nonbelief) coexist together stably, not as if partitioned apart, but as if united though distinct on the double-yet-single side of a möbius strip (79, 82–83). (Regarding madness specifically, the unresolvable oscillation is said by Anspach to block the self-awareness path to a cure.)

My agenda for this paper is an amalgamation of several lines of inquiry. After examining, in general terms, the gratuitousness of self-deception at-tributions, I cast doubts upon Davidson's arguments that lying to oneself is impossible and so cannot be what self-deception involves. This is fol-lowed by a rebuttal of Anspach's dismissal of partitioning accounts, and a critical analysis of his speculations concerning the "paradoxical" "oscilla-tory logic" (1998, 76–77, 81) of the self-deceiver's (or madman's) cognitive predicament. Finally, I provide two short appendices, the first clarifying one aspect of the distinction between self-deception and wishful think-ing, the second offering a detailed explanation of why belief in one's own self-deception need not be paradoxical.

1. Attributing Self-Deception

Self-deception is not merely the possession of logically inconsistent be-liefs, for these can be acquired and maintained innocently. Nor is it simply the adoption of a proposition as one's belief out of a desire for that event or state of affairs, for that may only be wishful thinking (see Appendix A). Self-deception seems to require that aversion to one already-present belief (that p, or that the evidence favors 'p') motivate action that produces adoption of a contrary belief (that not-p).[2]

---

2. For purposes of this essay, I stick rather close in some ways to Davidson's basic models of irrationality. On Al Mele's (1998) account, by contrast, self-deception can be initiated not only by an aversion to believing that p, but also by a desire to believe that not-p, and these cause self-deception by instigating biased processes of evidence gathering, interpre-tation, and evaluation—thereby producing a belief that not-p without any intentional ac-tions having been taken to bring this about. Thus, for Mele, wishful thinking may be only "a form of self-deception" (Mele 1987, 135) or perhaps a twin brother, by contrast with the wider Davidsonian distinction adopted in this essay.

But even that is not enough. For it is not self-deception if resistance to the original belief merely motivates a more thorough gathering or reexamination of evidence, and this then results in a change of belief. Self-deception demands that one's actions be *designed* to produce a change in one's belief, and that the reasoning process by which this is achieved be materially corrupted by this motive; for if one employs a scrupulously fair reasoning process that happens to achieve the intended cognitive outcome, one cannot be said to be self-deceived, even if one had been prepared to resort to underhanded methods if necessary.

Now, a threshold concern raised by these rather demanding conditions is whether self-deception actually exists—whether (as suggested by folk psychology and taken for granted by philosophers of mind) people really engage in such a thing, or, in other words, whether such attributions are ever either indispensable or at least the most fruitful explanatory hypotheses available.

In this section, I hope only to say enough about a 'perspectivist' alternative to impose upon philosophers a burden of justifying the attribution of self-deception, of explaining why this concept of folk psychology ought not be pared away by Occam's Razor. At the very least, there seems a disturbing readiness to diagnose self-deception prematurely, before exhausting other plausible but less epistemically unsavory possibilities.

Consider Anspach's paper as an illustration. He seems to reason that holding beliefs that strike others as "manifestly deluded" (1998, 60) entails being 'deceived'; and then, that unless someone else (or one's own DNA) has implanted these beliefs in one, one must be *self*-deceived.

This glib analysis of the concept of self-deception loses touch with the specific mental phenomenon described above. It also employs a spurious dichotomy, between extrinsically "implanted" versus "internally generated" beliefs (61), which subtly conveys the false notion that others' queer beliefs are insular fantasies and never reasonable responses to evidence.

Worst of all, the implicit criterion for self-deception (and *madness* for that matter) is disturbingly easy to satisfy: having beliefs that seem to other people, in light of the evidence as they interpret and evaluate it, to be obviously wrong or ridiculous. This alone is supposedly enough to make one self-deceived, and not just grossly in error or merely committed to a different cognitive framework or perspective. But as Davidson rightly insists (e.g., 1985, 348), one may simply have formed an interpretation of the world that makes sense given one's perspective (which may include strange beliefs and theories), rather than a view motivated by aversion to an already-possessed contrary belief.

It is not easy to keep in mind that deviant beliefs can, in this way, be explained by mere difference in perspective. In fact, even relatively widespread evidence of another's perspectival divergence is all too readily construable simply as chronic, or perhaps metastasizing, self-deception. Given the natural assumptions that there is a single True account of reality and that users of a language (dialect) all share the same concepts, people readily reason, when they encounter another's judgment that differs from their own confident one, that both cannot be right; but, surely, theirs is right, so the Other's must be wrong. And since it appears that the Other is not stupid and had access to all the pertinent information that led them to *their* view, the explanation must be some irrational kink in the Other's stream of thought.[3]

But this is quadruply misguided. (i) Other persons often use words with senses and usage criteria subtly different from one's own, which can lend their avowed beliefs a false appearance of absurdity relative to the other beliefs or evidence they seem to possess. (ii) Thinking isn't easy; it's far from trivial to bring to bear in each judgment all of one's relevant reasoning skills and memories. (These include one's standards of cogency and weightiness in reasoning, explanation, and argumentation.) Even those with admirably efficient habits of mind are beset by (unmotivated) blind spots and slip-ups, and sometimes forget or overlook relevant considerations. (iii) Those evaluating another person's beliefs are typically handicapped by an information disparity: he has evidence unavailable to

---

3. Typical self-deception attributions do, in this way, involve matters that seem perfectly obvious to the attributors, and this contributes to the ease of unwarranted attribution. On occasion, however, a judgment of self-deception is not a response to a particular patently absurd belief, but an adjustment of one part of a multifaceted understanding of someone's mind in order to improve the logical fit of *other* attributions to that person. In such cases (which include self-deception *self*-attributions), the reevaluated belief need not seem on its own to be misguided, let alone obviously so. (There are other possibilities as well. For example, one might hold an attributional principle 'Whenever people believe their mates are perfect for them, they suffer from self-deception' and apply it categorically, even where one has no other reason to think that the beliefs in question are deluded.)

The atypical cases appear to be parasitic upon the typical ones, though, in that if the latter were no longer accepted as meriting the label 'self-deception,' the use of the concept could no longer be sustained in the former (and not vice versa). Hence my focus upon the central cases.

the smug onlookers, and often lacks evidence they possess. (iv) Most important: given the variability of perspectives, a slice of reality can be given more than one rational interpretation.

In sum, if we do not see someone's construal as a reasonable employment of his mental resources, the source of the difficulty may be *our* mental limitations, not his. Interpretive "charity" (e.g., Davidson 1982, 302–3) does not preclude restraint or retreat in the face of bafflement. The deepest attainable understanding of another being is often an acceptance that one cannot understand him in depth, that his perspective cannot be specified in enough detail, and that bending the pieces to get them to fit is no solution to the attributional puzzle he poses.

The same issues arise for *self*-ascriptions of self-deception that respond to the now-unfathomable beliefs of one's own past self. And a parallel explanation obtains when one has a *current* belief that from another standpoint one considers indefensible.

That is, one thinks in differing ways in differing types of situations. A somewhat altered frame of mind gets elicited or composed whenever one perceives (usually not self-consciously) a change in one's 'pragmatic context,' hence in one's immediate mental task, purpose, or activity. The differing frames of mind, which we might call 'perspects,' do not all make available the same full set of mental resources and dispositions. Each affords access to only a subset of one's memory, and thus lacks some intentional states available in other perspects.[4]

Hence one person may in different situations (perhaps very close in time) innocently use inconsistent beliefs about the same subject-matter, each one rationally acquired and maintained in the context of its surrounding perspect. (The beliefs may stably coexist in a state of *compatible inconsistency* if each is useful within its contexts of usage, if these domains do not overlap, and if no applicable norm demands that the beliefs be reconciled.) While using *one* "structure... of interlocking beliefs, expectatations, assumptions, attitudes and desires" (Davidson 1982, 300), one may be reminded of a belief that is part of another, and from the current

91

---

4. Such a frame of mind is, roughly, a subset of one's 'perspective' or total mental endowment, and it functions to provide a particular point of view, guiding and constraining mental processes—thus the name 'perspect.' According to this conception, a perspective, like a hockey or football team, is at no time ever fully activated and available for use. It is only through the mediation of a single perspect at a time that a person engages the world, and in that sense perspects are psychologically and explanatorily prior to perspectives.

standpoint that belief may seem ludicrous. So here again, a perspectivist explanation—one overlooked due to assumptions about the mind's unity or integration that obscure its structural complexity—seems superior to an ascription of self-deception.

To posit a mind structured in this partly nonintegrated way is to posit a sort of mental partitioning, though one different from that proposed by Davidson.[5] However, Davidson's own account of self-deception may itself rely tacitly also upon some such organizational arrangement. A self-deceiver who promotes a belief by "pushing the negative evidence into the background" (1986, 90), say, is not merely turning attention away from certain of his beliefs (and other intentional states), for that would provide no assurance against their prompt return. He is placing them out of bounds, making them unintrusive upon reasoning for the duration of the self-deceptive project—hence the seeming aptness of a 'partitioning' idiom. Once the new belief is in place, they may well be readmitted without threat, given the remarkable tendency to reconstrue data so as to harmonize it with established beliefs—now including the induced one. (This prodigious reinterpretive capacity also casts doubt upon Davidson's insistence that the aversive original belief and its motivating power must survive the self-deceptive inducing of the contrary belief lest the latter be smothered in its crib by remembered or freshly encountered evidence (1986, 90).)

Now, a plausible self-deception hypothesis in a particular instance must involve a strange belief(-set) that is both isolated (for the more wide-ranging an attribution of irrationality, the greater the suspicion that the overall interpretation can be improved upon) and best construed as *motivated* to evade an uncomfortable realization. However, determining what beliefs are so aversive to someone as to bring about self-deception only expands the opportunity for interpretive arrogance and disregard of perspectival difference. The spottiness and ambiguity of evidence insures that some story can always be constructed *ex post* about what the agent is afraid of facing—his sadness or, contrariwise, his happiness; infidelity, or fidelity that he does not deserve.

---

5. John Heil (1994) mentions mental "compartmentalization" of this type, and seems to consider it a situation of "mental regions functionally circumscribed," but apparently resists conceiving it as involving "mental divisions" or "partitions." Bill Talbott (1995, 29,34), by contrast, states unequivocally that certain "innocent divisions" are required for "adequate explanation of non-self-deceptive phenomena."

At times, the search for independent evidence of motivation gets skipped altogether. Anspach, for instance, shows no interest in asking why someone would be so disturbed by suspecting he is not Napoleon that he would contrive to believe the opposite. The explanation would likely point to some alien-to-us reasoning—but then parsimony would dictate attributing the 'I am Napoleon' belief to that alien body of beliefs alone, without self-deception. Anspach, though, infers self-deception (hence that *some* suitable motivation *must* be in play) simply from steadfastness in an enigmatic belief in the face of efforts at rational persuasion (64):

> If… a reasoned attack on his deluded beliefs actually provokes the patient to cling to them all the more strongly, one might surmise that the patient is resisting recognizing something as true out of a belief, or at least a nagging suspicion, that it *is* true. This resistance would then qualify as self-deception….

Who is not vulnerable to such 'logic'? Are not our convictions commonly fortified in the process of being defended against reasoned criticism? Where opposing webs of belief confront one another, neither seeming flawed by its own standards more than its opponent seems to be, why *should* reasoned argument win one of them over? There are, moreover, many innocent reasons even for *emotional* responses to a reasoned attack upon one's beliefs. (For a start, one's interlocutor may reasonably strike one as tedious, arrogant, insulting, inconsiderate, self-righteous, simple-minded, dogmatic, or a threat to disseminate misinformed, harmful views.)

Diagnoses of self-deception can carry serious consequences, starting with distrust and disrespect for the target's viewpoint (and ending, in some contexts, with autonomy-infringing manipulations and controls). Perhaps some of the same leeriness now aroused by suggestions of group 'false consciousness' ought to be directed toward attributions of individual self-deception.

A cloud of suspicion lurks over such ascriptions even where the charge is 'confirmed' (and perhaps volunteered) by the target himself. His ignorance and unreliability aside, self-deception (if it exists) involves a complex configuration of mental states, not an isolable, introspectively discernible one. One can affirm the theoretical hypothesis, but cannot have special first-person means to validate it; self-consciousness of one's self-deception is not to be had.[6] Though such affirmations are commonly construed as true insights dispelling the fogs of self-mystification (see, e.g., Talbott 1995, 40, 58), these construals presuppose the truth of the self-deception hypothesis and thus cannot provide support for it. 'Confessional' affirmations may simply be alternative, perhaps false, readings of the evidence (and possibly themselves influenced by, say, wishful thinking).[7] Even where the hypothesis of self-deception produces searching self-scrutiny, and adjustments in outlook, it is not thereby verified, any more than is a charge of selfishness or racism that sparks reflection and change.

Suppose perspectivist psychological explanations obviate the need to attribute self-deception. They might still be thought to impute irrationality of a different sort, and thus to offer no great gain from the standpoint of interpretive charity. They ascribe to agents interpretations and evaluations that, in having been shaped to conform with already-existing beliefs, arguably have been illegitimately biased, even if this is the normal course that understanding takes. Psychologists have discussed a "primacy effect," whereby beliefs based upon earlier-encountered information cause later data to be interpreted to fit them, and hence are themselves "revised insufficiently in response to discrepancies in the later-presented information" (Nisbett and Ross 1980, 172). Now, even if such assimilation of new data to old were irrational, substituting a pervasive and ineliminable element of psychological explanation for the more dubious and dangerous self-deception concept could itself be an improvement. And *is* such assimilation

---

6. Where the overt, supposedly-self-deceptive belief is firmly held, it seems clear that introspective self-awareness of one's own self-deception is unattainable. Where weakly held (as shown, eg, in one's feelings toward it, or dispositions to use it), the weakness itself might be introspected, but there is no similar way to perceive that the belief was induced via self-deception and is not simply an ordinary belief about which one has serious reservations.

7. Compare Talbott's (1995) discussion of the Fox, who, after finding that he cannot reach the sweet-seeming grapes, reconsiders and decides that they are green and sour after all, and Mary, who, after her lover leaves her, reconsiders and decides that he had long been heartlessly taking advantage of her but that she had been too blind to see it. The former case is treated as a movement from rational to motivationally biased belief, the latter as a movement from self-deception to rational clarity. But it could be that none of the four beliefs is irrationally biased, or that it is the two that Talbott treats as rational that are in fact biased, perhaps by wishful thinking. Self-deception interpretations, even if offered by the putative victims themselves (e.g., Mary), are question-begging and do not provide independent evidence that self-deception exists.

of evidence really irrational? It does not violate the "total-evidence principle" (said by Davidson (1986, 91) to be a norm all rational agents must possess), which calls for choosing the hypothesis best supported by all the evidence. For a violation requires that the evidence be construed as favoring a competing hypothesis (1986, 82), and the putative self-deceiver seemingly does not do this, however much observers think he should.

Perhaps assimilating evidence to existing theory contravenes another norm of rationality. Now, there is surely no norm that requires that one *always* canvass for alternative hypotheses and interpretations of evidence. But Davidson (1985, 347–48) suggests one that demands considering alternative hypotheses upon finding oneself forced to "invent strange explanations" for observed data. Other principles belonging to the same family would demand considering alternative hypotheses upon finding one's judgments at odds with those of experts or the consensus of reasonable, intelligent people, or upon recognizing that one needs to make a high-stakes, irrevocable judgment. Still, if one either does not comply with such norms (which are only 'optional' for rational agents), or does entertain the alternative hypotheses yet reaffirms one's original view, allegations of irrationality seem to be left without basis.

So what, then, do we say of someone who consistently takes himself to be Napoleon?–That he has an abnormal perspective, and need not be thought self-deceived.[8] The bizarreness of his beliefs may be due to isolation from the people around him, rather than due to a narrowly motivated process like self-deception. Most people rely upon others far more than he in forming their judgments; they handle the inherent difficulty of understanding the world by making thinking in effect a collective activity. Two heads *are* better than one. Cooperative communication lessens neglect of relevant factors, provokes frequent corrections–and limits how far different people's perspectives can drift beyond the limits of mutual comprehensibility. (Some deviant patterns of construal and reasoning

8. He might, for instance, use 'Napoleon' idiosyncratically, reflecting an eccentric metaphysical view. 'Napoleon' could, say, denote for him not a unique individual (as it does for us), but something closer to a type–to him, he is not numerically identical with the Napoleon we all know, but is *another* Napoleon with similar properties. If we allow philosophers and physicists to believe in possible worlds and branching universes, and heed anthropologists' and historians' accounts of other cultures and of the deviants and innovators within our own, we must concede that psychotics' languages and metaphysics may differ from ours.

may be underlain by neurochemical factors. But the interpretations may nevertheless be reasonable *given* the abnormal brain processes, and quite free of any motivated irrationality.)

2. The Intentions of Liars

Whatever self-deception is, Davidson contends that it is not lying to one-self (1998, 3; 1986, 88). But his main arguments do not appear to compel this conclusion.

Only two intentions are indispensable for any liar, he says (1986, 88). First: "to represent himself as believing what he does not." This seems needed because a liar achieves his aim by exploiting the victim's reliance, in his own (the victim's) belief-formation, upon what he takes the liar to believe. Typically, the liar is granted epistemic authority by the victim, so that the latter comes to believe that p because he (wrongly) takes the former to do so. (Atypically, the victim may think that the liar forms sys-tematically and dependably false judgments in this area, and so when the liar appears to believe that p, the victim believes that not-p.)

Now, Davidson's construal of this first requirement seems to need some slight modification, as he apparently takes 'representing oneself as believ-ing that p' to involve communicating some sign whose literal meaning is 'p' (1998, 3). But when one represents oneself as believing something, one takes into account and makes allowances for the conventional nonliteral interpretations that one's audience is likely to place upon one's words. Surely one represents oneself as believing that p when one utters 'Not-p' in the knowledge that one's hearer will detect the obvious irony or face-tiousness in one's tone and manner. Under such circumstances, it would be a feeble and ridicule-worthy defense to maintain that one didn't actual-ly lie because one believed that not-p and, after all, one *said* that not-p.

The objection to Davidson's argument, however, does not turn upon the precise characterization of what it is to represent that one believes something. The more important feature of his statement of the first in-tention of the liar ("to represent himself as believing what he does not") is that it is formulated in abstract terms of which the liar need not be aware. The liar need not think of his own 'representing' or 'believing.' He may simply intend, for example, to say that p (which he does not believe), in order to get the victim to believe that p; he need not grasp that lying has anything to do with a victim's perception of and reliance upon the liar's state of belief. A liar must *in fact* represent himself as believing what he does not, and must intend to do something that (perhaps unbeknowst to him) *can be described as* such a representing; but he need not intend 'to represent myself as believing something that I do not.'

The second intention that Davidson considers essential, "to keep this [first] intention... hidden from his hearer," seems to makes lying *to one-self* impossible and hence an untenable interpretation of 'self-deception.' But while a successful lie does demand that any intention to (in effect) misrepresent one's belief not be found out by the victim,[9] this need not call for intentional action on the liar's part. He may just, for example, off-handedly assert a knowing falsehood, without any concern that his mis-representational intention (or simply the fact that he does not hold what he says to be true) might be discerned. (If it seems that a liar *must* be concerned with this, think of liars who do not think their lying is wrong, or do not care whether it is, or have unquestioning confidence in the ease with which they will con their victims.) If later the possibility of being found out comes to the liar's attention, he can *then* take steps to hide the original misrepresentational intention, forming an intention to do certain things or to improvise so as to keep it hidden.

From the fact that success in an activity requires that not p, and maybe that one not intend that p, it does not follow that one must intend that not-p. For example, though in order to use a tool one needs for it not to break, it does not follow that one uses it intending not to break it or have it break, unless and until there is a specific concern about that possibility. Again, one's bridge hand may need to stay hidden from opponents, but one need not intend to keep it hidden if one was trained to hold one's cards in a way that happens, as an incidental and nonfocal feature, to keep them hidden. Know-how obviates the need for explicit control over various aspects of an action.

And consider feinting, which like lying involves intentional action de-

---

9. By contrast, a liar's more general intention to deceive can be found out without this invariably undermining the lie. The victim may still miscalculate what the liar really believes and end up in the belief state sought for him by the liar. Indeed, a cunning liar might intentionally have his victim discover the intention to deceive. (For example, though I believe that not-p, I tell you that p; I then (without you knowing that I planned this) let you discover elsewhere that I intended to deceive you and that I expected or contrived for you to discover this; you then figure that I sought to induce you to believe that not-p, and that I really believe that p; so you accept that p.)

signed to produce a belief that one does not share. A basketball player's fake (e.g., a step toward the basket, when he really intends in a moment to jump out and receive a pass) must be communicated to the defender, while the misrepresentational intention must be hidden. Yet the player need not actively hide anything; his routinized action pattern keeps the crucial facts hidden, but it can be initiated and executed without this feature being intended (or noticed). And if a player *is* aware that discovery of his intention would be disastrous, he typically will not take that possibility seriously enough to form a second intention expressly to hide the first.

98

So, any general impossibility in lying to oneself apparently lies not in "doing something *with the intention that* that very intention should not be recognized by the intender" (Davidson 1986, 88; emphasis added), for the italicized intention need not exist.

Might it lie, then, in the impossibility of doing something with an intention (the misrepresentational one) that *is in fact* not recognized by the intender? Stated so generally, this hardly seems capable of rendering lying to oneself impossible in principle, for people seem often to perform actions without at the time being aware of their intentions or later recalling them. True, some aspect of an intention may need to be retained over time, lest the action go off the rails, transmute into something else, or simply be abandoned. But it can suffice to remember what one is doing, without also remembering why. All but the most narrow of one's aims can safely be forgotten (at least in many cases, and at least until a decision arises that requires consideration of higher-level aims), as can the background precipitating circumstances of the original intention to act.

Thus, if the original intention is to do something with the aim or hope of getting oneself to believe that not-p—treating 'not-p' as one's working premise in reasonings, for instance, or gathering a body of strong evidence to support it—it seems that one might pursue this activity effectively without retaining awareness of one's broader aims or of the precipitating circumstances, such as an initial aversion to the thought that p (or the thought that one ought rationally to believe that p). If so, one can retain as much of the intention as is needed to sustain one's actions, without also retaining a project-imperiling awareness of the misrepresentational aspect of the original intention.

That an intention to lie to oneself has distinct aspects that can be given different psychological treatments also supplies the reply to Davidson's new impossibility argument (1998, 3). The supposed impasse is that in lying to oneself, the liar must intend (or simply need[10]) both (i) that his intention—to misrepresent what he believes, by asserting that p—go unrecognized by the victim, lest the victim see through the deception, and also (ii) that the intention be recognized by the victim, insofar as any lie requires that the liar be taken as making an assertion that p.

If this is a fair synopsis of the new argument, it seemingly cannot be valid, for if valid it would show the impossibility of lying *to others*, too. The problem appears to reside in a failure to distinguish two different aspects of the intention—assertion and misrepresentation—one of which could be (intended to be) recognized, while the other could be (intended to be) not recognized. Reconsider how a liar's primary intention could simply be to say that p (which he does not believe), in order to get the victim to believe that p. The intention to say that p might be (intended to be) discovered, with the non-belief in 'p' (or belief in its falsehood) (intended to be) not discovered. (Such a distinction was also noted above regarding feinting.)

The second Davidson argument, then, seems to fare no better than the first. Does the analysis of self-deception as lying break down elsewhere? If yes, perhaps it is where lying demands that the victim accept the proposition *because* he thinks the liar believes it; for where liar and victim are one, it is not clear how such (granting of and) reliance upon epistemic authority, and upon one's own apparent belief, can take place.

On the other hand, a scenario like the following seems possible. One intends, as suggested earlier, to accept 'not-p' as a working premise in one's reasonings and to find support for it. Later, once certain aspects of the original intention have been forgotten, one then accepts 'not-p' because one remembers oneself using and trusting it. Even a brief time separation might in this way allow one to bifurcate functionally into 'relier' and 'relied upon.'

The case against the possibility of lying to oneself thus seems yet unproven.

99

---

10. Davidson frames his argument in terms of states of affairs the liar "intends"—here, that his (the liar's) intention in making his lying assertion be both recognized and not recognized by the victim. But this focus upon intending seems superfluous, as it is the factual impossibility of the victim's recognition-plus-nonrecognition that is the crux. It also seems misleading. Davidson apparently infers (1998, 3) that a liar "must intend" that p from the fact that p happens to be a precondition for the successful execution of his action; but this does not follow. (When one asserts something, one need not, e.g., intend that one's hearer not have a deafness-inducing stroke as one commences).

3. Partitioning as an Explanation for Self-Deception

Anspach approvingly reiterates Sartre's flawed argument that where there is motivated resistance to acknowledging one of two opposed beliefs–as in ordinary self-deception[11]–partitioning cannot be what is at work.

Sartre (1956, 90) assumes a partitioning model that includes a *censor*, an "autonomous consciousness" (94) who polices the mental boundary, keeping hidden beliefs hidden and turning the conscious mind away from evidence in their favor. The censor itself would need be self-deceived, he argues, thus only displacing the problem of explaining self-deception, not resolving it. But Sartre never does establish that there need be any entity beyond the distinct mental subsets themselves. For instance, the unconscious mind itself might somehow monitor its conscious counterpart, instigating resistance when necessary. Neither the censor (which would not exist) nor unconscious (which would be unconflicted) would then itself be self-deceived.

Partitioning theories do need to explain the precise mechanics of how a hidden belief could cause an opposite manifest belief to be maintained. But, *contra* Anspach's extension of Sartre, such accounts need not "call for a censor to keep the agent from surveying the whole" (Anspach 1998, 67, n. 5); nothing Anspach or Sartre says shows that "one cannot limit the scope of consciousness by positing... a wall inside the mind without also positing... an independent consciousness to mind the wall" (Anspach 1998, 67). A 'censoring' effect might be produced by the structural organization of the mind, such as a system of transition rules or switches regulating the activations of the partitioned areas.

Even if one were for argument's sake to accept the censor's existence, and that it "must know what it is repressing" and "apprehend... [it] *as to be repressed*" (Sartre 1956, 93), Sartre's argument would not go through. For it would not follow that this mental module must have "an awareness of its activity." Sartre relies upon the premise that "[t]o know is to know that one knows," but an animal may know what it is stalking, and know it as something to be stalked, yet without self-consciousness at all. Sartre's argument seems to entail that we have self-conscious awareness of doing every activity we do–which seems false. (Absorbed in driving, one appre-

100

---

11. Sartre is actually discussing 'bad faith,' which he views as lying to oneself. Anspach sees lying to oneself as only (an ingredient in) one kind of self-deception, but treats Sartre's comments as sometimes applying to self-deception in general.

hends the road reflectors as objects to be skirted without thereby gaining an awareness of this activity.)

But assume that there *is* a censor, conscious of its own activity. Now, its self-awareness is supposedly "the consciousness (of) being conscious of the drive to be repressed, but precisely *in order not to be conscious of it*" (Sartre 1956, 94), with the crucial upshot that the censor itself is in bad faith. Yet however this climactic quotation is paraphrased–e.g., 'The censor must have awareness of being conscious of the repressed matter, and yet it is also crucial [for the self-deception to succeed] that the censor not be conscious of that matter'–the second clause seems simply false. It makes no difference what the censor knows. The repressive activity is aimed at keeping the conscious mind (or rational ego)–not the censor–in the dark.

Anspach's borrowing from Sartre thus does not come close to establishing that partitioning cannot account for ordinary self-deception.[12] Sartre's interesting but convoluted account is rife with missteps, builds upon a dubious premise about "the total translucency of consciousness" (1956, 89),[13] and is a shaky basis from which to draw conclusions about self-deception. (See also Pears (1986, 74) and the thorough discussion by Allen Wood (1988).)

4. The Supposed Paradoxes of Self-Deception

4.1 The Self-Aware Madman

Anspach uses the plight of a self-aware psychotic to argue that no escape from self-deception is offered by the flickering self-awareness of that con-

---

12. Anspach also objects (1998, 73) that a posited mental "dividing line cannot explain… [the fact of inconsistent beliefs] if its own existence is deduced from the fact to be explained." Rather than being "circular reasoning," however, this is simply normal 'abduction' or 'inference to the best explanation.'

13. Sartre's idealization of the mind imputes self-awareness where none exists (given his "dogma that *all* mental activity must be conscious" (Wood 1988, 211))–sometimes even where the propositional attitudes said to be known do not themselves exist. Thus, he criticizes as in bad faith those who avoid facing their knowledge of their absolute self-determining freedom. Yet most people do not actually have beliefs that they are totally free, beliefs that they can then in bad faith ignore; at best (and even this is doubtful), they have only 'implicit beliefs,' which are not actual thinkings at all but only potential ones (e.g., propositions easily inferable from actual beliefs and memories).

dition supposedly guaranteed by "the reflexivity of consciousness" (1998, 73). This awareness is what makes it true that "self-deception involves a pragmatic paradox in one's relation to oneself," a "double bind" (74). The self-deceiver's "psychic system... oscillates indefinitely in the manner of the liar's paradox" (81).

Anspach's premise of self-awareness is itself suspect, and founded upon dubious Sartrean positions that will not be rebutted here. Moreover, the supposed self-awareness, as exemplified by the statements of a French proto-psychiatrist's mental patient, does not show the paradoxical oscillations that Anspach supposes.

102

The alleged sufferer from madness (S) is quoted as saying

<1> If I could believe with you that I am mad, I would soon be cured, but I cannot acquire this belief. (79)

<2> ...I follow quite well your reasoning,... and if I could convince myself, I would no longer be crazy, you would have cured me. (82)

On Anspach's reading, "on the one hand, he believes he is crazy, and yet... he does not believe he is crazy" (79). Note first that in stating that the psychotic both *believes and does not believe* he is crazy, Anspach makes what Davidson considers a common, but inexcusable, error. To Davidson (1986, 79–80; 1998, 5), such talk asserts 'p and not-p,' and so cannot make sense.

Yet it seems to be Davidson who is in the wrong here, for he discounts an implication of partitioning accounts. These allow that a person might in part of his mind believe that p, while in another part believe that not-p; so it should be possible in one part to believe p, while in the other to have no belief regarding p. If the parts are to some degree self-contained and independently usable thinking systems, this picture seems entirely reasonable. Then, just as 'X believes that p, and X believes that not-p' – which, on its face, looks nonsensical given the ordinary notion of person-level belief, the evidence supporting each of the conjoined ascriptions undermining the other – actually makes sense, due to tacit semantic subtleties deriving from the background picture of mind, so might 'X believes that p, and X does not believe that p' make sense in similar fashion. In minds that are partitioned into sequentially activated, and sometimes inconsistent, perspectives, 'believes and does not believe that p' ascriptions may not be simply self-negations (i.e., 'X believes that p, and it is not the case that X believes that p') or colloquial ways to express 'believes that p and believes that not-p.'

That is, an excessive concern to avoid seemingly self-contradictory attributions may be inhibiting theorizing in this area. A further consequence of this is neglect of the reasonable possibility that some self-deception might involve driving oneself to or from a state of *non*-belief. If self-deception is an escape from an uncomfortable state of belief into a more tolerable one, then might it not sometimes involve fleeing from a disturbing state of undecided non-belief (about whether God exists, say, or whether one's parent really loves one) into a state of belief, or from a state of belief into a state of nonbelief?

In any event, it is dubious to impute to S a belief that he is crazy. He never directly expresses such a belief, of course. To Anspach (1998, 79), however, S's "I would /soon be cured/no longer be crazy" in <1, 2> implies the belief 'I am not yet cured'; and then, "to believe he is not yet cured is to believe he is still crazy." Hence, paraphrase <3>:

<3> *I am crazy,* and would cease to be if I were to come to believe that I am—but, I do not believe that I am.

If a fair paraphrase, this would not serve Anspach, because it would be an instance of Moore's Paradox, which generally is thought to be absurd and not believable at all, rather than to involve oscillatory beliefs. Yet the best reading of <1, 2>, given a proper reluctance to attribute paradoxical belief or belief in contradiction, finds the more strongly counterfactual

<4> *If* I *were* crazy, I would cease to be, if I were to come to believe that I am—but, I do not believe that I am.

S may, as Anspach states (79), "believe[] he *should* believe he is crazy" (and even wish he *could*), at least while conversing with his therapist, because he comprehends the latter's reasoning and finds it intellectually appealing. But S cannot be said to believe he is crazy (as well as not crazy). This is no "mystery" (79)—it is commonplace to evaluate an entertained idea without finding grounds for objection, even while being precluded from also *believing* it by a subconscious recognition of conflicts between it and unspecified cognitions within one's perspective (see Dennett 1978, 308).

103

Even were there evidence of the overt contrary beliefs 'I am crazy' + 'I am not crazy,' this would indicate *ambivalence,* not self-deception or paradox. It might also be straightforwardly explicable via partitioning, the two beliefs being available and supported in different regions of mind. Vacillation could occur, as Anspach notes—but due merely to alternating activations of the different parts, and in a way likely not to be "perpetual" (83) (as a change in either part, perhaps spurred by the discomfort of vacillating, could end the divergence in beliefs). (The same analysis holds if S is taken to have, not two contrary beliefs, but one belief ('I am crazy') and one state of nonbelief.)

Self-awareness of ambivalence ('I seem both to believe that p and to believe that not-p') does pose a further puzzle: how does partitioning provide a habitat for contrary beliefs if during reflection the segregation can be undone enough to allow such self-description? (The contradictory propositions still could not be used simultaneously in reasoning.)

The (non-Davidsonian) kind of partitioning mentioned above, with the mind activated one perspective at a time, ultimately may offer an answer. If one thinks with different networks of intentional states in different contexts of thought and action, one might sometimes accept that p, at other times accept that not-p, and in either type of context perhaps access a memory of the other. So when pondering an issue, one might shift back and forth between perspectives and consider the issue in their different lights. If no reconciliation of the standpoints is apparent, one may simply remain knowingly ambivalent for the time being.

But whether this story is convincing or not, the self-awareness of ambivalence does not entail paradox. Even an ensuing belief in one's own self-deception or madness—'I'm crazy because I believe that p and believe that not-p; yet I'm not crazy'—would only return one to (self-aware) ambivalence, though now with the different routes to judgment giving conflicting beliefs about *oneself.*

Real paradox requires the proper logical interlocking of propositions. How about (see Anspach 1998, 82)

<6> 'I (believe I) am crazy *because* I believe I'm not crazy'

<6'> 'I (believe I) am crazy *because* I don't believe I am crazy'

Suppose there were clear evidence of agents firmly believing (and not just entertaining) <6> or <6'> due to a commitment to the (false[14]) theory expressed by the connective 'because.' Still, <6, 6'> must be construed as nonparadoxical, the second 'believe' referring to periods of time different from the first (e.g., times other than this very moment of utterance) or to a nonconscious belief running in parallel in some partitioned-off part of mind. Here is where Davidson's admonition against ascribing belief in plain contradiction has its bite: the idea of having *conscious* occurrent beliefs 'p' and 'not-p' simultaneously just makes no sense.

This is not to say that no one can ever have oscillating beliefs. For example, one who believes he's not crazy, realizes what he believes, and holds 'Whoever does not believe he's crazy, is crazy (and inversely),' may come to believe he's crazy, then believe he's not crazy, and so on (though only until his concern or attention withers). What of it? At any time, he will have at most one of the beliefs—not contradictory beliefs contained in some special mental structure. Oscillation between two individually coherent beliefs is not tantamount to believing a paradox, which is incoherent and cannot be believed.

Belief in one's own self-deception is evidently not paradoxical or self-imprisoning, no matter how many rungs of self-mistrust one climbs. For example, I may believe I am self-deceived about my developing baldness, yet come to think that that second-order belief (about the corrupt nature of my first-order baldness-related belief) is itself corrupted, underlain by another, hidden second-order awareness that the first-order one is *not* a product of self-deception. This may seem perverse, but it might occur.[15] The upshot, however, will tend to be the annihilation of my original concerns about the legitimacy of my baldness beliefs. There need be no oscillation—merely the conviction that I am not, after all, self-deceived about my hair, but am self-deceived about the epistemic status of my hair-belief. (See Appendix B for greater detail.)

---

14. (Dis)belief in one's sanity is no indicator of mental health: sane people, too, believe they are not crazy, and both sane and crazy people believe they *are* crazy. Further, while belief in one's insanity can increase receptiveness to treatment, it can also itself play a causal role in insanity. (These matters, however, are relevant only to madness and its cure, and not to self-deception and whether it involves paradox.)

15. Maybe facing the belief that I am not self-deceived about my baldness would require recognizing that I may lose the caring attentions of my therapist. (The newly uncovered second-order self-deception fails to strike me as likely to elicit her care.)

5. Lying to Oneself, the Liar's Paradox, and Double Binds

We have not yet encountered paradoxical beliefs that are 'möbiused,' rather than partitioned, within the mind. Anspach ultimately makes recourse to lying to oneself for the postulated element of paradox, but this tactic, too, is unavailing.

For even supposing that lying to oneself is present in self-deception, the idea that one who lies to himself is confronted with the liar's paradox (Anspach 1998, 80) is based upon a confusion. The liar's paradox applies only to reflexive assertions like 'I am *now* lying,' or '*This* sentence is false' – and obviously not to an "I am lying" or "This statement is false!" remark (Anspach's example) that refers only to assertions other than itself. In a lie *to others*, such a disclosure is taken as a truthful warning, challenge, or confession, or perhaps a false joke or bluff. A hearer might reasonably scratch his head over the utterance's intended purpose, but not over whether its substance is self-referential and hence paradoxical. And it is clearer still that if an 'I am lying' belief is part of lying *to oneself*, it applies to the particular falsehood to be swallowed (e.g., 'I am not bald') and not also to *itself*. It is thus simply false that "the person on the receiving end [of a disclosure of an intention to deceive] is confronted with the liar's paradox" (Anspach 1998, 80).

Similarly, a psychotic's 'I am crazy' (83) need not itself be infected with madness. Anspach himself emphasizes that the mad are partly sane: "the most deluded lunatic can be quite rational" (63). If 'I am crazy' is a reflection upon other thought or behavior and not self-referential, talk of paradox is inapt.[16] Not even 'All my beliefs, including *this* one, are delusions' would be paradoxical, for it could simply be that this belief *is* delusional (i.e., false) while some other(s) are not. (Compare: 'I always lie' can simply be false.)

It takes something quite peculiar to effect a liar's-like paradox. S asserts nothing of the sort. While the words 'I cannot acquire this belief' appear in <1>, "this belief" there refers not to those five words (or to <1>), but to *another* belief that <1> is about ('I am mad'). And if S's assertion *had* been

---

16. Anspach does take himself to have established that an 'I am crazy' judgment "applies not to any particular deluded belief external to itself, but to the very consciousness doing the judging," and that because it imputes "craziness as an overall outlook" it ought to be rephrased "This statement is untrue" (1998, 84, 84 n.12). His justification for this position is not at all clear.

self-referential? No matter. Liar-type propositions, though utterable, as sentences to create paradoxes for interpreters, cannot be *believed* by those who fully understand them. One believes a proposition only when one holds it to be true, and if its content states that it is false, there is a psychological impossibility, and neither paradox nor oscillation. The 'if it's true, it's false, if it's false, it's true' nature of a liar's paradox has no clear relevance to lying to oneself.

Anspach, perhaps appreciating the force of this objection, has supplemented his discussion with remarks on Gregory Bateson's 'double bind,' which supposedly presents "an actual pragmatic dilemma" unlike the "purely semantic" liar's paradox (Anspach 1998, 74).[17] He tells (74–76) of Bateson's example of a child and its unconsciously hostile mother, both of whom want to believe that the mother loves the child unreservedly. (The same dynamic can also exist within other relationships, and does not require hostility but simply a degree of feeling not as great as both wish to believe.) But Anspach never establishes his claim that (mutually dependent and mutually threatening) self-deception, rather than innocent, unmotivated misinterpretation is at work.[18] More important, he never does

---

17. Anspach's examples arguably present no such dilemma. "Don't always do what I say" can be obeyed, while not thereby disobeyed as well: one need only disobey some future order out of compliance with this one. "Love me because you want to [or, Do D out of motive m], and not because I tell you to" can be obeyed: subsequent *D-ing-out-of-m* may be due to compliance with the order, but *D-ing* will even then be due not to compliance but to m, and hence will not constitute disobedience.

Other orders will naturally be construed as applying only henceforth, thus not to themselves (e.g., "Be spontaneous," "Think for yourself"). Even on reflexive construals, the results may again be only "semantic," descriptive paradoxes for observers, not actual pragmatic dilemmas for actors. "Disobey this order" is absurd, and affords no true alternative responses. As for "Disobey all orders, starting with this one," while obeying it does involve disobeying it, the converse can be escaped. If one chooses simply to disobey that order (by obeying some subsequent order), one has not thereby also obeyed it–though an observer might describe one as *in effect* having done so–because obedience to an order requires a motivation to comply with it, and that is, by hypothesis, absent. Receiving such an order, then, one faces no actual practical dilemma in forming an intention to act.

18. That is, it is not clear that either party ever realizes, in order to provide the initial motivation for self-deception, that the mother feels hostile toward the child (or that the evidence suggests that she so feels), despite Anspach's claims (76) that both "must" be aware of the truth; nor is it clear that the subsequent process of judgment is corrupt. And if they were truly self-deceived, would we not expect an end to the oscillation, as they would contrive a nonthreatening construal for the mother's periodic withdrawals?

show that in self-deception (and lying to oneself) one is caught in a double bind (76, 81).

Indeed, for all the eye-catching superficial resemblances among the various phenomena in Anspach's curiosity shop, it is not apparent that any of them really casts useful light upon self-deception.

Appendix A: 'Negative Cases'

One way in which Davidson distinguishes wishful thinking from self-deception is that supposedly in the former "belief takes the direction of positive affect, never of negative; the caused belief is always welcome," while "[t]he thought bred by self-deception may be painful" (1986, 87). Further distinctions, however, can clarify the contrast. The scale of absolute affect, from pleasurable to painful, ought not be confused with that of relative preferableness of states of affairs (or events) in the world, or of relative preferableness of states of belief.

Believing that is painful in an absolute sense – that 45 people have perished in an accident, that a lover's rejection was callous and selfish – can still be wishful thinking precipitated by "a desire or wish that a proposition be true" (Davidson 1998, 8) – but only if some more-dreaded scenarios have also been contemplated (as well, perhaps, as none that seems substantially preferable and reasonably likely). If the alternative is that 150 have died, or that the lover's rejection was honorable and caring, thus making the loss more unbearable, the thinking may be wishful despite being distressing.

Jealously believing that one's spouse had an illicit sexual encounter during a business trip thus may be wishful thinking, if one has contemplated a worse alternative state of the world that would explain one's evidence (say, that the spouse has been conducting a long-term affair) – but otherwise is not, even if one *has* sensed that another state *of belief* would be less preferable (e.g., if one feels relief at not taking one's spouse to be faithful and thereby leaving oneself maximally vulnerable to devastating later disappointment and humiliation.) So, in this case, the jealous belief may perhaps be innocent, or might involve some kind of irrationality such as self-deception or fretful thinking (see below); but it is not a wishful thinking.

Corresponding observations may apply, with the polarity of terms reversed, to 'fretful thinking,' a counterpart phenomenon that seems recognized by folk psychology despite not being named. Just as some beliefs are taken to result directly from *wishes* that certain propositions be true, and not indirectly (and self-deceptively) from aversion to other existing opposed beliefs, so do some beliefs seem to be produced directly (without rational evaluation of evidence, and without self-deception) by *worries* or *fears* that certain propositions are true. Though these new beliefs depict relatively undesirable states of the world, they may or may not be pleasurable in an absolute sense. In either case, by hypothesis they are not desired states of belief–hence the explanation for their production cannot be intentional self-deception or nonintentional 'wishful belief' (Talbott 1995, 59).

109

If this is right, it would then seem not to be the case that, "If a pessimist is someone who takes a darker view of matters than his evidence justifies, every pessimist is to some extent self-deceived" (Davidson 1986, 87). For pessimism might be produced by fretful thinking alone.

Appendix B: Believing in One's Own Self-Deception

Does believing that one is self-deceived plunge one into paradox? Consider the example in the text (pp. 104–105). At the outset, my relevant belief is

<a> I am not growing bald.

To which gets added

<b> I am self-deceived; <a> is the product of self-deception.

From <b> it follows that

<c> I *really* believe/know that I *am* growing bald.

So when <b> is in mind, I also employ as a belief the proposition

<a'> I am growing bald.

At this stage, there is no paradoxical indeterminacy. Speaking loosely, there may be an 'oscillation' of sorts, because whether I use <a> or <a'>

will vary with the perspect then in place. If <b> is not in mind at the time, I will freely use <a>. If <b> is present, I will use the epistemically untainted <a'>, however much <a>'s intuitive appeal. (Of course, if the appeal grows so strong that I forget about <b> for the time being, I will revert to <a>.) Thus it seems quite possible to acknowledge one's self-deception without remaining mired in it.

The next, more perverse stage of self-doubt adds:

<d> I am self-deceived regarding <b>; i.e., <b> is the product of self-deception.

From which it follows that

<e> I *really* believe/know that I am *not* self-deceived regarding <a>, i.e. that <a> is *not* the product of self-deception.

So when <d> is in mind, I also employ as a belief the proposition

<b'> I am not self-deceived regarding <a>; i.e., <a> is not the product of self-deception.

With an added layer of self-skepticism, then, there is again a non-paradoxical variation in belief state. If the perspect of the moment includes <a> but neither <b> nor <d>, I will use the proposition <a> in thought. If it includes <b> but not <d>, I will use <a'> as discussed above. If, however, it includes <d>, I will use <a>, because <d> undermines the perceived validity of <b> while <b> has no reciprocal impact upon <d>.

References

Anspach, M.R. 1998. "Madness and the Divided Self: Esquirol, Sartre, Bateson." Paper presented at the Symposium on Self-Deception, Stanford, California, February 1993. In J. P. Dupuy, ed., *Self-Deception and Paradoxes of Rationality.* Stanford: CSLI Publications (this volume).

Davidson, D. 1982. "Paradoxes of Irrationality." In R.A. Wollheim and J. Hopkins, eds., *Philosophical Essays on Freud.* Cambridge: Cambridge University Press.

———. 1985. "Incoherence and Irrationality." *Dialectica* 39:345–54.

———. 1986. "Deception and Division." In Elster, ed. (1986).

———. 1998. "Who Is Fooled?" Paper presented at the Symposium on Self-Deception, Stanford, California, February 1993. In J. P. Dupuy, ed., *Self-Deception and Paradoxes of Rationality.* Stanford: CSLI Publications (this volume).

Dennett, D. C. 1978. *Brainstorms: Philosophical Essays on Mind and Psychology.* Cambridge, Mass.: MIT Press.

Elster, J., ed. 1986. *The Multiple Self.* Cambridge: Cambridge University Press.

Heil, J. 1994. "Going to Pieces." In G. Graham and G. L. Stephens, eds., *Philosophical Psychopathology.* Cambridge, Mass.: MIT Press.

Mele, A. R. 1987. *Irrationality: An Essay on Akrasia, Self-Deception, and Self-Control.* New York: Oxford University Press.

———. 1998. "Two Paradoxes of Self-Deception." Paper presented at the Symposium on Self-Deception, Stanford, California, February 1993. In J. P. Dupuy, ed., *Self-Deception and Paradoxes of Rationality.* Stanford: CSLI Publications (this volume).

Nisbett, R. and L. Ross. 1980. *Human Inference: Strategies and Shortcomings of Social Judgment.* Englewood Cliffs, New Jersey: Prentice-Hall.

Pears, D. 1986. "The Goals and Strategies of Self-Deception." In Elster, ed. (1986).

Sartre, J.-P. 1956. *Being and Nothingness.* Trans. H. Barnes. New York: Philosophical Library.

Talbott, W. J. 1995. "Intentional Self-Deception in a Single Coherent Self." *Philosophy and Phenomenological Research* 55:27–74.

Wood, A. W. 1988. "Self-Deception and Bad Faith." In B. P. McLaughlin and A. O. Rorty, eds., *Perspectives on Self-Deception.* Berkeley: University of California Press.

Rationality and Self-Deception
Jean-Pierre Dupuy

France's Nobel Prize winner in economics, Maurice Allais, under whom I was lucky enough to study, used to say: "When it comes to rationality, the fundamental maxim is: *only the future matters.*" Obviously, he did not mean that the past is not important. In a certain way, the past makes us what we are: if the past had been different, we would be different and, in particular, when faced with a given problem, we would certainly not make the same decision. No, what Allais's maxim asserts is that the past will always be what it was and, specifically, our present decision cannot change it. This metaphysical principle of the fixity of the past with respect to free action is what underlies Allais's maxim. What could be more obvious or less controversial? When I compare a number of possible actions, I consider only the impact their foreseeable *consequences* will have on me, the others and the world. This word must be taken in its etymological sense: that which accompanies the action but occurs *after* it. Whether I do this or that might have an effect on the future of the world, but certainly not on its past.

Again, we seem to be in the domain of the obvious. Moreover, violating Allais's maxim truly seems to lead to characteristic irrationalities, of which we will soon see several examples. However, the nub of my argument is that this maxim cannot be universally valid. I will, of course, be talking in terms of reason and not of psychology. Most of us break Allais's principle in a good many minor, everyday decisions. We also break it when we are faced with choices concerning the way we most deeply define ourselves, or even our "salvation," or whatever takes its place. Rational Choice Theory (like Philosophy of Mind, to which I will often resort in the following analyses) has always been uneasy when faced with what it holds to be irrational and which is a paradox or challenge for it. However, here we will not be concerned with the actual practices of agents, but with what those practices should be.

I will begin by examining several cases of violation of Allais's principle which, it seems, it should be uncontroversial to consider irrational. I will establish a certain progression that will lead us to a rupture: suddenly, the diagnosis will no longer be taken for granted, and we will have to ask why.

114

1. Irrationalities

1.1

Suppose I notice that a certain private club is very highly rated by my friends and acquaintances. Many people are ready to incur non-negligible costs of all kinds in order to be admitted. From this I infer that admission to the club is an extremely desirable goal. I set it for myself and strive hard to achieve it.

Is it irrational for me to *believe* that admission to the club is a goal that merits being pursued? Would my *behavior* be irrational if I accepted to pay a high price to be admitted?

Not necessarily. We are dealing here with an unobservable, quasi-metaphysical entity: the value associated with being a member of a closed, exclusive group of people. When a value is uncertain and difficult to estimate, it can be rational to imitate the behavior of others in their efforts to obtain it. To be sure, this is a heterodox view in the small world of rational choice theorists, where imitation is generally considered to be an element of irrationality. Rationality implies independent preferences, absence of mutual influences and, more generally, absence of all phenomena associated with crowd or fashion behavior. However, this excessively incomplete vision of things must be resisted, as Keynes made especially clear in the context of financial markets and speculation. The argument can be made as follows. The others may have clues or information to which I have no direct access: by imitating them I can benefit from their knowledge. Of course, they might be just as ignorant as I am, but I know nothing about even that. I thus lose nothing by assuming they know something. (A Bayesian argument can be made to support this line of reasoning; see Orléan (1990).)

1.2

After deliberation, I decide to pay the price (in the broad sense) of admission–and I am admitted. What a disappointment! The members, the ambience, the conversations, the activities all appear to me to be mediocre, ordinary, vulgar. I have now two sets of evidence available to me, or so it seems. On the one hand, there is my direct perception that the club is worthless; on the other hand, there is the fact that it was expensive to join. I place more weight on the latter than on the former and draw the conclusion that the club is not so bad after all.

I have been influenced here by an article by the late Stanford cognitive psychologist Amos Tversky, whose work on rationality has hit hard at the rational choice edifice. It has shown, in effect, that the axioms of the theory are in practice violated massively, universally, and, undoubtably most troubling of all, systematically. Far from being chaotic or random, these violations seem to obey rules, as if they were subject to what one hesitates to call their own rationality (Quattrone and Tversky 1986). I believe that these results must be taken seriously, but on the condition that one go beyond psychological analysis. I will thus depart from Tversky's analysis when the time comes.

Let us go back to our club. Amos Tversky takes a fraternity on an American campus as his example. I prefer an illustration that is more literary and more Gallic. Marcel, the narrator of *La Recherche*, made many sacrifices in order to win his heart's desire: to be received in the Guermantes Salon. He had to wait until *Sodome et Gomorrhe* to finally be invited. Once there, however, he found none of his expectations fulfilled. Yet, he resisted the obvious and resorted to this astonishing rationalization: on that particular occasion the salon was not in its normal state *because he was there!* The physics of Proust's time was already open to the idea that the observer's presence disturbs the system being observed.

This is a case of what psychology calls *cognitive dissonance* between a previous, *a priori* belief (that the club or salon was desirable) and uncontrovertible evidence (which proves the mediocrity of the object in question). Rational revision of the belief, which would satisfy Bayes's rule,

115

does not take place. Why? Because the subject takes another piece of evidence to be indisputable: the high price paid for admission.

Yet this is clearly irrational. The fact that in the past I incurred costs to obtain X should not come into play in the judgment I make as to the desirability of X—in other words, as a reason for me to think that X is desirable. Or so it seems. How can this form of irrationality be described? According to Tversky and Quattrone, we are dealing here with an inversion of the causal link between desirability and cost, or a confusion of causal and diagnostic contingencies. One is ready to pay a high price for X *because* one believes X to be desirable. The costs one is thus ready to assume are only the *evidence*, the manifestation of the desirability that one grants to X. These costs do not, and should not, play a role in the evaluation of X.

There is another way to express what appears to us to be irrational in this "behavior" (which is in this case not an action but a mental process). In the first step, we saw that the fact that *others* incur or have incurred heavy costs in order to obtain X can reasonably play a role in my evaluation of the desirability of X. Here we see that the fact that *I* incurred similar costs should not play a role in this evaluation. What is the difference between me and the others that explains this asymmetrical treatment? The others' belief that X is desirable provides me with a reason to believe that X is desirable, but my past belief does not. My *past* belief cannot in itself constitute a *reason* for my present belief if elsewhere I have acquired a good and decisive reason to abandon or revise it. However, my past belief may be the *cause* of my present belief if we suppose that the mental process responsible for the evolution of beliefs brings into play auto-reinforcement mechanisms or hysteresis phenomena. One would then have a case of a mental event (the past belief) causing another mental event (the present belief) without counting as a reason for the latter.

This is precisely the way in which Donald Davidson characterizes irrationality in general. Going against many philosophical traditions, Davidson has argued that the reasons we have for acting must be treated as causes of our actions (1980). However, some mental causes cannot be considered to be reasons: the case we are examining is an example of this. Under such circumstances, we must speak of irrationality. Davidson has studied the conditions of possibility of this type of case (1982). It is significant that his point of departure is the case we examined at the beginning: the influence one mind has on another. This makes it clear how a mental event (the one that occurs in the subject's head, his belief for ex-

116

ample) can be the cause of another mental event (the belief of the imitating subject) without constituting a reason for it. (I have argued that the belief of the other *could* under certain circumstances be a reason for my own belief, not that this is always the case.) The case of many minds is paradigmatic for Davidson. If there is, in a single mind, a mental cause that is not a reason, we must grant, he concludes, that this mind is separated into relatively closed compartments, after the fashion of Freudian structures. This argument is not among the most solid, but let us apply it to the case in question nonetheless. Everything occurs as if my past belief, a cause of but not a reason for my present belief, were isolated from my self, the self that now forms a belief. I, my present self, imitate my past belief: I use it as a model, as if it were the belief of some one else.

1.3

The third step is an irrationality well known to economists, and often denounced by them. Maurice Allais likely had it in mind when he formulated his principle. It is known as the sunk cost fallacy. In rational choice theory, unlike accounting, all expenses must be considered written-off at the very moment they are incurred. This is a direct application of Allais's principle. This time the irrationality of the sunk cost fallacy no longer concerns belief formation, but action itself. It would be better to say: action in the service of belief.

I have acquired some expensive equipment. I judged it rational to make this investment because I thought it probable a certain event would occur. I was, however, mistaken. For example, I naively believed that television programs would amuse and instruct me, and I acquired a highly sophisticated television. I have been awakened to my error. What should I do? Use the equipment or get rid of it? In principle, rationality requires that I not take into account the cost of the investment when I make this choice. This expense is a sunk cost, it will always belong to the past and "only the future matters." In other words, my decision should be the same as that which would be rational if the equipment had been *given* to me. Thus, the costs and benefits of my decision to use the equipment considered as a gift must be compared with the costs and benefits implied by all other options open to me. Although this principle of comparison tends to favor the former option, I could be led to consider that it would be best to discard the television, which implies writing off the purchase cost and acknowledging the *a posteriori* irrationality of the original decision.

Most of us do not act like this, and the sunk cost fallacy is one thing people everywhere have in common. This equipment was expensive, so the costs must be recovered. The more paid for it, the more it seems indispensable to use it, even if doing so is very expensive and provides few returns compared with other options. We are prodded into acting in this way by a concern for internal coherence between our past and present selves ("demonstrating one's wisdom to oneself," as Davidson (1998) puts it in his contribution to this volume). This concern must be better analyzed. According to Allais's principle, we are engaging in perfect irrationality, but we nonetheless feel that there is a kind of logic behind it. By committing the sunk cost fallacy, I am in fact acting according to the rules of imitation, as in the first two steps. This time what I am copying or imitating are neither the beliefs or actions of others, nor my own past beliefs as if they belonged to some one else—it is the behavior which would have been mine if the circumstances had been those I was expecting and my decision to make the investment had been *a posteriori* justified. In Tversky's terms, this is once again a confusion of a causal issue with a concern for diagnosis. My action targets not its causal consequences, but the diagnosis which it will allow me to make of the situation. The television completely satisfies my needs, the proof is that I am using it right now. Thus, I am now reassured of the coherence of my choices, and of my rationality.

Things can also be presented in the following way. My behavior *symbolically* aims to *change the past* through imitating what would have been the causal consequences of a different and more desirable past. On this view, we can see the logic of vengeance in the sunk cost fallacy. An act of vengeance also aims to change the past. In fact, it attempts to abolish it by claiming to annul one act of violence by a new one, when all it does is add to the first one. The sunk cost fallacy consists in adding operating costs to an unjustified investment cost as if this would provide revenge for the latter.

1.4

The fourth and last step along our way is the class of common cause Newcomb problems.

Consider the following classic example from the great statistician R. A. Fisher. We know that there is a strong correlation between tobacco smoking and lung cancer. Suppose that it is discovered that the reason for this correlation is not, as was thought until now, that tobacco smoking *causes* lung cancer. The cancer is caused by a certain gene which also predisposes people to smoke. Let's take the case of an individual who enjoys smoking. Does this person now have a reason to quit? (As was the case under the interpretation that prevailed until now: smokers were guilty of "weakness of the will.") Her decision will in no way alter the fact that she has, or does not have, the lethal gene. It would be irrational for this person to deprive herself of the pleasure she feels, by hypothesis, when she engages in her vice.

Yet, if this case is made subject to the golden rule of rational choice theory – namely, always act so that you maximize your mathematical expected utility – we must conclude that it is rational to refrain from smoking. So, if we are convinced (as are most authors) of the contrary, we must explain what is wrong with rational choice theory in its traditional form (which dates from Leonard Savage and John von Neumann). This question, and the class of problems in which it arises, are at the origin of a schism within the world of rational choice theorists. The vast majority of authors assert the irrationality of the behavior which, in this example, consists in quitting smoking. Their argument leads back to Allais's principle: whatever the subject does, her action will not change the past, which, here, means the presence or absence of the gene. They must thus amend the golden rule in order to make it compatible with their conviction. A small minority opposes this orthodoxy. Its members follow the golden rule in its original form and conclude that refraining is rational. According to the orthodoxy, they are committing a grave mistake. They reason as if quitting smoking were the price, relatively small compared with what is at stake, that the agent accepts to pay in order to acquire the *evidence* that she does not have the fatal gene. This behavior is perfectly irrational, protests the orthodoxy: it consists in taking the evidence for the thing. It is *magical*, in the proper sense of the word.

[For the sake of brevity, here I will skip the strategy open to the heterodoxy which consists in dodging a head-on confrontation with the orthodoxy, by noting that quitting smoking, in this case, obviously has no evidential value. I have shown elsewhere that this strategy backfires (Dupuy 1992)].

Fisher's problem is characterized by a double relation between the action (here, the decision to refrain or not) and the state of the world (the presence or the absence of the gene). There is a (strong) *probabilistic dependence* between the action and the state of the world although the action is not the *cause* of the latter. This double relation of probabilistic dependence and causal independence characterizes the class of Newcomb problems. This configuration is permitted here by the existence of a *common cause* of the action and the risk of lung cancer. This is why Fisher's problem is said to belong to the subclass of common cause Newcomb problems. All problems belonging to this class have the following form: a state of the world C causes, at the same time, a very favorable state of things X and a moderately costly decision x:

120

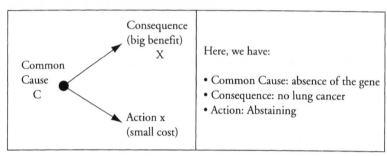

For this class of problems, maximization of the expected utility according to the usual procedure—namely, through the intermediary of conditional probabilities (of the states of the world given the action) weighing the outcomes—leads to a decision considered irrational (by the orthodoxy).

Why is this? Conditional probabilities are indifferent to the nature of the links they make manifest—indifferent to the fact that these links are or are not causal. The orthodoxy holds that when I decide between several possible actions, I must consider only the *causal consequences* of my action and their more or less desirable characteristics. The more or less desirable character of the state of things manifested by my action, or for which my action would only be *evidence*, should not be taken into account. When an agent maximizes his expected utility in the usual way, he acts as if he had an external vantage point on himself, as if he were someone else. He discovers his decision in the same way we do and his strategy is to act in such a way as to make the news that this discovery brings as favorable as possible. The subject reasons that if he does this, then his action will make manifest the presence of such and such desirable features in the world. I would like these features to be the case, thus I act in this way. The orthodoxy concludes that this is irrational, magical behavior. Things are actually even worse. If the action makes manifest the state of the world, that is here because it is caused by it. In consequence, to act in a given way because what can be inferred from one's action is a favorable diagnosis of the state of the world, which is a state determined in the past, is to give oneself an unimaginable power: the power to *choose one's past.*

Decision theory as reformulated by the orthodoxy is known as the *causal* decision theory. It is now clear why this is so. The traditional theory, to which the minority clings, is rechristened the *evidentialist* theory. From the preceding, it is clear that the evidentialists have their work cut out for them if they want to be taken seriously.

Evidentialism presents features that we have learned, in the earlier stages of our discussion, to associate with irrationality: looking at oneself from the outside as if one were someone else; giving oneself power over the past. I would, however, like to propose a defence and illustration of evidentialism in what follows. This does not imply that I wish to do this *against* the orthodoxy, in other words, the causal theory. My thesis (Dupuy 1992) is that rationality is not univocal. There are two forms of rationality that are irreducible to one another. Since it puts them into conflict, the class of Newcomb problems has the merit of revealing and identifying them. These two types of rationality correspond to two different, though inseparable, conceptions of time–better expressed as two authentically human experiences of time.

Before presenting a whole series of arguments in favor of this thesis, I would like to take up an example with considerable theoretical and historical importance. The present debate seems unaware that this example is the paradigm case that has inspired, to varying degrees, all the others. Here I am referring to the famous thesis, in the form of a paradox, advanced by Max Weber, on the "correlations" between the "Protestant ethic," or more precisely the ethical consequences of the doctrine of predestination, and the "spirit of capitalism" (Weber 1930). Tversky and Quattrone are an exception. They address the issue, but unfortunately without referring to Weber's analysis. This may account for our differences in interpretation.

Here I will examine only the logical structure of Weber's argument, not its empirical validity. In virtue of a divine decision taken for all eternity, each person belongs either to the camp of the elect or to that of the damned, without knowing which. No one can do anything about this decree, and there is nothing anyone can do to earn or merit salvation.

However, divine grace manifests itself through *signs*. Here what is important is that these signs cannot be observed through introspection: *they are acquired through action*. The principal sign is success obtained through *testing* one's faith in a worldly profession (*Beruf*). This test is costly. It requires one work continually, methodically, without ever resting secure in, without even enjoying, one's wealth. "Unwillingness to work," Weber notes, "is symptomatic of the lack of grace" (159).

Here we again find the logical structure of a common cause Newcomb problem:

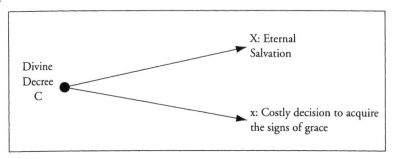

Divine Decree C

X: Eternal Salvation

x: Costly decision to acquire the signs of grace

The "logical consequence" of this *practical* problem, Weber points out, should "obviously" have been "fatalism." Here fatalism means the "orthodox" choice, Non-x, the choice of the "dominant" strategy, as it is known in game theory: whatever the state of the world—here, whether I am one of the elect or not—it is better for me to lead a lazy life. (This "fatalist" choice is equivalent to, in the Fisher problem, continuing to smoke.) However, Weber's whole book attempts, as we know, to explain why and how "the broad mass of ordinary men" made the opposite choice. We are perhaps more or less, whether we like it or know it or not, the inheritors of this choice—the evidentialist choice.

The Calvinist doctrine of the masses held it "to be an absolute duty to consider oneself chosen, and to combat all doubts as temptations of the devil, since lack of self-confidence is the result of insufficient faith, hence of imperfect grace" (111). The means of acquiring this self-confidence, the means of assuring oneself of one's state of grace, was "intense worldly activity" (112).

The debate between the Lutherans and the Calvinists is extremely interesting. The former accused the Calvinists of reverting to the dogma of "salvation by works," to the great dismay of the latter, outraged that their doctrine could be identified with what they most scorned: the Catholic doctrine. This accusation amounted to saying that she who chooses x reasons *as if* x were the cause of X—magical behavior, insist the accusors, since it consists in taking the evidence for the thing (x for C). This accusation is no other than the one causal theorists today make against their adversaries, the "evidentialists." From this we can see that the present debate is more than it claims to be: a defence of rationality, and that it has theological roots. This should surprise no one who, taking the point of view of the Durkheimian tradition, is convinced that what we call Reason has its origins in religious thought.

I have just used the expression "as if." It is ambiguous. If it is interpreted to mean that the two lines of thought lead to the same result, then the accusation has good grounds since in practice both doctrines, the Calvinist and the Catholic, are indistinguishable—and in an extremely paradoxical way the Calvinist doctrine even reveals itself to be much more meritocratic than the Catholic doctrine (Weber, 115–16). However, if the interpretation is that the Puritans *really* took the sign to be the thing, the accusation then becomes incomprehensible and completely unjustified. For Weber shows that, as is well known, ascetic puritanism constitutes the final stage of the vast movement of "elimination of magic from the world" which rejects "all magical means to salvation as superstition and sin" (105). He emphasizes that this Puritan view is what "stood at the cradle of the modern economic man" (174), "gave birth to economic rationalism" (259, n. 4) and transformed the "calculating spirit" of capitalism "from a mere means to economy into a principle of general conduct" (261).

Of course, one could place the derogatory label "irrational" on the Puritan choice, in other words, the evidentialist choice. However, one should be aware of the risks one would be taking. Economic rationality—it is important to note here that I am referring to the rationality of economic *actors*, not of economists—represents for many the pinnacle of Reason in history. Weber's analysis incites us to think that this rationality belongs to evidentialism's camp. Are we ready to face the paradox of judging it... irrational?

1.5

In order to move ahead in this discussion of the presumed irrationality of evidentialism, I would now like to introduce the topic that concerns us in this volume: self-deception. Weber dubs the Calvinists "saints overflowing with self-confidence" and "self-proclaimed saints." The issue I would like to examine is: did they also deceive themselves, were they self-deceived?

Tversky and Quattrone give a positive answer to this, and that same response can be given to any evidentialist choice. Their argument can be put in the following terms. Propositions (1) and (2), used in the situation under examination, are both true:

(1)   The Calvinists believe that they have placed themselves among the elect by choosing x;

(2)   The Calvinists believe that they have not placed themselves among the elect.

(1) and (2) express contradictory beliefs. Furthermore, one could think that:

*   The Calvinists find a way to hide (1) from themselves

*   because they want to believe they were chosen by God.

If we further postulate that the first belief is the *cause* of the second, without, obviously, constituting a reason for it, we obtain a pure case of self-deception as described by Donald Davidson (1986). He takes the example of a man preoccupied by growing baldness who manages, using various cosmetic and, especially, psychological means to deny the obvious, but whose efforts have perhaps more successful effects on his own beliefs than they do on those of others. This man believes that he is bald *and* believes that he is not bald at the same time. He manages to hide from himself the fact that he has the first belief because he wants to have only the second. Yet, it is certainly *because* he has the first belief that a mental mechanism of wishful thinking sets in and leads him to have the second belief.

I do not want to deny that this is an acceptable interpretation of the evidentialist choice. At Stanford, Quattrone and Tversky have done a series of impressive experiments in which they place their subjects in situations which have the structure of a common cause Newcomb problem. The remarkable result is that not only do the great majority of subjects make the evidentialist choice, they deny (to the experimenter and it seems likely to themselves) having *intentionally* chosen x in order to make a favorable diagnosis about themselves. I simply want to propose another interpretation that reveals the *rationality* of the evidentialist choice.

In my view, the Calvinists can be said to have the following two beliefs, which are not (necessarily) incompatible:

(3) The Calvinists believe that they did not place themselves among the elect because they believe God chose them;

(4) The Calvinists believe that they were free to choose x or Not-x when they chose x.

From the beginning I have been telling essentially the same story, with a few variations: is it worthwhile to pay the price of admission to a very exclusive club? However, common cause Newcomb problems have one fundamental difference with those mentioned above. The critical decision is no longer made by the agent: someone or something, God or Nature, has already chosen for him. My thesis is that this difference weighs heavily in the question of rationality. Under Tversky's interpretation, the belief described by proposition (2) is irrational: the Calvinists adopt the belief that they themselves are not responsible for their believing that they are among the elect because, in their deepest hearts they know very well that they have acted to give themselves the signs of the elect and they want to hide this truth from themselves. Under my interpretation, the Calvinists believe that they have not proclaimed themselves saints simply because they take seriously the premises of the problem as they have been submitted to them or as they have internalized them: God has proclaimed them to be this way. They nonetheless face a formidable problem: they must consider it to be not incoherent to believe both that God has chosen for them (proposition (3)) and that they are free to choose (proposition (4)).

Certainly, one might object that (4) is not really one of the givens of the problem. However, what would be the sense in questioning the rationality of the agent if she does not have, or does not give herself, free choice, understood in its minimal sense as the ability to act in a way other than the way in which one does? In terms rooted in an extremely old philosophical tradition, for an agent to be able to take seriously a common cause Newcomb problem, he must first be convinced that it is reasonable to be "*compatibilist*:" in other words, to believe in the compatibility of determinism (here, causal) and free will.

I will now show that there are two ways to defend compatibilism, according to the degree to which determinism menaces free will. Furthermore, the solution given to the compatibilist problem *determines* the solution to the Newcomb problem. The distinction between two forms of rationality and two forms of temporality to which I referred above is thus rooted in the distinction between two conceptions of determinism.

2. Two Temporalities, Two Rationalities

2.1

Like all occurrences in the world, actions leave traces, such as memories in the minds of people. In favorable cases, these traces can be *followed back* to the events of which they are the reflections, copies or representations. If this were not possible, disciplines as diverse as archaeology, history and psychoanalysis would be unthinkable. Generally, less attention is paid to the inverse possibility because our conviction that time flows irreversibly in one direction is so strong. Yet, it can sometimes be legitimate to treat an event that *precedes* another as the trace *in the past* of the latter. Consider an event that occurs at t_2: at $t_1 < t_2$, this event could have been preceded, announced if one likes, by its cause (causal determinism); or it could have been predicted correctly (theological determinism if the predictor is God); or else it could have been true at t_1 that the event would occur at t_2: "it was written" (logical determinism); and if the event is an action there are yet other possibilities. The subject could have formed at t_1 the intention to carry out this action at t_2; or this action could have been announced through threats (deterrence) or promises (commitment, contracting). It is sometimes possible to trace the event occurring at t_1 *forward* to the event occurring at t_2. If the latter is the action of a subject, one can argue that the existence of these traces in the past, or if one prefers, these memories of the future, render the agent incapable of taking any action but the one she took. This is the classical argument of those who deny free will and who are known as *incompatibilists* because they assert the incompatibility of determinism (of any sort: causal, theological or logical) and free will. I will now sketch out the incompatibilist argument in the condensed form which contemporary authors have given it. I will then examine the possibility or possibilities of refuting it.

2.2

Let us call "C" the event that occurs at t_1 and "x" the action at t_2 which C announces. "S" designates the subject. We can write:

A1:   C occurred at t_1

A2:   If C occurred at t_1, then S does x at t_2

Thus A3: S does x at t_2

We should note the role played by A2: this proposition expresses the temporal chain that links C to x; it characterizes C as that which announces x.

The incompatibilist argument applies an operator of necessity which is generically represented by the symbol $\square$. When this operator is applied to a proposition, it asserts that the proposition is true in all possible worlds. More specific to our problem, we will call $\square^S_t$ the operator of necessity such that:

$\square^S_t(p)$ means: p is true and S is not free at t to perform an act such that, if he performed it, p would be false.

The incompatibilist argument can be written thus:

N1: $\square^S_{t2}$ (C occurred at t_1)

N2: $\square^S_{t2}$ (If C occurred at t_1, then S does x at t_2)

Thus N3: $\square^S_{t2}$ (S does x at t_2)

N1 expresses the principle of the *fixity of the past*. At time t_2, A1 is necessary, not because it has always been necessary but because it has become so. It was contingent that it become necessary. It is "accidentally necessary," according to scholastic terminology.

N2 expresses the *fixity of the temporal link that unites events C and x*. Depending on the case, we could be dealing with the fixity of the laws of nature; or the fact that the predictor is omniscient in all possible worlds; or indeed any other constraint, depending on the nature of the temporal link which makes C the announcement of x. We must note that N2 is equivalent to:

(5) (C occurs at t_1) $\prec$ (S does x at t_2)

in which the symbol $\prec$ expresses strict implication (or entailment) in logic. The meaning of (5) is that in *all* possible worlds in which C occurs at t_1, S does x at t_2. It is fundamental to understand that A2 is not sufficient to imply (5). Indeed, this is the point of origin of the bifurcation between the two forms of temporality that we will be led to distinguish. A2 is an indicative conditional the validity of which is limited to *our* world. A2 does not exclude that in a possible world *other* than ours, in which C occurs at t_1 as in our world, S does not do x at t_2.

The conclusion N3 says that S does in effect do x at t_2, as was "announced" at t_1, but that S does not act freely because it is not in his power to act other than as he does.

Can one be compatibilist? Can the above argument be refuted? The thesis I am defending is that, depending on the nature of the problem, the agent has two possibilities, neither of which has greater *a priori* legitimacy than the other.

a) The agent could accept N1, in which case he would have to reject N2. The past is fixed, thus the subject, who considers himself to be free, must give himself the power to invalidate the fixity of the temporal chain which links C to x. The nature of this power must be made clear. Obviously, it is not that *in our world* the subject can act so that the link between C and x will be violated: this would be contrary to hypothesis A2, which indeed remains valid. Rather, it is that the subject reasons in this way. Suppose that C took place at t_1 and, thus, that I will decide to do x at t_2. While I do perform x at t_2, I know that it is in my power to perform Not-x. It is thus in my power at t_2 to do something (namely, Not-x) such that *if I were to do it*, the link between C and x *would* be invalidated. This is because, since the past is fixed, the fact that C occurred at t_1 would remain unchanged. By acting other than the way I do, I would enter another *possible* world (since I am free), in which the relation expressed by A2 would not hold. This power is called *counterfactual*.

This option corresponds to the orthodox view. It rests on Allais's principle: the past is fixed in relation to my present action. Consequently, "only the future matters." If, as in the case of common cause Newcomb problems, there is a dominant strategy, it must be chosen, as we have seen. By convention, we have called "C" the favorable common cause (the absence of the lethal gene in the Fisher problem, or, in Weber's example, being among those chosen by God), and "x" the evidentialist strategy. Non-x is thus the dominant strategy, and it is endorsed by the orthodoxy. Since the agent decides to do Not-x and he believes A2 to be valid, he must infer that at t_1 Not-C existed, not C. He must claim that it is rational to continue smoking with the knowledge that this choice proves he has the fatal gene. The ungodly Calvinist must convince himself it is better to indulge in idleness life even though this choice reveals that he is among the damned! It is too easy for the evidentialist to reply that if such is the case, she would willingly seem "irrational" if doing so would ensure her good health or even her eternal salvation. While it is troubling, this argument is not entirely convincing, and I will not use it because I have, I believe, a better one.

129

b) The agent's other option is to accept N2, but then he can only reject N1. This time the temporal chain A2 is held to be fixed (in other words, as true in all possible worlds). The agent, considering himself to be free, must thus give himself a *counterfactual* power to invalidate the past. Let us examine this: obviously this is not a *causal* power over the past, which would be completely inconceivable unless we were writing science (or rather philosophy) fiction. More reasonably, the agent thinks in the following way. Suppose that C occurred at t_1 and thus that I will decide to do x at t_2. While doing x at t_2, I know that it is in my power to do Not-x. It is thus in my power at t_2 to do something (namely Not-x) such that *if I were to do it* C would not have occurred at t_1 since the fixed link between the past and my action entails that if C occurred at t_1, x is what I would do. By acting in a way other than the way I do, I would enter another *possible* world (since I am free), in which the past would be different from what it was in my world. This is the nature of the power which Alvin Plantinga (1986) named the *counterfactual power over the past*.

It can thus be shown that by giving herself this power over the past, the agent in the common cause Newcomb problem is rationally led to choose x—in other words to make the evidentialist, or Calvinist, choice. (Dupuy 1992; the demonstration, however, requires the additional hypothesis that Non-C causes Non-x).

At this crossroads, we are faced with a metadecision. The great majority of professional philosophers who reflect on these problems resolutely take the orthodox path: they unhesitatingly adopt Allais's principle. In contrast, "the broad mass of ordinary men" (at least in the Californian, therefore strongly Puritan, population in which Tversky performed his experiments) take the other route. Is this crowd "irrational"?

At this point it should be clear that two conceptions of time are in opposition. Their essential difference has to do with the past. The fixity of the past with respect to our free actions seems to be very much a part of the very essence of what we call rationality. Allais's principle gets its strength from this intuition. However, three remarks are pertinent.

a) The class of Newcomb problems is responsible for revealing that there is a thorny problem here. Now, it is certainly not for nothing that in these problems, the past is not known and is unknowable except through signs of various kinds (causal consequences, predictions coming true, etc.), which it leaves in the form of actions performed by free agents. Is a past that is unknown, and impossible to know directly, fixed to the same degree as a known past?

b) Moreover, there is much to say in favor of the fixity of the law or rule that characterizes the evidentialist choice. We will soon see that it offers a way out of pragmatic paradoxes that commonly occur in life in society. The risk of "superstitious rule-worship," i.e. of making the rule, or law, sacred, promptly denounced by the orthodox camp, certainly does exist. However, we will see that a similar risk menaces the principle of the fixity of the past. This principle can also become the object of quasi-religious devotion. An illustration of this will be provided below.

c) One very important result of the preceding analyses is that there is no need to resort to an inconceivable power to change the past, or to choose it, in order to found the evidentialist choice. There is thus no reason to reproach the Puritans for giving themselves a power, which belongs only to God, to save or damn themselves. A much more "innocent" power, as the analytic theologian Plantinga (1986) says, suffices: a counterfactual power over the past.

Firmly adhering to the principle of the fixity of the past, the orthodox theorists place themselves in what I call the *temporality of history* or *occurring time* (Dupuy 1992). I call it the temporality of history because, as a discipline, history treats the past as an object and also because, in a certain philosophical tradition, events spring up in history without shedding any light on the past insofar as they are pure beginnings. In the terminology we are using here, events seen as *Ereignisse* play no role as *evidence*.

I hold that as humans we experience another form of time, which I call the *temporality of projects* or *projected time.* Let us go back to the strict implication (5), which is its characteristic formulation, and not shrink from reading it according to the classical metaphor. C is the *inscription* in the past of the agent's future free action ("future contingent"). Everything is already "written." As Diderot said, "It is like a Great Scroll which is unrolled little by little" (*Jacques le Fataliste*). The agent acts according to a previously prepared scenario, but because she is free, she can raise herself to the level at which this scenario is written and exercise a kind of power over it–the power we call counterfactual.

The temporality of projects is one of the forms of human experience of time. This experience is that of the subject who executes a plan he has devised for himself, of which he is both author and actor. This doubling or "bootstrapping" clearly reveals the demiurgic character of projected time. Significantly, the French language uses reflexive expressions such as "se décider" and "se déterminer" to express the moment of choice when the agent creates a new determinism of which she herself is both the subject and the object. Projected time is clearly more "paradoxical" than the temporality of history. In it we find two features which we have learned to associate with irrational behavior: the subject giving himself a form of power over the past, and the subject looking at himself from outside, as if he were separated from himself. I hope I have succeeded in showing that these two features are not *sufficient* conditions for irrationality.

131

3. One Paradox of Backwards Induction: The Problem of the Credibility of Promises

3.1

Rational choice theory and game theory, two of the principal actors in the rationalist paradigm, are now undergoing a foundational crisis. This is openly acknowledged by some of their most eminent representatives (for example, Aumann 1988). The class of paradoxes we will discuss constitutes one of the most serious symptoms of this. These are known as paradoxes of backwards induction. For any decision problem with a finite horizon, whether it involves an isolated actor or a strategic dimension, backwards induction consists in first solving the last step of the problem, the one which, by hypothesis, has no future implications. Then, sticking to the solution thus determined, a decision is made on the next-to-last step, which at this point in the reasoning has no *undetermined* future. Working backwards in time, step by step, the complete solution is in principle reached. Since the invention of dynamic programming, this method has become *the* rational way for dealing with this sort of problem. More than one subject in economics and game theory owes its existence to this method. Yet, in the last few years its very foundations have come to appear less solid than once thought. My claim is that there is no other foundation for the pretended obviousness of backwards induction than Allais's principle. I will show that the general framework I have built to contest the universality of this principle is sufficient to resolve the difficulties posed by the method in question. More precisely, I will establish that the paradox of backwards induction is a Newcomb problem.

This last result, aside from its intrinsic interest, has important consequences for the meaning we should give to the type of intellectual exercise in which we are engaging here. We might have thought that the common cause Newcomb problems, which we have analyzed, were fantasies of philosophers or theologians. This they are, no doubt, even though (let us consider the Calvinist choice) these imaginary constructions have shaped the world in which we live. The various forms that the paradoxes of backwards induction take are quite another story: the possibility of reciprocal exchange; the stability of agreements, promises, and contracts; the effectiveness of threats and deterrence are only a few examples, and it must be admitted there would be no viable human society if people had not succeeded in ensuring the stability of these raw materials of social relations. That these paradoxes turn out to be equivalent to problems with a theological aspect or source is thus in itself heavy with meaning.

Here I will limit myself to one case: the credibility of promise. I have shown elsewhere that the issue of the effectiveness of deterrence can be dealt with in the same framework, but that it is appreciably more complex than the problem of promising.

3.2

The credo of those who champion free trade is that the economy is not a "zero-sum game." Exchanges can benefit everyone and, if such is the case, nothing put in their path can last (except that undesirable, the State, with its finicky regulations and policies of redistribution). All we need to do is to give free rein to the famous "invisible hand," and all will be for the best in the best of all possible worlds. In theory, however, there is one condition, rarely made explicit, necessary for things to work out this way. The two actions that make up the reciprocal exchange, which is supposed to benefit the two parties, must be *simultaneous*. In principle, the least time lag is fatal. Let us consider the following situation between Peter and Mary:

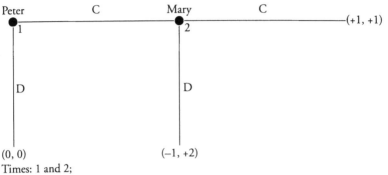

Times: 1 and 2;
C: Cooperation;
D: Defection

A mutually advantageous exchange between Peter and Mary is in principle possible. It would lead them from their present situations—or the vector (0, 0), of which the first component represents the "utility," or any other indicator supposed to order the preferences, of Peter, and the second that of Mary—to a state (+1,+1) which both prefer. The problem springs from the fact that for some reason the exchange will only take place if Peter takes the first step (C), in which case he runs the risk that Mary will not take the second step, thus pocketing what Peter gives her without giving anything in return (Mary would thus do D at time 2, ending up with +2 and leaving Peter with -1).

Backwards induction quickly convinces us that the exchange cannot take place even though it would benefit both parties. Let us begin with the last step, in other words, at time 2, in which it is Mary's turn to act. It is rational for her, according to the orthodoxy at least, not to reciprocate because she obtains +2 by defecting, against +1 by cooperating. Note that this reasoning—that of Mary as well as that of the orthodox theorist—is independent of the way that she came to have her turn to act at time 2. "Only the future matters." Again the obviousness of Allais's principle rules.

What should Peter do at time 1? Let us assume that Peter's mind is able to *simulate*, or reproduce the reasoning that the orthodox theorist lends

133

to Mary at 2. Note in passing that this implies that Peter believes Mary is rational, or, more precisely, that she is rational in the orthodox way. Peter thus has the choice between taking the first step in which case he anticipates that Mary will not take the second, and that he will end up with -1; and not moving, in other words, doing D, in which case he will obtain 0. Therefore he does not move and the exchange does not take place.

Perhaps this disastrous result could be avoided thanks to the institution of promising. Before the game begins, because it is just as much in her interest as it is in Peter's, Mary promises her partner that she will cooperate at 2 if he cooperates at 1. A waste of time, according to the orthodoxy! Mary knows very well that when the time comes, at 2, it will be in her interest to break her promise. Peter, reading her mind, knows this too. Even if she swears by all the gods, Mary is not *credible*. Therefore Peter does not act.

Could Peter not *trust* Mary? Trust: this is certainly a notion smelling of religion that economic rationality should hold in suspicion. Yet, in these times of "crisis," this is the word on the tongue of every economist, those who determine policies and, even more remarkably, theorists alike. It is as if the play of egoistic interests were no longer sufficient to power the economic machine. It now requires a good dose of this virtue or elixir: trust. I suspect that this need or lack has to do with the admittedly schematized problem we are discussing.

The market economy vitally needs trust. The principle of rationality (that of the theorists or the orthodoxy) demonstrates its irrationality and thus its impossibility. Should we content ourselves with merely contemplating this abyss separating economic practice and economic rationality? Luckily we can see a way out. Today this rationality is no longer so self-assured: it has been shaken in its very foundations. It could be that another conception of rationality can bring the real and the rational closer together. It might even be able to reconcile them. It is time to go back to the paradoxes of backwards induction.

After all, what is so paradoxical about the orthodox analysis of the Peter and Mary example? The fact that interacting rational actors mutually condemn themselves to a situation which is disastrous for both? Rational choice theory is full of this type of situation, beginning with the famous prisoner's dilemma. If the opposite impression prevails, it is due largely to the considerable influence on economic thought of the Walrassian model of general equilibrium, seen as the formalization of the idea of the "invisible hand."

No, the fact that a growing number of authors are tempted to see a paradox in the very principle of backwards induction is because it seems to suffer from an insidious illness: self-refutation. This reasoning appears to repudiate itself in its conclusion. How so? Let us consider the intermediate result we believed we established: if it is Mary's turn at 2, she will defect. This is the result on which we built the following, conclusive step that permits us to assert that Peter himself would defect at 1. But this means that Mary will never get her turn at 2! Our reasoning has kicked away the ladder that allowed it to climb up to its conclusion, and now it is suspended perilously in the air with nothing left to support it.

If this can be considered an argument, it provokes two opposite kinds of reaction. The orthodoxy rejects it with a simple shrug of the shoulders. Others, and I am among them, have the impression they are facing a serious difficulty but that it must be completely reformulated. Contrary to most of those who share this intuition, however, I do not think that this obstacle can be avoided through technical means. What is at stake is much more fundamental and concerns our relation to time.

There are good reasons to reject the argument that this is a case of self-refutation. If this argument were taken seriously, it would strike right to the heart of decision theory, with perhaps fatal results. As Shafir and Tversky noted (1992) in a text on "thinking through uncertainty," when one reasons through a decision tree, one is led to "assume momentarily as true something that may in fact be false" once the overall line of reasoning reaches an end. In the example discussed, this is exactly what happens in the case of the hypothesis that Mary gets her turn at 2. As cognitive psychologists, these authors observe that people are extremely reluctant to think in this way, unlike Artificial Intelligence devices for which it is child's play. Tversky and Shafir even suggest this may be one of the crucial points where the essential difference between natural and artificial intelligence comes into play.

The self-refutation argument is significant, to some of us at least, not only because it resounds with the psychological structure of our faculties of reason: there are ethical reasons. In Voltaire's tale, when Zadig sees the hermit murder the nephew of their hostess of the previous night, he is aghast. What, he cries in outrage, could you find no other way to thank our hostess for her generosity than to commit this terrible crime? To this, the hermit, who is none other than the angel Jesrad, the spokesperson of Leibniz's system, replies that if that young man had lived, he would have killed his aunt a year later and, a year after that, he would have murdered Zadig himself. How do you know that? demands Zadig. It was written. Peter refuses to trust Mary because he "knows" that she will not keep her promise. His refusal makes the falsification of his certainty impossible. Thus, as they say in philosophy of science, his strategy is auto-immunizing. Like Zadig-Voltaire, we might want to rebel against such arrogance. According to more than one moral tradition, if Peter hopes for trust to reign between Mary and him, he has no choice but to "prove motion by walking," to jump in, to trust Mary by taking the first step. However, I would not much want to create the impression I am taking Voltaire's side against Leibniz. In effect, I will soon suggest that trust may, to a certain extent, be vindicated, if not proven, and I will do this using the metaphor of writing, the same metaphor to which the Leibnizian messenger resorts.

I have two goals. I want to show that it is possible to make rigorous the argument according to which the orthodox solution self-refutes; and, at the same time, that reciprocal exchange is both rational and possible. First we must review a few points.

3.3

Most authors accept that the Peter and Mary problem can be solved in terms of *precommitment*: there are a thousand ways for Mary to "tie her hands" in Peter's eyes and with his knowledge so as to convince him that if he takes the first step, it would be impossible, or at least very costly, for Mary to not take the second step. Literature is full of stories like this, some of which are utterly fantastic. Thus, Mary could contract a murderer to kill her if she did not keep her promise. She could also make a bet with a third party that she would remain faithful to her commitment regarding Peter so that losing her bet by reneging on her promise would cost more than whatever she could gain at Peter's expense. Such solutions carry risks and are, in any case, very costly in themselves. Most importantly, however, they come up against some apparently well-established ethical principles. Is it thus only by alienating her freedom to a third party or a mechanism that Mary can become free? This paradox is, in the eyes of many, untenable. Perhaps a solution in terms of commitment, rather than precommitment, could be devised? Could Mary not *commit herself* towards herself when she commits herself towards Peter—with a pure translucent conscience, without this relation to herself and the reflexive doubling or bootstrapping which it presupposes implying she be in any way opaque to herself, in bad faith, or self-deceiving?

A very small number of philosophers (in the Anglo-American tradition I am considering here) think this is possible. Among them are Edward McClennen (1990), with his notion of "resolute choice" and especially David Gauthier (1984), with his notion of the "rationality of plans." I will concentrate on laying out the latter's argument, as I interpret it. At least for the type of problem we are now studying, rationality must be evaluated at the level of plans and not directly at that of actions. Mary's choice is *a priori* between four plans, each one consisting in an intention formed at time 0, before the game begins, and an action at time 2. Suppose, as above, that since Mary's intentions are transparent, Peter can "read" her thoughts. If Mary intends to reciprocate at 2, Peter sees it and concludes that it is in his interest to cooperate at 1. The four plans are as follows.

Mary:

      Plan 1: Intends to reciprocate; defects;

      Plan 2: Intends to reciprocate; reciprocates;

      Plan 3: Intends to defect; defects;

      Plan 4: Intends to defect; reciprocates.

From all points of view, Plan 4 is a nonstarter. For Mary, Plan 1 would be the ideal if it were possible, but it is not, Gauthier argues: it is certainly possible to form the intention to x at one time and to not-x a minute later, but one cannot form the meta-intention (the plan) to do that (Gauthier does not develop the justification for this argument which would require some refinement). Two possibilities remain and it is clear that, given Peter's reaction, Plan 2 is better for Mary than Plan 3. Thus, she adopts Plan 2 and this is possible for her because she is convinced it is rational.

The orthodox reply is that Plan 2 is "dynamically inconsistent." At time 2, Mary will not reciprocate because doing so would be against her interest. She knows this at time 0. It is impossible for her to form the intention to do something which she knows will be, when the time comes to do it, irrational for her to do. As David K. Lewis (who places himself in the orthodox camp) notes critically, Gauthier can only claim the contrary because his thesis is that rationality must flow "from the rationality of intention to the rationality of action, rather than vice versa" (Lewis 1984). For Gauthier (1984), the fact that Mary was able to establish the rationality of Plan 2 gives her a *"reason to act"* (according to the plan) at time 2, which overrides her preferences at that time. This "holism of plans" is unacceptable to the orthodoxy.

In this debate internal to American philosophy, the defence of my position requires finesse because it finds itself, as it were, caught in the crossfire. On the one hand, I wholly share the conviction of Gauthier and McClennen that one can and should save the possibility, rationality and effectiveness of promises in situations like Peter's and Mary's. On the other hand, I hold that there is a high philosophical price to pay for this, a price much higher than that which these authors are ready to pay. If the orthodoxy accepts my demonstration it will certainly be delighted, but for the wrong reason: it is equivalent, according to them, to the proof by *reductio* that reciprocal exchange is impossible. More precisely, Gauthier's method remains a form of consequentialism, a consequentialism of plans as it were, in opposition to that of actions. My claim is that if one is to save the rationality and possibility of reciprocal exchange, one absolutely must renounce consequentialism and put oneself in "projected time." This is what I will now attempt to show.

3.4

In the first stage, I will present a demonstration that is very unsatisfactory from at least three points of view: (1) it is purely formal and syntactic; (2) it retains only the metaphorical characterization of the concept of projected time, in other words, the image of the Great Scroll on which everything "is already written"; (3) it resorts to the concept of "rational expectation," which carries a heavy metaphysical load and, more importantly, as we will discover in the end, suffers from incompleteness because it is fundamentally ambivalent. In the second stage, I will attempt to deconstruct the metaphysical residue and give meaning to what will have been nothing but a formal exercise.

Let us call "rational expectation path" or, for short, "rational path," any path in a decision tree that satisfies the two following conditions:

a) It is temporally consistent. This means that it corresponds to what could be an actual sequence of events, each one leading to the next.

b) It is compatible with the assumption of rational expectation. The expectations of the agents are compatible with the "true" model of the problem and their behavior is rational given these expectations.

In the Peter and Mary example, we see that there are three temporally consistent paths:

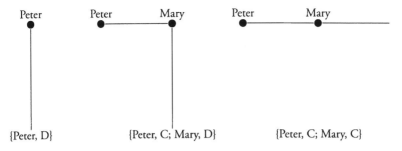

{Peter, D}   {Peter, C; Mary, D}   {Peter, C; Mary, C}

If we consider condition b), we see that the second of these paths obviously does not satisfy it. The orthodox and the heterodox cannot but agree on this: at 1 Peter is supposed to know that Mary will defect at 2; it is thus irrational for him to cooperate at 1. There are thus *two candidates* to the status of rational path: (Peter, D) and (Peter, C; Mary, C). The rational path is necessarily one of these two possibilities: everyone agrees on this. Which of the two is *the* rational path, that is where views are at odds. For the heterodox it is the second, to which the orthodox object that it violates condition b); but the heterodox reply that one can say that only on the basis of the Allais principle, the universal validity of which is precisely in question. For the orthodox, the rational path is (Peter, D); the heterodox object that this result rests on the claim that it is true at t=1 that Mary defects at 2 even though Peter chooses at 1 to defect (self-refutation argument). Before delving into this controversy, let us set out formally what we have just discovered.

Suppose that (Mary defects at 2)—or (Mary, D) for short—is part of the rational path. From this we deduce:

(Peter cooperates at 1), due to temporal consistency;

(Peter defects at 1), due to rational expectation.

Thus, a contradiction. We conclude that (Mary, D) is not part of the rational path. It follows that the following property is valid for the rational path, whatever it is:

Either (Mary does not get to play at 2) or (Mary reciprocates at 2)

This proposition is equivalent to:

(6)   If Mary plays at 2, then she reciprocates at 2;

or:

(7)   If Peter cooperates at 1, then Mary cooperates at 2.

At this point we might be tempted to cry victory. It seems we have succeeded, using a self-refutation argument, in doing away with the possibility Mary might defect at 2 if she gets a chance to play at that time. Nothing seems to stand in our way to concluding that Peter, knowing (7), concludes that it is rational for him to cooperate.

This would be all too easy. We must not forget that (6) and (7) are only properties of a rational path. They tell us nothing about what it would be rational for Mary to do at 2 if she should have her turn at that time. The orthodoxy has no trouble accepting (6) and (7) insofar as they are properties of the rational path. Their path, or (Peter, D), satisfies them perfectly, in other words trivially, by falsifying the antecedents of these conditional propositions. In their oecumenism, these propositions provide absolutely no way to decide between the two camps.

Obviously, the orthodox theorists do not stop here. They have another fundamental concept in their toolbox: *equilibrium*. It is inherent to the concept of equilibrium in game theory that it specifies a choice at each node of the decision tree, even at those nodes that will never be reached by a sequence of events constituting a rational path. The information contained in the equilibrium is thus very rich since it includes, as well as the specification of a path actually followed in time, a whole set of counterfactual propositions. Thus, the set of choices that constitute an equilibrium will generally not satisfy the condition of temporal consistency (but it will obviously respect, by construction, the condition of rational expectation).

In the case of the example given, the equilibrium is, according to the orthodoxy, (Peter, D; Mary, D), or:

Backwards induction provides the justification for this particular equilibrium, which is clearly not temporally consistent. In the name of Allais's principle, the orthodox theorist can assert:

(8)   If Mary got to play at 2, she would defect at 2.

The orthodox theorist, rightly, feels no contradiction in asserting both (6) and (8). Again, (6) simply expresses a property satisfied by the rational path, and the rational path for the orthodox theorist is (Peter, D). (8) is a "subjunctive conditional" which expresses a counterfactual proposition.   141

We will now attempt to draw out the implications of the Great Scroll metaphor, which characterizes projected time. Since everything is "already written," there is no way, not even a counterfactual way, to escape the rational path that appears on the scroll in question. More precisely, any subjunctive conditional expressing such a counterfactual will immediately be reduced to an indicative conditional describing a property of the rational path. A question like:

(9)   What would it be rational for Mary to do if she got to play (at 2)?

is translated as follows:

(10) What does Mary do at 2 on the rational path if she gets to play at 2 (on the rational path)?

Since proposition (6) is true of the rational path, whatever it is, it provides the answer, which we hurry to translate into the language of counterfactuals:

(11) If Mary got to play at 2, then she would cooperate at 2;

which is equivalent to:

(12) If Peter cooperated at 1, then Mary would cooperate at 2.

Peter is rational and anticipates (12): from this he concludes that it is rational for him to cooperate at 1. Therefore, he cooperates, and so does Mary. Reciprocal exchange is both rational and possible.

Remember that we do not claim to have shown anything here. We have given ourselves a syntactic rule (the translation operation) and we have applied it mechanically, without attempting to endow it with meaning. Now we must interpret what we have done.

3.5

We must return to the origin of the bifurcation of the two temporalities (see section 2.2.). Projected time, we note, corresponds to the option of taking the temporal linkage to be fixed (in other words, valid in all possible worlds), and "sacrificing," in a certain way, the fixity of the past. Propositions (11) and (12) thus express a *necessary* relation, valid in all possible worlds. This can also be written as:

(13) (Peter cooperates at 1) $\prec$ (Mary cooperates at 2),

and expressed in the following way: the fact that Peter cooperates at 1 is the "writing" in the past of the future fact ("future contingent"): Mary will cooperate at 2.

This is the option that allows counterfactual questions regarding the rationality of choices to be reduced to factual questions concerning the rational path. Once again, using the metaphor of the Great Scroll, what is "written above" has the authority of an intangible rule. One might object that this turns the rule into a sacred object: in other terms, this is "superstitious rule-worship" (J.J.C. Smart). Before justifying this approach by analyzing its conditions of possibility, I would like to remark that the orthodoxy is not safe from a similar objection. It, too, must pay a high metaphysical price. The orthodoxy arrives at the subjunctive conditional (8) in virtue of the principle of the fixity of the past: *no matter what* past path led Mary to have her turn at 2, only the (future) consequences of her present choice have any relevance (Allais's principle). Very well! Yet is not the domain of validity of that principle stretched beyond reasonable limits when, as in this case, it is applied even to decision situations to which *no* past path leads? This too strongly resembles the sacralization of a principle.

The syntactic exercise in which we engaged above took for granted the concept of rational expectation, which plays such an important role in economic theory today. The concept is in no way above suspicion, and our little exercise will at least have the merit of revealing that it is not well formed since it is unable, alone, to separate the two rational paths, the orthodox and the heterodox. This ambivalence springs from the ambiguity of the notion of "perfect foresight." In our model, Peter is both a predictor and an actor. His action is closely linked to his prediction: in a certain way, his action writes his prediction in the material world since if Peter predicts that Mary will cooperate, he cooperates himself, and if he predicts that she will defect, he, too, defects. He is supposed to predict Mary's action perfectly. What does this mean? This can be understood in two ways, which differ as N2 differs from A2 at the point where the two temporalities branch apart. Peter could be essentially omniscient, in other words, omniscient in all possible worlds, or he might be so de facto, in other words, only in our world (Plantinga 1986; Dupuy 1992). This is determined by Mary when she reasons, before the game starts, about what she should do at 2.

143

In the first case, she reasons as follows. If I was to cooperate at 2, Peter would have foreseen it at 1 and, being rational, would have cooperated himself. If I was to defect, we would be in another *possible* world (since I am free), in which Peter would *also* be omniscient. He would thus have foreseen that I would defect and he would have defected too. But in that case I would not have been able to have my turn at 2, contrary to my premise: I must thus set aside this possibility. This is where the self-refutation argument appears. If it is here validated, it is because Mary's hypothesis of the *essential* omniscience of Peter automatically leads her, as we can see, to give herself, as she reasons, a counterfactual power over the past. Mary logically concludes that, if she were to have her turn at 2, she would cooperate. Since her cooperating at 2 entails no such contradiction, we have a ground for the cooperative solution. This reasoning is strictly equivalent to that which we performed in section 3.4. It also shows that the Peter and Mary problem is equivalent to the Newcomb paradox in its original form, which brings in an omniscient predictor who is capable of acting on the state of the world according to his prediction (Dupuy 1992).

If Mary attributes Peter with the power to predict perfectly, but only in our world, her reasoning develops quite differently. Peter foresaw what I was going to do, and he recorded this mental act in the material world by acting in consequence of it. What I, Mary, will in fact do at 2 will in no way alter this past occurrence. I thus take the past to be fixed when I act.

Mary cannot seriously attribute Peter with an omniscient power, essential or de facto. Fantastic hypotheses like this are found only in economics textbooks. We must get rid of this metaphysical residue. Peter has no privileged access to the future, but he has certain access to Mary's mental state at the time preceding the moment at which he must act. He can "read" Mary to see if she has the *intention* or not to cooperate at 2. This is certainly far from providing him with a sufficient guarantee. It could be that at 0, Mary had the intention to cooperate at 2 but when the time comes she does not act in conformity with this intention. It could even be that Mary only "has" this intention, or manifests it, strategically, in order to bluff Peter. Peter thus needs much more than this. He must convince himself that Mary's intention at 0 to cooperate at 2 is the writing in the past of the future contingent: Mary will cooperate at 2. Mary's task is to convince him of this. It must be granted that she will only succeed insofar as she can convince herself. The question therefore becomes: can she do it without deceiving herself? Alas, the answer is negative, as the following argument shows.

3.6

Gregory Kavka (1983) challenged the philosophical community with a particularly cunning puzzle. Kavka, a specialist of the moral and political philosophy of Hobbes, is known for the positions he has taken in the American debate over nuclear deterrence. His puzzle is known as the "toxin puzzle." A billionaire, who has made his fortune in cognitive science, comes to you and proposes the following exchange. "You see this vial," he says, "it contains a toxin which, if you swallow it, will make you as sick as a dog for two days but will not kill you and will leave no after-effects. If you swallow the contents of this vial, I will pay you a million dollars." You are already rejoicing over this unexpected deal because you consider that the physical discomfort will be greatly dwarfed by the fortune you have been offered, when your eccentric acquaintance adds: "I am not even interested in whether or not you actually drink the toxin. I will be satisfied if you form the intention to do so. I have brought along this machine I have invented, which is able to detect intentions precisely. You will attach it to your brain tonight at midnight and it will then record whether or not you have the intention to drink the toxin tomorrow at noon. And, since I am generous, I won't even wait for you to drink it to give you your reward. If the machine detects a positive intention, you will find the million dollars in your bank account first thing tomorrow morning." On this, the billionaire leaves you to your bitter thoughts because, as a well-informed philosopher of mind, you have quickly understood that the pot of gold, which appeared to be at your fingertips, or rather your lips, has slipped away forever.

Let us reason like the orthodoxy. Tomorrow at noon, whether or not you have found the million dollars in your account, you have no reason to drink the toxin, and you have a very good reason not to drink it. The past is what it is, and your decision will not change it (Allais's principle). There is a dominant strategy, not to drink the toxin, and it is the rational strategy. You know this from now on, and thus also tonight at midnight. Since you cannot will yourself to form an intention, it is impossible for you to form the intention to do X if you know that when the time comes it will be unreasonable for you to do X. It is thus impossible, tonight at midnight, to form the intention to drink the toxin tomorrow at noon. The true poison is not that in the vial, as you thought, but indeed the billionaire's generosity.

It is easy to see the isomorphism of the toxin puzzle and the promise problem. Whatever the dominant views in cognitive science, which include belief in the *reality* of mental states such as beliefs, desires and intentions, the machine for detecting these states is, and it seems will remain, fictional. In contrast, the "machines" for *attributing* mental states to various cognitive systems, be they human, living, artificial or collective, have been around a long time and are in abundant supply: they are human minds. The translation of the promise problem into the terms of the toxin puzzle is crystal clear. The toxin is Mary's renunciation of the advantages of her dominant strategy, defection. The million dollars is the gift Peter gives her by letting her have her turn, and the link between the intention to drink the toxin and what appears to be the reward has its equivalent in Peter's deciding to cooperate if he detects Mary's intention to do the same. The conclusion is the same in both cases. At 0, Mary cannot form the intention to cooperate at 2 because she knows that when the time comes it will be irrational for her to do so. Thus she will not have her reward.

That was the orthodox argument. Can it be refuted using the projected time approach? Alas, we must give up this hope because of the nature of intentions. Remember that in order for us to be in projected time, the portent—the event we label C—must appear as the writing in the past of the future contingent which it announces. In other words, the temporal link between these two events must be considered as valid in all possible worlds. However, the link between the intention at o to do x at t, and the action of doing x at t, cannot be held to be fixed in this sense. The analysis of the toxin puzzle brings this out. The subject is free to do Not-x rather than x, but this in no way endows her with a counterfactual power over the past (here, the past intention) which defines projected time. Suppose, in effect, that the subject determines that one of the options is rational and that this option is, say, x. It would not be reasonable for her to do Not-x at t, therefore she cannot form the intention to do it at o. Consequently, the fact that she is free to do Not-x gives her no power to form the intention to do Not-x at o.

3.7

Should this failure be the end of the line for our inquiry? I think not. The analysis of what differentiates the promise problem from the toxin puzzle will allow us to move on. In the latter, the subject is connected to a machine; in the former she is interacting with a person. The link between the intention and the reward is, on the one hand, a mechanical condition imposed by the capriciousness of a being whose interest in the affair is opaque; on the other hand, the link *can* be an agreement, contract or convention in the form of a *fixed rule* (always in the sense of: valid in all possible worlds) between the actions of the subjects concerned. I repeat that my ambition is not to *prove* this possibility (this would, it seems clear, be bound to fail). In the framework set up here, and more particularly concerning the issue of the scope of Allais's principle, which we have been studying since the beginning, I simply want to bring out the formal conditions of this possibility.

Ethical issues have no bearing, in principle, on the toxin puzzle. This makes it even more significant that certain subjects claim to be able to hit the jackpot because they spontaneously introduce a parasitical notion which did not figure among the givens of the problem: *merit*. There is a way out for he who considers that, in spite of the billionaire's apparent, deceptive laxity on this point, he has the right to the million only if he pays what seems to him to be the price: the discomfort caused by ingesting the toxin. A world in which he does not drink the toxin at noon is a world in which there is no possibility he will have received the million. We can try as hard as we want to show him that he will have *already* received or not the million when it will be the time for him to decide to drink or not, but he sticks to his guns. He is not affected by the argument according to which he inverses the order of time. This determination is what saves him. In effect, he now has a good and decisive reason to drink the toxin: if he does not do it, he *forbids himself* to have the million. This is his reasoning when his intentions are detected, thus *before* he knows if he has passed the test. Since now he has a good reason to drink, he is able to form the intention to do so, and thus pocket the million. Contrary to what Gauthier asserts concerning his own solution, here there is no inversion of the usual relation between the rationality of the action and that of the intention—the rationality of the intention determining, according to Gauthier, that of the action. Rather, there is simultaneous, reciprocal determination of the rationality of the action and the rationality (and thus the possibility) of the intention through a *bootstrapping* operation which frees the heterodox solution from the orthodox trap.

147

It seems as though we solved the toxin puzzle thanks to ethics. Ethics would be like a *deus ex machina* whose miraculous intervention would solve an otherwise intractable problem. This is the kind of solution, or rather dissolution, that David Gauthier plainly rejects. And he is right. The challenge is, as he puts it, to show that "in order to choose rationally, one must choose morally," or, in other terms, there is a rational requirement to choose morally. Morality is rational, and not super-rational, as it were. I agree on that. Where I depart from Gauthier is in this. The rationality that corresponds to morality—defined as a set of rational constraints on the pursuit of individual interest or advantage—is *not*, I claim, and cannot be, the orthodox conception of rationality, ie. the conception that respects the principle: "Only the future matters."

Gauthier's concern is to *generate* morality as rational principles for choice, and so without introducing prior moral assumptions, without incorporating into the premises of the argument any of the moral conceptions that emerge in the conclusions. I believe that this is an impossible task. My claim is much more modest. Let us take the traditional, deontological understanding of morality for granted. People are endowed with freedom—in the Kantian (and Rousseauian) sense. Liberty is "obedience to a law that we prescribe to ourselves." Let us see in what sense this can be said to be rational. Deontology *is* rational, I claim, but not in the orthodox sense.

We want to show that at time o, Mary can reasonably make a promise to Peter and, through him, to herself to cooperate at 2; and, if Peter makes the first move, to make the second, thus fulfilling her promise. The action that constitutes this promise is the inscription in the past of the future contingent: I will cooperate at 2. The temporal link between these two actions is fixed, or valid in all possible worlds. A world in which Mary defects at 2 is a world in which it is excluded that she promised at 0 to cooperate. At 0, Mary thinks thus: if I were to defect at 2, then I would not have promised at 0 to cooperate. But then Peter would not have given me my turn, and I would not be in a position to make any decision at 2. Therefore, Mary now has a good and decisive reason at 0 to cooperate at 2: if she does not do it, she forbids herself the benefits of the exchange by not giving Peter any reason to make the first move. With this decisive reason to cooperate, she can make the intention at 0 and express it to Peter in the form of a sufficiently firm promise to incite him to embark on the adventure of trust. The self-refutation argument is thus perfectly legitimate here. We are obviously in what I call projected time. Two of its features are clearly visible. Mary takes distance from herself, inferring the state of the world through the observation of her actions. She gives herself, within her reasoning, a counterfactual power over the past.

Let us call this a "Kantian promise." In effect, its bootstrapping form evokes the Kantian (and Rousseauian) concept of autonomy: the ability to limit one's individuality by giving oneself a transcendent, fixed law or rule, and following it. This self-limitation, we should note, is radically different from a solution consisting in "tying one's hands." The former (commitment) is an act of free will: it in no way suppresses liberty. Rather, it is the highest manifestation of freedom. Having made the Kantian promise to cooperate, Mary nonetheless remains perfectly "free" (in the sense of free will) to defect. This is why this promise requires projected time in order to be effective. The fact that one has tied one's hands (precommitment), in contrast, implies that one limit, in the temporality of history, one's freedom of choice. The Kantian promise is undoubtably one of the summits of ethics. Yet, we detect at its very heart the two features we have learned to associate with the irrational: the subject attributing himself with a power over the past and observing himself from the exterior like another self. It seems to me appropriate, in conclusion, to paraphrase the last phrase of Donald Davidson's classic article on irrationality (1982): "A theory that could not explain irrationality would be one that also could not explain our salutary efforts, and occasional successes, at self-binding and self-transcendence." (The original ends with the words: "self-criticism and self-improvement.")

References

Aumann, R. 1988. "Preliminary Notes on Irrationality in Game Theory", a paper presented at the IMSSS Summer Seminar on Economic Theory, Stanford University, July 1988, mimeo.

Davidson, D. 1980. "Actions, Reasons, and Causes." *Essays on Actions and Events.* Oxford: Clarendon Press.

———. 1982. "Paradoxes of Irrationality." In R. Wollheim and J. Hopkins, eds. *Philosophical Essays on Freud.* Cambridge: Cambridge University Press.

———. 1986. "Deception and Division." In J. Elster, ed., *The Multiple Self.* Cambridge: Cambridge University Press.

———. 1998. "Who Is Fooled." Paper presented at the Symposium on Self-Deception, Stanford, California, February 1993. In J. P. Dupuy, ed., *Self-Deception and Paradoxes of Rationality.* Stanford: CSLI Publications (this volume).

Dupuy, J.-P. 1992. "Two Temporalities, Two Rationalities: A New Look at Newcomb's Paradox." In P. Bourgine and B. Walliser, eds., *Economics and Cognitive Science.* Oxford: Pergamon Press.

Elster, J. 1979. *Ulysses and the Sirens.* Cambridge: Cambridge University Press.

Gauthier, D. 1984. "Deterrence, Maximization and Rationality." In D. MacLean, ed., *The Security Gamble. Deterrence Dilemmas in the Nuclear Age.* Totowa, New Jersey: Rowman and Allanheld.

———. 1988–1989. "In the Neighbourhood of the Newcomb-Predictor (Reflections on Rationality)." In *Proceedings of the Aristotelian Society.* Vol. 89, part 3. London.

Kavka, G. 1983. "The Toxin Puzzle." *Analysis* 43, no. 1 (January): 33–36.

Lewis, D. 1984. "Devil's Bargains and the Real World." In D. MacLean, ed., *The Security Gamble. Deterrence Dilemmas in the Nuclear Age.* Totowa, New Jersey: Rowman and Allanheld.

McClennen, E. F. 1990. *Rationality and Dynamic Choice: Foundational Explorations.* Cambridge: Cambridge University Press.

149

Orléan, A. 1990. "Le rôle des influences interpersonnelles dans la détermination des cours boursiers." *Revue économique* 41, no. 5 (September):839–68.

Plantinga, A. 1986. "On Ockham's Way Out." In *Faith and Philosophy* 3 (July):235–69.

Quattrone, G. A. and A. Tversky. 1986. "Self-Deception and the Voter's Illusion." In J. Elster, ed., *The Multiple Self.* Cambridge: Cambridge University Press.

Shafir, E. and A. Tversky. 1992. "Thinking through Uncertainty: Nonconsequential Reasoning and Choice." In *Cognitive Psychology* 24, no. 4:449–74.

Weber, M. 1930; reprint 1985. *The Protestant Ethic and the Spirit of Capitalism.* Trans. Talcott Parsons. London: G. Allen and Unwin.

Cooperation and Time
John Ferejohn

1. Rationality, Cooperation, and Morality

Jean-Pierre Dupuy's essay, "Rationality and Self-Deception" (Dupuy 1998) takes up an issue of profound significance both for moral theory and for decision theory, which has divided philosophical opinion for centuries. On the one side are those who see moral action as a variety of rational action, as acting rationally in certain restricted contexts. For these writers–those who share what might be called the "reduction project"– both the content and the force of morality can, in principle, be given a complete rational choice explanation. On the other side are those who see moral requirements as independent of rationality, who believe either that existing moral norms cannot be accounted for by rational choice theory, or that rational choice analysis cannot provide an adequate account of moral motivation. For such writers, morality is seen as a constraint on rationally chosen actions.

In recent writings, this issue has often been posed in a game theoretic setting in which moral (or cooperative) action is sharply distinguished from (narrowly) self-interested behavior. Typically this is done by examining games in which self-interested behavior cannot support a cooperative outcome as equilibrium play. Some writers like David Gauthier (1984) focus on prisoner's dilemma games, in which noncooperative behavior is actually a dominant strategy (i.e., a best response to any strategy the other may play) for all players. Jean-Pierre Dupuy's one-shot exchange game also exhibits the appropriate contrast because one player has a dominant strategy of not cooperating and, so, anticipating that this player will play her dominant strategy, the other player would not cooperate either. Thus, the only equilibrium is one in which cooperation does not occur.

Within such strategic settings the goal of reductionists–those who see moral action as a specie of rational action–is to provide some conception of rationality that has the property that cooperation can be made consistent with equilibrium play. Like Gauthier and Edward McClennen (1990), Dupuy has proposed such a revised conception of rationality, one that rationalizes cooperative behavior in a one-shot exchange game. Dupuy's conception differs greatly from Gauthier's and McClennen's at the "semantic" level–the way the players reason about the game–while producing a similar analysis of the rationality of cooperative play. I want to say that it is, in this sense, functionally similar to Gauthier's and McClennen's proposals.

However, while Dupuy manages to construct a sense of rationality for which cooperation is possible in the exchange game, the applicability of the rationality concept rests on a deeper moral notion: the idea of a "Kantian promise." Dupuy's project is not to derive morality from rationality, as it is commonly understood, but instead to show a way in which rational creatures may be able to cooperate even in a one-shot exchange game. This way is to construct a temporal setting in which a certain kind of "promise" can be made, a promise whose occurrence can be inferred in the course of the play of the game.

It should be clear at the outset that the games Dupuy studies are very sharply defined in that cooperative play is inconsistent with all orthodox rationality concepts. In this model–one in which players meet for a one-shot interaction–which is taken as the background model of the "state of nature," it is very hard to see how cooperation could "emerge" among rational players, according to any of the traditional definitions of rationality. By seeking to give a rational account of cooperation in this game, therefore, Dupuy has posed himself the very difficult problem of defining a persuasive new notion of rationality. If he fails to do so, and I think he and others do fail, this failure might be taken to undermine the "reduction" project and to suggest that morality and rationality must be seen as independent spheres. While I have some sympathy for this conclusion, I think it is probably a mistake to associate the success of the reductionist project with showing that cooperation is rational in the Peter-Mary game (or in the one-shot prisoner's dilemma).

Alternatively, to take a familiar example, we may envision individuals meeting sporadically and interacting in circumstances in which their actions can be observed and remembered by others. If one player fails to reciprocate another's offer, someone else may be able to see and remember this failure and so may condition her subsequent behavior on this information or may pass the word on to others who may do the same. In view of this possibility, actors may reasonably choose to behave cooperatively. In this circumstance, orthodox game theoretic analyses show that it is possible (though hardly inevitable) to support cooperative behavior in equilibrium. Moreover, one might expect a specific set of normative standards to emerge in such a setting and expect that individuals might even internalize these standards in deciding how to interact with others.

Moral standards in this setting might be seen to emerge from rational behavior and to be at least partly reducible to it. We would not, of course, have a complete reduction of the kind that Gauthier seeks because (due to the multiplicity of equilibria) there would be no account of the specific content of the emergent norms. There would be many distinct forms of play—both cooperative and noncooperative—that could be supported as equilibria. But, by showing how moral behavior is supportable as equilibrium play, we would at least have a "compatibilist" account of moral motivation. Thus, at a general level, this account of moral motivation would also apply to societies such as the Ik, who seem to have evolved an extremely uncooperative set of moral norms. The only difference is that their norms are supported by a different equilibrium in the same game.

Of course, depending on the extent to which emergent norms are internalized and employed generally, we still would not expect frequent cooperation in genuine one-shot settings. Indeed, it seems wise to distinguish the strong reduction project—the one shared by Dupuy, Gauthier and McClennen, in which rationality can account for cooperation in one-shot play—from the weak reduction project that sees moral action arising from circumstances of interaction over time. For the weak reductionist, time (in the form of the anticipation of future play) permits cooperative play, whereas for strong reductionist, time (the fact that exchanges must be organized in time) is an intransigent obstacle to moral interaction.

153

While the strong reduction project is intellectually appealing, I think that it must fail. Specifically, I shall show that each of the proposed projects rests on an arbitrary elimination of temporality, which has the effect of importing moral premises into the rationality concept itself. Each solution effectively permits the players to commit themselves to courses of action and the source of this commitment ability is unaccounted for. The effect of this importation is question-begging for the strong reduction project. It shows only that moral creatures can act morally.

In any case, it is misleading to develop our conception of rationality on "hard" cases like the prisoner's dilemma or the Peter-Mary exchange game. The resulting conception of rationality is likely to be too tailored to the stringent demand that the single play problems pose to provide a useful general theory of rationality. Indeed, by making cooperation either possible or necessary in such circumstances, such a rationality notion would make cooperative play possible or necessary in virtually every circumstance. Such a notion would, it seems, surrender the possibility of explaining how variations in choice situations can influence the extent of cooperative play—surely an important descriptive project (and perhaps one with important normative aspects as well).

2. Evidential Rationality and Cooperation

Dupuy proposes a novel solution to a class of puzzling problems in the theory of rational choice. In particular, he shows how a version of evidential decision theory can permit rational players to cooperate to achieve outcomes that would be insupportable under the causal decision theory that lies at the heart of classical game theory. I shall say in advance that I do yet not find this solution convincing—perhaps I am too attached to the orthodox conception of rationality and to consequentialist thinking.

The idea of an evidential, as opposed to a causal, decision theory is that evidentially motivated agents treat their actions as diagnostically related to some external fact rather than as having independent causal force. In the context of one of Dupuy's examples, an evidentialist, who believed that both smoking and lung cancer were brought about by some common cause, would refrain from smoking in order to support the diagnosis that she was unlikely to have lung cancer. Evidential theories might be seen as aimed at securing for an actor the best set of beliefs, while causal theories would aim at securing for her the best possible outcome.

154

Dupuy's evidentialism seems novel because, in addition to positing the "common cause" structure of Newcomb problems, he interprets the common cause as occurring only in some of the possible pasts. Thus, rather than taking it as a fact that the common cause has occurred, and then choosing the action that would produce the best beliefs possible, Dupuy permits the actor to "choose" in some sense which past has in fact occurred. By taking a current action the agent brings about a past in which *that* action was predicted (or, equivalently, a time t-1 at which it is true that the agent takes the specified action at time t).

The key ideas of the paper can be simply illustrated by considering the simple exchange game between Peter and Mary that occupies the central part of Dupuy's essay. Here, Peter acts first, possibly offering something to Mary in the hope of receiving something else in return. If he offers nothing, the outcome is (0,0); if he offers something and Mary reciprocates, the outcome is (1,1); if he offers and Mary fails to reciprocate, the outcome is (-1,2). Classical game theory notes that, if offered anything, Mary would always find it best not to reciprocate. Peter would anticipate this and fail to offer anything in the first place. The (0,0) outcome is the only (classical) Nash equilibrium in the game and so, from the classical point of view, rational players would not be able to exchange.

155

Dupuy proposes a different concept of rationality by shifting attention from the choices among strategies to choices among projects they could execute. This shift in the definition of the alternatives for choice resembles the reformulations of Gauthier and McClennen, each of whom require actors to choose among feasible plans for playing the game rather than among classically defined strategies. For Gauthier, there are four plans that Mary could conceivably adopt:

Intend to reciprocate; defect
Intend to reciprocate; reciprocate
Intend to defect; defect
Intend to defect; reciprocate.

Gauthier regards only the second and third plans as feasible on the grounds that it is not possible to plan to intend one choice and make another. If this step is granted, it is easy to see that Mary would rationally choose the second over the third plan and that Peter would anticipate this and offer to exchange.

Dupuy's proposed solution is similar. He defines the notion of a *rational (expectations) path* as a sequence of play in which each agent has correct expectations as to the "true" model of the problem (13). He then says that while the path in which Peter offers nothing is rational in the classical sense, the path in which Peter offers to exchange and Mary reciprocates is rational in *projected time*. The path in which Peter offers to exchange and Mary reneges is irrational in both the orthodox and Dupuy's senses. For the orthodox game theorist there is only one rational path: Peter (predicting that Mary would not reciprocate) does not offer and Mary never gets to move. For Dupuy the only rational path, in projected time, is the one in which Peter (predicting that Mary will reciprocate) offers and Mary reciprocates.

Dupuy, in explaining why Peter offering and Mary defecting is not rational, says "if Peter knows that Mary is going to defect, he will not cooperate" (13). The reason that he will not cooperate is presumably that, if he does offer (cooperate), he will receive -1 rather than 0, which he would get if he offered nothing. In other words, cooperating if Mary is going to defect is not maximizing behavior. Conversely, if Peter expects that Mary will reciprocate his offer, his best response would be to make the offer. The two ideas of rational play rest on distinct views as to which expectations agents would form.

In the orthodox view, the agents are not taking maximal actions on a Dupuy-rational path. The path on which Peter offers to exchange and Mary reciprocates has Mary failing to maximize when her turn to choose arises. Then, too, the path on which Peter offers nothing involves a maximizing choice by Peter because he expects Mary to defect if she gets the chance. In the orthodox view, Peter believes that Mary prefers more money to less and that she will take the best action available to her when her turn comes: if she gets the chance to defect, she will do so.

For Dupuy, being on a rational path entails being on a path in which expectations are fulfilled. This means that if Peter offers, he must have the expectation that Mary will reciprocate, and this expectation must be fulfilled on the path: Mary must in fact reciprocate. If Mary ever gets to make a choice, under the assumption that only a rational path may be followed, she will choose to reciprocate. Stating the matter this way, rather than the way Dupuy does, makes clear the resemblance of his solution to Gauthier's. The idea that play is restricted to rational paths amounts to giving the players a capacity costlessly to commit themselves to actions in the future. This is just what Gauthier's restriction of choice to plans rather than to strategies does. And, of course, this restriction is precisely what critics of Gauthier object to.

This is not at all the story that Dupuy tells. He wants to give an interpretation, according to which Peter and Mary are carrying out a project implicitly arranged or "agreed to" prior to any play actually occurring. But, as I understand it, the "agreement" on a project has occurred only in certain possible pasts. Dupuy insists that which past has occurred depends on the choices taken in the present. By offering an exchange, Peter is both providing evidence as to which past has preceded the present moment (i.e., the past in which Mary "promised," in the Kantian sense, to reciprocate), and is in effect selecting which past has occurred. Peter either has or has not predicted that Mary will defect when her time comes and has made his choice conditional on this prediction. This means that if and when Mary gets to choose she can, by choosing to reciprocate, make it true that Peter predicted that she would cooperate. In this sense, the agents are said to have a "counterfactual power over the past."

It is not known to either one what they will do in advance of play; instead their choices are evidence of what has been arranged. In deciding which actions to take, they engage in deliberation or reasoning in "projected time." The key move here is given on page 141:

A question like:
(9) What would it be rational for Mary to do if she got to play (at 2)?
is interpreted as
(10) What does Mary do (at 2) on the rational path if she gets to play (at 2 on the rational path)?

In an orthodox game theoretic account of expression (9), Mary would choose maximally if she got to make a choice (i.e., defect). In Dupuy's "projected time" account, Mary is restricted to remaining on a rational path (this is the effect of the fulfilled expectations condition) and so "must" cooperate. Peter, knowing this, will choose to offer to exchange, knowing that Mary will reciprocate. This, of course, is a consequentialist reading of projected time reasoning: Peter, knowing that Mary will cooperate, must rationally choose to exchange. But, if we are to maintain the evidentialist interpretation that Dupuy prefers, I think we need to weaken his conclusion.

I imagine that Peter's offer to exchange is taken to be evidence of the fact that it is arranged in some possible past that the two agents are cooperating. Mary would, on Dupuy's account, then reciprocate. Peter could, I suppose, choose not to offer an exchange, thereby providing evidence that the two are not cooperating. This would not seem to be maximizing behavior, if we take Peter's action as signaling which past has occurred, since he would do better by offering and having Mary reciprocate. But Dupuy seems not to want to endorse either consequentialist reasoning or the idea that an agent has causal power over the past, and so it seems likely that not offering is rationally admissible.

Indeed, this possibility seems required for an evidentialist interpretation. If Peter were not free to do this, then both parties would already know they are cooperating before Peter does anything, so that any evidence he provides would either be redundant or contradictory. Thus, the most that can be said, on the evidentialist interpretation (as opposed to the consequentialist interpretation of reasoning in projected time), is that cooperation is possible in one shot interactions of the sort described.

Dupuy (1997) objects to this conclusion by arguing that it is impossible that Mary defects (there is no possible world in which Mary defects), so that Peter's failure to offer would not be rational. In this argument Dupuy provides what I think is the key to his account. He notes that "...the *determinations* of Peter's and Mary's actions at the equilibrium occur simultaneously: indeed it is only when Mary acts that Peter's prediction and action are determined—even though in the sequence of events, they took place prior to Mary's action" (Dupuy 1997). The strategic problem is transformed into a decision theory problem in which Mary is the only *actor*: her choice to reciprocate brings about Peter's expectation that she will reciprocate and, therefore, his offer.

It seems to me that there are two problems with this account. First, how can we understand the relationship between Peter's and Mary's actions and the past? Dupuy is required to provide a noncausal account that can, nevertheless, ground the idea that the past is not fixed in relation to current actions. Second, assuming such an account can be given, how can we understand Mary's choice to reciprocate if given the chance to act? In most of his work, Dupuy posits that Peter is essentially omniscient, so that the relation between Mary's action and his beliefs go through his capacity to make correct predictions in counterfactual worlds. He worries (in Dupuy, 1997), plausibly, that this assumption may seem a "sleight of hand" and so he notes, correctly, that *omniscience* is not actually required for the argument. But while Peter need only be a pretty good predictor of Mary's actions, he must be *essentially* pretty good: that is, he must be pretty good in all counterfactual worlds. Actually, while he does not say this, it seems only necessary that this property hold locally—for nearby possible worlds, of the kind that could be realized in the course of play of the particular game being analyzed. If Mary were to choose to defect, Peter must be sufficiently likely to have predicted this that he would not cooperate, thus "deterring" her defection. Personally, I find this weaker assumption nearly as implausible and as inexplicable as the former, and so I cannot see that Dupuy has provided a convincing account of the interaction. Why would Mary believe, if she were, at the last instant before choosing, to change from reciprocating to not reciprocating, that Peter would have predicted that change with high probability?

The fact is that the reinterpretation of expression (9) into (10) plainly imposes a restriction on Mary's choice, and it is this restriction that permits Peter rationally to offer to exchange. The problem Dupuy faces is in explaining and motivating this restriction on Mary's choice. Whether or not he meets this test, Dupuy's solution seems very like Gauthier's and McClennen's, in which agents' choices are restricted to plans. I think it is here, rather than in the metaphysical interpretation that he offers, that Dupuy's solution clashes most sharply with the classical approach. The game theorist wants to know how it is possible that Mary can be restrained—or restrain herself—to rational paths even if she wishes, *ex ante* to impose such a restriction on herself.

I think that Dupuy's account, by failing to provide a convincing answer to this question, is deficient in the same way as those offered by earlier writers. Specifically, the idea of a rational path does not yet appear to be well defined. Finally, it is not clear that the evidentialist interpretation is really essential to the basic idea (which is, on my account, the restriction of play to rational paths); it may be merely one interpretation among many that support the restriction on future action that is critical to Dupuy's account. I doubt that evidentialism—a metaphysical solution—is really necessary to the problem of explaining cooperation in one-shot interactions. Three other routes, within the broad contours of the reduction project, might still seem available. Perhaps rational players (and most real people) do not cooperate in such settings insofar as they understand the situation (the orthodox solution). Perhaps, if real people actually do cooperate in one-shot settings, it is because they are not rational in the orthodox sense but instead have some hard wiring that disposes them to cooperate in certain circumstances, in which defection would be rational (pace sociobiology). Or, perhaps, as Gauthier argues, people choose (or, are able to choose) courses of action or dispositions rationally and (for some reason) tend to stick to them. This suggestion seems very close to saying that people are hard-wired to be able cooperate or that they are, for some reason, disposed to do so for other (possibly moral) reasons. Either way, morality is bought at the price of rationality and the strong reduction project fails.

160

3. Descriptive and Normative Decision Theory

Theories of rational action or decision theories function as both normative and descriptive theory. This duality is part of what makes for the production of paradoxical examples, from Bernoulli through Allais, Ellsberg to the Newcomb examples. These examples are sharply drawn to appeal to strongly held but conflicting intuitions. This is the source of their appeal. Not surprisingly, when people are confronted with these difficult choice problems, their behavior and their reasoning reflect these conflicts. But it seems to me to be important to recognize that these examples are delicately constructed to highlight the internal tensions in the notion of rationality. An adequate theory of rationality must, on the other hand, have general applicability in a very wide range of circumstances and it must "work" both at a normative and a descriptive level. It strikes me, therefore, as unlikely that we will develop a satisfactory rationality concept of such generality by focusing on philosopher's examples of the kind that Dupuy and Gauthier study. And, I think we have not.

I have argued that Dupuy, like Gauthier, essentially "solve" the cooperation problem in one-shot play by building a primitive capacity for agents to commit to courses of action chosen in advance—either by choosing among plans (Gauthier, McClennen) or among rational paths (Dupuy). They provide very different interpretations of the source of this capacity but none offers a persuasive account of why rational agents, in actually playing the game, would not defect if, when the time for taking action arrives, that is the best act for them in the sense of causal decision theory.

Obviously, I doubt that moral action is rationally required in the strong sense that Dupuy and others (seem to) seek to show. In a world of ongoing interaction, cooperation and morality make for better and more satisfying lives, and that may be part of the explanation for the fact, if it is a fact, that we generally choose to act cooperatively and morally. But, it seems to me a mistake to think it is the whole explanation, since in any model of continuous interaction, there is a multiplicity of equilibria. There must be something else that explains why we end up playing the equilibrium we do. Moreover, it is by no means clear that we would behave in this way in briefer exchanges.[1] Indeed, it is not clear that anything important actually turns on this issue. Genuinely one-shot interactions are rare in the real world, and so we have neither much reliable intuition nor observed facts to guide us as to how such interactions would proceed. What we do know is that ordinarily (i.e., in circumstances of repeated interaction) most people act morally and cooperatively quite frequently, and it is this fact that needs explaining.

References

Dupuy, J.-P. 1997. "Philosophical Foundations of a New Concept of Equilibrium in the Social Sciences: Projected Equilibrium." Paper presented at the Conference on Reasoning, Language and Cognition, University of Arizona at Tucson, February 1997.

———. 1998. "Rationality and Self-Deception." Paper presented at the Symposium on Self-Deception, Stanford, California, February 1993. In J. P. Dupuy, ed., *Self-Deception and Paradoxes of Rationality* Stanford: CSLI Publications (this volume).

Gauthier, D. 1984. "Deterrence, Maximization and Rationality." In D. MacLean, ed., *The Security Gamble. Deterrence Dilemmas in the Nuclear Age.* Totowa, New Jersey: Rowman and Allanheld.

McClennen, E. 1990. *Rationality and Dynamic Choice: Foundational Explorations* Cambridge: Cambridge University Press.

---

1. The experimental evidence offers only weak encouragement for the notions that humans behave cooperatively with strangers. While experimental subjects often cooperate if such an experiment is run once (with low payoffs), this behavior is rapidly extinguished when the experiment is repeated a few more times and subjects come to understand the protocol.

(Apparent) Paradoxes of Self-Deception and Decision

Kent Bach

Self-deception and decision are separate topics, but they do overlap. And they both give rise to paradoxes, or at least seem to. Self-deception, a kind of motivated irrationality, is paradoxical insofar as it involves a scheme that cannot be coherently undertaken or even coherently described. But does it? Paradoxes of decision stretch the limits of rationality, by identifying rational decisions that principles of rationality cannot justify or by exposing conflicts in principles of rationality themselves. The two topics overlap in connection with certain decision problems that seem to give rise to self-deception. In the first part of this essay I will take up various questions about self-deception, including what it is, what distinguishes it from other sorts of motivated irrationality, and why it is not as puzzling as it seems. In the second part, I will take up certain puzzling decision problems, particularly those taken up in this volume by Jean-Pierre Dupuy, and then examine Dupuy's diagnoses of them. In this way I hope to pin down what is and what is not puzzling about them. More importantly, I will suggest that the semblances of paradox ultimately depend on neglecting a certain basic feature of the human condition.

1. What Self-Deception Is (Not)

As philosophical topics go, self-deception has something for everyone. It raises questions about the nature of belief, intention, reasoning, motivation, attention, self-knowledge, the unity of the self, self-esteem, psychic defenses, the unconscious, personal character, and interpersonal relations. There are two basic questions about self-deception itself, which take familiar philosophical forms: What is it? How is it possible? These basic questions have both an analytic and a psychological side (this is recognized in Alfred Mele's and Donald Davidson's essays in this volume). Is self-deception, as its name suggests, literally a case of lying to oneself? If not, how different can it be from other-deception and still deserve its name? Psychologically, what processes does self-deception involve and how is it motivated?

If we simply analyze what the term "self-deception" means and ignore the question of whether it has any application to real pheonomena, we risk falling into the skeptical position of doubting that there is such a thing. Any analysis should encompass a range of intuitively acceptable examples of self-deception (the analyst should take care that his choice of examples not be influenced by any self-deception about self-deception itself) and exclude such distinct phenomena as wishful thinking, denial, repression, and fanaticism. Mele's analysis, at least as it stands, does not appear to do this. Also, insofar as the meaning of "self-deception" is a function of the meanings of "self" and of "deception," an analysis cannot be oblivious to the meanings of the words making up the phrase. Now there are different ways in which the word "self" can make its contribution, not all of which are operative. Not just any way of causing oneself to be deceived counts as self-deception. Similarly, self-deception need not be deception *about* oneself. The occurrence of the term "self" in the phrase implies, rather, that one is both agent and victim. But exactly how?

1.1 Self-Deception and Intention

A rich old man thinks his young mistress loves him, an alcoholic thinks he takes but "a little nip now and then," and a frustrated careerist thinks his talents are too subtle to be appreciated by the bosses who have fired him. The self-deceiver in each case thinks something contrary to what he believes ("deep down") or at least contrary to the weight of the evidence. Although we tend to regard self-deceivers like these as somehow aware ("at some level") of what they're doing, indeed as somehow deceiving themselves intentionally (as Davidson maintains), perhaps this is only because what they are doing is so obvious to us. I have argued (Bach 1981), as does Mele, that there is no need to regard self-deception as intentional just because it is motivated and purposeful. And, as Mele points out, self-deception can involve intentional activity without itself being intentional. Davidson's view, that it is intentional, leads to Mele's "dynamic" paradox: what could the self-deceiver's intention be, such that he could keep it in mind and still manage to execute it? Brian McLaughlin (1988) argues that although one can intentionally mislead oneself, as in what he calls "self-induced deception," which typically involves a "memory-exploiting strategem," this is different from self-deception properly so-called. Mark Johnston (1988) argues similarly against the "time-lag theory" that self-deception is an intentional scheme of now causing oneself to be deceived later. If self-deception were intentional in that way, it would involve practical reasoning, but that seems far-fetched. It is not like calculated "positive thinking" or Pascal's wager, which do involve deliberate scheming. But to deny that self-deception is intentional is not to deny that it is motivated. Johnston warns against the tendency of theorists to "over-rationalize mental processes that are purposive but not intentional" and offers several convincing examples of motivated yet unintentional action.

Some theorists, while seeing the error of viewing self-deception as straightforwardly intentional, proceed to compound the error by insisting on intentionality anyway, within a partitioning or even homuncular model. The idea here is to dissociate the victim from the intending agent. It is difficult to take such a model as anything more than a metaphor for the fact that some of the self-deceiver's states are inaccessible (Davidson regards it as a metaphor but does not say exactly what it is a metaphor for). Johnston argues against the homuncularist ploy by showing that if self-deception really were a matter of one subperson deceiving another, its motivation would be a mystery. For even if there were identifiable subpersons of the required sorts—culprit and victim—why should one's deceiving the other even be relevant to the *person's* being deceived? Moreover, we can grant that "as a result of his own activity [the self-deceiver] gets into a state in which he is misled, at least at the level of conscious belief" without accepting the presupposition, which generates the paradox of self-deception, that this is the "reflexive case of lying." As Johnston makes clear, the homuncular model, which drops the reflexive condition but still assumes that self-deception is intentional, just replaces one set of problems with another. And, as McLaughlin observes, one can intentionally act and act on a motive without intentionally acting on that motive.

As I see it, the massive over-rationalization that Johnston speaks of—on the part of theorists, not self-deceivers—stems from a levels confusion of the kind endemic to philosophy: one that is both psychologically implausible and viciously regressive. Lewis Carroll (1895) showed what happens if it is supposed that for the conclusion of an inference to follow from the premises, the principle that licenses the inference must be included among the premises. A related levels confusion, it seems to me, is to suppose that the self-deceiver has second-order awareness of his unpleasant belief and of its conflict with how he would like things to be and therefore must deliberately intervene to mitigate this conflict. If that were so, then resolving the conflict would require adopting the incoherent strategy of getting things in mind in order to get them out of mind. No wonder theorists are tempted to invoke a subperson, be it a censor, the unconscious, or a homunculus, to do the trick.

1.2 Thinking and Believing in Self-Deception

Much of the mystery surrounding self-deception is lifted once we abandon the assumption that the self-deceiver must be acting intentionally if he is to be acting purposefully. But what *is* he doing? What does he accomplish and how does he manage to accomplish it? The question of means—rationalization and other ploys—will be taken up later, but as for ends, in typical cases the self-deceiver wants to avoid facing up to some unpleasant and lingering truth. If there is an orthodox view of what this involves, it is that he gets himself to form a contrary belief. He does not change his mind, in the sense of replacing one belief with a contrary one, but adds the contrary one to his stock of beliefs. And, while the original belief retains its epistemic support, he forms this new belief without having adequate evidence, even by his own standards. No wonder paradox looms, for the orthodox view has it that the self-deceiver incoherently intends to form a belief that conflicts with another belief that he does not abandon. Some philosophers have tried to avoid paradox (Mele's "static" paradox) by claiming that the two beliefs are segregated, each belonging to a different subperson or perhaps with one confined to the unconscious, but such a claim produces mysteries of its own.

Both Georges Rey (1988) and I (Bach 1981, 1992) reject this orthodox way of looking at self-deception. Although our accounts differ, we agree that self-deception involves the functional equivalent of giving up or replacing the unpleasant belief, at least as far as one's ongoing thinking is concerned. That is, whereas a belief about something normally causes one, at least at appropriate times, to think the very thing one believes, in self-deception this tendency is inhibited. Rather than adopt a new, contrary belief (as on the orthodox view), what the self-deceiver does, in my view, is to keep himself, at least on a sustained and recurrent basis, from thinking what he believes. No contrary belief is needed to suppress or inhibit the effect that the unpleasant belief normally has on his thinking, although the self-deceiver may need to clutter his mind with reasons against the unpleasant belief and with thoughts to the contrary. So, for example, the rich old man can be self-deceived even if he does not believe that his mistress loves him, provided he avoids the sustained and recurrent thought that she does not. In the next section we will consider the means by which this is accomplished.

Rey thinks I'm "on the right track" but insists that the self-deceiver does hold a pair of contradictory beliefs. He departs from the orthodox view by cleverly proposing that these opposing beliefs are of two different kinds: the unpleasant one is a "central belief" and the self-deceptive one is an "avowed belief." What is the difference? A central belief is a functional state that tends to play a certain role in reasoning. Avowed belief is, as the name suggests, what one admits to believing (Rey does not mean a speech act but a mental endorsement). Ordinarily, what one centrally believes and what one avowedly believes are the same, but in special cases like self-deception the two can pull apart. It is important to understand here that Rey is not claiming that self-deception is a matter of getting oneself to believe that one does not hold the unpleasant belief and that one holds some contrary belief instead. That is, holding an avowed belief contrary to a central belief does not require, though it may involve, a disavowing second-order belief. An avowed belief is merely a first-order belief contrary to some central belief. It explains what we mean when we describe a self-deceiver as refusing to admit or to face up to something; we are referring not just to what he is willing to say but to what he is willing to think.

The obvious objection to Rey's view is that there just are not two kinds of belief. Avowed belief is no more a kind of belief than a putative fact is a kind of fact. People do not always believe what they sincerely avow; a belief does not have to be possessed to be sincerely expressed. So it seems that Rey's two labels ("central" and "avowed") point merely to two different roles both normally played by beliefs: to enter into reasoning, and to come to mind and thereby be in a position to be avowed. Sometimes these roles pull apart, as in self-deception, for a belief can become activated without being explicitly thought (a belief is a complex, persisting disposition, whereas a thought is a momentary occurrence). That is, beliefs can play a role in reasoning, inquiry, recall, and association without needing to come to mind. They can do this even if one denies that one has the belief. If, as Rey contends, sincere avowal were constitutive of some kind of belief, then sincere avowals could not be mistaken. But they can be mistaken.

168

In my view the self-deceiver avoids the sustained and recurrent thought that p (here I distinguish thinking *that p* from the broader notion of thinking *of p*, which can include rejecting or just entertaining it as well as accepting it). It is precisely the sustained and recurrent thought that p that provides a person with evidence that he believes that p. One effect of self-deception, then, is to suppress the subjective evidence that one believes that p, hence to make it seem to one that not-p. That is how it is with the rich old man when he avoids the sustained and recurrent thought that his mistress does not love him.

What is the status of the belief that self-deception suppresses? McLaughlin (1988) has suggested that the belief is "inaccessible." This seems plausible but needs to be qualified, in a way suggested by Allen Wood. In contrasting self-deception with ideological and other kinds of prejudicial thinking, which too are blind and riddled with rationalization, Wood observes that in self-deception "the psychically upsetting awareness is dangerously close at hand" (1988, 359). This also distinguishes self-deception from trauma-induced repression. So the above requirement must be qualified to say that the suppressed belief cannot be "too" unconscious or inaccessible. I am not certain just how to formulate this qualification on the requirement—it would not do, for example, to appeal to something as metaphorical as the distinction between a state's being "near the surface" rather than "deep in one's unconscious"—but some such restriction must be imposed or else repression would count as self-deception.

1.3 Rationalization and Other Techniques

In my view being self-deceived involves a disposition not to think what one believes (or what one takes there to be strong evidence for). If so, what does it take for that disposition to be exercised? That is, what keeps one from thinking the nasty thought about the touchy subject and leads one to think other thoughts in its place? There is a general consensus that the primary means of self-deception is rationalization, but that is not the only means. Rationalization can involve distorted weighing of reasons or evidence and even fabrication of plausible but phony reasons (or motives, when one's own actions are involved). I identify two other processes that self-deception can involve, ways of keeping a nasty thought from coming to mind or for stopping it when it does. This can be accomplished by evasion: one avoids the thought *that p* by avoiding the thought *of p* (avoiding the thought that *p* does not count as self-deception unless one would be disposed to avoid the thought that *p* even if one did not avoid the thought of *p*). There is also what I call "jamming," so-called because of the radio/radar analogy. Whereas with evasion one keeps one's attention off the touchy subject simply by focusing it elsewhere, in jamming one clutters one's mind with thoughts contrary to the unpleasant belief or contrary to evidence one has in support of that belief (jamming is where Rey's "avowed beliefs" come into play, though for reasons given above, I do not regard them as beliefs). For example, the rich old man thinks of his mistress's sweet words and other displays of affection but not of her motives, which are obvious to others.

What about rationalization? Mele nicely illustrates various aspects of it, including positive and negative misinterpretation, selective attention, and selective evidence-gathering, and makes the useful distinction between internal biasing and input control. Robert Audi (1988) offers some interesting ideas about how, with its uncanny ability to operate against the weight of the evidence, rationalization connects to self-deception. The connection goes both ways: self-deception can lead to rationalization, and rationalization that is initially not self-deceptive can lead to self-deception. In both cases Audi distinguishes three variables: the occasions favorable to the process, the agent's threshold for engaging in it, and the measures of its success. For example, the agent's threshold of proceeding from rationalization to self-deception on occasions favorable to it is lower in proportion to the strength of his desires or needs as well as to the extent that he can rationalize convincingly, evade systematic exploration of his own thoughts and behavior, marshal favorable information, and focus his attention accordingly. As for the measure of success in self-deception produced by rationalization, Audi distinguishes such interesting parameters as "accessibility, entrenchment, resilience, stratification, systematization, and integration," which all make reference to broader aspects of the self-deceiver's cognitive and motivational psychology. Finally, the rationalization in self-deception may involve the complicity of other people. Others can, as William Ruddick (1988) puts it, help the self-deceiver "dismiss evidence, not just linguistically launder it," and thereby "believe his own false advertising." We make this easy for them when we exercise "evasive, as well as persuasive, linguistic skills," like using socially sanctioned jargon or euphemism to discourage others from making us face up to what we are too anxious to face up to.

170

1.4 Exclusionary Categories and Selective Attention

Worth special mention is a kind of cognitive device that can facilitate self-deception. It is important because of its pervasive role in everyday life (see Bach 1994 for further discussion), not just its self-serving role in self-deception. Given our limited attentional and cognitive resources, we must be selective in what we consider in a given situation. Obviously, we cannot spend time and effort on each thing that might come to mind just to determine that it is not worth considering. Indeed, at every moment we implicitly but effectively judge that certain things are not worth considering simply by not considering them, either not at all or not for long. This is essential to the default reasoning that characterizes our everyday thinking (Bach 1984). Furthermore, I suggest, we each possess an arsenal of "exclusionary categories" that we apply to topics, doctrines, actions, and persons (among other things) in order to justify not taking them into account in our thinking. Applying such a category plays the role of keeping one from considering something any further, and having applied it may keep one from considering that item at all. Here is a sample of familiar exclusionary categories: *absurd, crazy, dangerous, extremist, impossible, incoherent, incompetent, inconceivable, irrelevant, ludicrous, misguided, obscene, offensive, superstitious.* For better or worse, everyone has some such categories in their repertoire. People differ as to which ones they use and as to the conditions (epistemic or emotional) under which they use them. Indeed, people's diverse habits of mind even suggest a basis for classifying different character types. For example, those who use certain of these categories to excess may be bigots or zealots. Others, by excluding from consideration certain matters that really do need to be faced up to, may suffer from repressive neuroses. On the other hand, people who lack an adequate arsenal of exclusionary categories may, because they let in too much that is not worth considering, be flighty or impulsive; and those who cannot apply exclusionary categories to some salient subject matter may develop either an inhibition or an obsession and compulsion about it. Yet despite their often misguided use, most exclusionary categories normally play a legitimate role. They help us manage our cognitive resources and protect our view of the world from radical change in the face of pressures that are more efficiently and reasonably felt as marginal. Better, at least in general, to ignore or explain away recalcitrant data than to make massive readjustments. Epistemic conservatism has its virtues.

If the use of exclusionary categories is pervasive and often justified, what is their specific role in self-deception? When applied, an exclusionary category serves to exclude something from (further) consideration, and does so justifiably, at least from the agent's perspective. When such a category is applied unreflectively, its target can be dismissed from consideration without having to be considered any further. Thus, one does not have to think about something, at least not seriously, in order to justify not thinking about it (any further). This is generally a legitimate process, but in self-deception it is typically self-serving in some way. If something is too painful to consider, "to hard to deal with" as we say, one has a practical reason for not considering it. However, as McLaughlin and Johnston both show, in self-deception avoiding the touchy subject is not the result of practical reasoning. One does not reason: this is too hard to deal with; therefore, I will not deal with it. Nevertheless, given one's anxiety about it, one is motivated not to deal with it. Efficiently finding ostensibly good reasons for not dealing with it may have precisely the effect of keeping it out of mind. Or, if it keeps coming back to mind, at least one can keep getting rid of it by jamming, by cluttering one's thoughts with reasons against it and alternatives to it.

The use of exclusionary categories is not inherently irrational. Provided one is reliable at knowing when things are worth considering, in preventing one's mind from being cluttered with things that are not worth considering one justifiably keeps one's processes of reasoning and deliberation from getting needlessly bogged down. Of course, the misapplication of exclusionary categories can deprive one of opportunities to correct errors in one's thinking and to entertain new possibilities. And uses of them are not merely defective but irrational if they are the result of dogmatism and closed-mindedness. The irrationality is motivated, as in wishful thinking

171

and blindness, if the application of the exclusionary category serves an emotional purpose. And the motivated irrationality is a case of self-deception if its use serves to facilitate avoidance of the sustained and recurrent occurrence of a certain thought. The thought in question is something one believes (or by one's own standards has good reason to believe), and so in this case, the case of self-deception, there is a cleavage between what one believes and what one occurrently thinks. This cleavage is possible because, contrary to Descartes's dictum that "there is nothing in my mind of which I am not in any way conscious," beliefs do not have to be conscious to be held. Recognizing this cleavage and why it is possible removes the semblance of paradox in self-deception.

172

2. (Ir)rational Decisions

Documenting the frailties of human reasoning has become a cottage industry (see Osherson 1990, for a short survey). Amos Tversky in particular made a brilliant career of identifying and characterizing areas of human intellectual weakness. Most of the examples for which he is known are not cases of *motivated* irrationality but of unmotivated ignorance or stupidity. There are all sorts of mistakes that people make because they do not know better or because they do not think very carefully, or even because of inherent cognitive limitations. Much of Tversky's later research, as reported in his talk at the Stanford conference on self-deception, focused on putative cases of motivated irrationality. For instance, the phenomena studied in Quattrone and Tversky (1986), which Dupuy takes up in this issue, illustrate reasoning that confuses diagnostic with causal contingencies: people do things even when they regard their actions not as furthering their goals but merely as signs that their goals will be fulfilled. This seems irrational because, since the action is completely under the person's control, it cannot constitute the evidence it is taken to be. That would be like taking an amphetamine to prove that one is an energetic person. Even so, is it always irrational to reason in this way? In the circumstances of Newcomb's notorious problem, perhaps it is not.

2.1 Newcomb's Problem

There are two boxes, the transparent Box A, which contains $1000, and Box B, which may or may not contain $1,000,000, and you can take either the contents (if any) of Box B alone or the contents of both. You are told that a highly reliable predictor has placed $1,000,000 in Box B if, and only if, he predicted that you would not choose both boxes, and he knows that you are told this. What should you do? (If Newcomb's problem is unfamiliar, think about it before reading on.)

For over twenty-five years a dispute has raged between one-boxers and two-boxers. Their dispute instantiates the dispute between evidential and causal decision theory. Two-boxers, reminding you that what you do cannot affect the contents of Box B, which is already filled if it ever will be, rely on a dominance argument: whether Box B contains $1,000,000 or is empty, you will do $1000 better taking both boxes. One-boxers, observing that those who take both boxes generally end up with only $1000, argue that whatever you do, the predictor is likely to have predicted that, so that if you take only Box B, he is likely to have placed $1,000,000 there, otherwise not. Two-boxers reply that you would have become $1000 richer if you had taken both boxes. But, one-boxers insist, in that case the predictor wouldn't have put the $1,000,000 in Box B in the first place. Two-boxers point out that whatever he did he already did and nothing you do now can change that. One-boxers, amused by the two-boxers' historical lack of wealth, ask them, "If you're so smart, why ain't you rich?" Such is pretty much how the debate has gone for nearly three decades, a veritable stalemate (Horgan 1985).

What is the broader significance of Newcomb's problem? It reflects a tension between two kinds of decision theory. Two-boxers generally rely on causal decision theory, which discounts considerations that do not make a causal difference. They reject the one-boxer's appeal to the counterfactual conditional, "If you were to take both boxes, the predictor would have predicted that," because what makes this conditional true cannot be a causal relation between the antecedent, which concerns one of your possible actions, and the consequent, which concerns the prior prediction of what your action would be. The one-boxer insists that Newcomb's problem is a special case, in which noncausal considerations are appropriate. He realizes that you can convince yourself that your choice will not affect the contents of Box B and that you can even imagine peeking into Box B and thinking (like the two-boxer) that regardless of what you see you will be $1000 better off taking both boxes. But he urges you to remind yourself of the predictor's past performance. You do not know how the predictor does it, but he does, you do not want to end up poor like almost all of the two-boxers.

2.2 Unratifiable Decisions

In "Newcomb's Problem: the $1,000,000 Solution" (Bach 1987), not only did I argue for taking Box B only, I went on to recommend a strategy for resisting any last-minute temptation to take both boxes: make a firm commitment, such as a side bet, to keep yourself from second-guessing yourself and changing your mind. For the decision to take just Box B is not "ratifiable" in Richard Jeffrey's (1981) sense: it is not a decision you can "live with," i.e., see as rational once you have made it and up to the time of the action. This is clear if you suppose that others can look inside Box B while you are waiting to find out what is in it. But your decision, I argue, does not have to be ratifiable to be rational. Compare the situation of someone who imposes a threat that is more costly to carry out than not to, such as nuclear retaliation. Assume the "game" is played only once, so that there are no considerations of future deterrence. That is not like the case of the parent who sincerely believes, when he punishes a child by carrying out a threat, that "this will hurt me more than it will hurt you," but punishes the child anyway so as to make the threat credible the next time. In nuclear warfare there is no next time. Part of the problem of nuclear deterrence is to make the threat of retaliation credible even though, after being attacked, one would do oneself more harm than good by carrying out the threat. Threats of this sort are more credible, hence more effective, hence more rationally posed, if one gives the appearance of being a little crazy, say, if you are robbing a bank while wielding a glass of clear liquid you claim to be acid (Ellsberg 1968). The voice of reason is too easy to persuade. No wonder the mutual threat of retaliation during the Cold War was known as MAD (mutually assured destruction).

Then there is the paradox of mutually beneficial exchange, as discussed by Dupuy. In general, a rational exchange is possible when two self-interested parties can each do something that benefits the other and at a net gain to both. Then it is rational for each to do his part on condition that the other does his. The paradox arises when circumstances are such that one party must act before the other and cooperation by the second is unenforceable: the second party will have no reason to reciprocate (unless, contrary to what is being assumed, there is independent value attached to being, or to being regarded as, cooperative and trustworthy), because the benefit will already be there for the taking; therefore, the first party, who has reason to act only on condition that the second will reciprocate, has no reason to act. This is in effect a temporally asymmetric prisoner's dilemma. As in the famous Prisoner's Dilemma, it seems that there is an indispensable need for trust, but in the circumstances of the problem such trust cannot be based on purely self-interested grounds.

There is an important one-person counterpart to the paradox of mutually beneficial exchange. Let us call it the commitment problem. We are often faced with the dilemma of choosing between small near-term values and larger long-term ones. One may have to choose between eating a nice snack now and enjoying a fancy dinner later, or between spending money now and saving it for something more important later. Such dilemmas can arise repeatedly with a "bad habit," like smoking, but in this case the situation is more complicated – repeated, not isolated, acts of smoking do the damage, and one needs a strategy for giving up the habit and not backsliding. It might seem that these are not dilemmas but merely conflicts – between tempting short-term desires and more valuable long-term goals – whose resolution requires overcoming temptation. In fact, they are genuine dilemmas, for it is reasonable (and natural) to discount the future (see, e.g., Nozick 1993, 14–21). Orthodox decision theory does not have the resources to explain how the expectation of later regret justifies refraining from present gratification. George Ainslie (1992) suggests that in such cases people need to make pre-commitments or adopt personal rules in order, to parody Rousseau, to be free to be forced. This is a case of what Dupuy calls "bootstrapping of the self."

A temporal mirror-image of the commitment problem is the reputed "sunk cost" fallacy. Economists generally assume, as in the dictum "Don't throw good money after bad," that one's present utilities should not be affected by past losses. Robert Nozick (21–25) argues, however, that counting on one's later valuing of sunk costs may be strategically necessary for making an investment now. Only thus can one count on oneself to follow one's plans through and not give up should prospects dim.

2.3 Noncausal Dependence

If there are solutions to the problems of costly threats and mutually beneficial exchange (including its one-person counterpart just mentioned), ratifiability is not required for rational choice. As Paul Horwich shows (1987, chap. 11), it is easy to construct choice situations in which the rational choice, once made, provides the agent with information that favors making the other choice. Horwich goes on to give four arguments against causal decision theory. In his defense of evidential decision theory, he points out that the counterexamples generally served up by its critics are not in fact cases in which the obviously irrational choice is justified by its diagnostic value. In the case of R.A. Fisher's smoking example (mentioned by Dupuy), where it is imagined that smoking does not lead to cancer but rather that a common genetic factor causes both cancer and the tendency to smoke, the usual claim is that evidential decision theory advises one to refrain from smoking. But Horwich points out the obvious fact that no evidence for one's not having the cancer gene is provided by one's decision not to smoke when this decision is made under the circumstances just described. Because one's decision is not a reflection of one's prior inclination in regard to smoking, the evidential import of one's decision is "screened off." There is also an information screen in the case of the Stanford students whose willingness or unwillingness to tolerate additional pain depended on how they took tolerance of such pain to be correlated with having a potential heart problem. What is irrational about their behavior is not that they implicitly (and unconsciously) rely on evidential rather than causal considerations but that their actions provide no evidence. Then there is Dupuy's example of incurring a big cost to join a club that you eventually deem to be lousy, resulting in cognitive dissonance. Once the evidence of your experience outweighs the prior evidence of other people's enthusiasm for membership, it is irrational to resolve the cognitive dissonance by convincing yourself that you're having a great time at the club. Avoiding the additional cost of acknowledging your error ("to sustain the belief in one's own rationality") just compounds the error—unless your ego is worth more than your time.

Newcomb's problem is different. As is implicit in my defense of the one-box solution and as Horwich says explicitly (1987, chap. 11), in this case one's act is not deprived of its evidential implications. One's action provides evidence for the prior prediction of it. Now it is often objected that if one acts so as to provide oneself with such evidence, one is magically trying to affect the past. But this objection, by describing the action as an attempt to affect the past, just begs the question against the evidential theory. The evidentialist is claiming that there is a dependence between the action and the prior prediction—but not a causal dependence. This noncausal dependence is described by the following two counterfactual conditionals:

> If I were to choose one box (probably) the predictor would have predicted that I would choose one box.

If I were to choose two boxes (probably) the predictor would have predicted that I would choose two boxes.

In the theory of counterfactual conditionals these are called "back-tracking" conditionals. Causal theorists disallow them out of hand, but evidential theorists do not. Evidentialists permit reasoning from one's choice to the prior prediction (with a probability determined by the predictor's reliability) on the grounds that the predictor, in order to be as reliable as he is, must be able to identify whatever factors contribute to determining one's choice, including the reasoning that leads to it.

To appreciate what's going on in the Newcomb situation, consider the importantly different cases of Michael Scriven's (1964) counterpredictor or Alvin Goldman's "Book of Life" (1970, chap. 6). In the first case the agent is highly motivated to prove a highly reliable predictor wrong. If told the prediction about his next act, he acts otherwise. This is easy to do, assuming the only alternative is not too costly or dangerous, i.e., does not offset the benefit of foiling the predictor. In Goldman's example, reminiscent of Diderot's Great Scroll, an agent comes across a book detailing his life, starts reading it, finds it uncannily accurate, and then turns to the page for the current date. He reads the words, "You are reading your Book of Life." He pauses a moment, wondering whether he should read on. At just that moment he remembers an important appointment and puts the book down. But what if he kept on reading? Well, consider again the case of the counterpredictive agent, but this time assume that the predictor does not announce his predictions (it is too easy to falsify announced predictions). Instead, the agent attempts to replicate the prediction by figuring out exactly the information on which the predictor relied (this information includes general psychological laws and particular facts about himself to plug into those laws). He replicates the prediction and acts otherwise. But surely the predictor would have taken into account that the agent would be trying to replicate his prediction. So what would the predictor have predicted? Nothing that the agent couldn't have figured out that he would have predicted. But anything the agent could have figured out that the predictor would have predicted is something the agent could have refrained from doing. So the predictor could not have predicted it. In short, if the agent has as much information as the predictor, the predictor cannot make a prediction that the agent cannot replicate and falsify, in which case the predictor has insufficient information to make a reliable prediction. On the other hand, if the predictor can make a reliable prediction, the agent cannot have sufficient information to replicate the prediction and thereby be in a position to falsify it. So there can never be parity of information between the agent and the predictor. Similarly, there can never be parity of information between the Book of Life and its subject (unless that person likes everything he reads in it!).

In these cases, as in Newcomb's problem, there is no issue of changing the past. Rather, as we will see in the next section, the issue concerns, in the peculiar circumstances of these cases, one's access to information about the past. The peculiarity is that one cannot possess the relevant information while being in a position to act on it.

2.4 Dupuy's Dualities

Dupuy presents a fascinating analysis of several decision problems. In my opinion, however, his discussion is needlessly complicated by a number of philosophical red herrings, upon which neither the problems nor their solutions depend: (1) changing the past, (2) determinism, (3) two kinds of temporality, and (4) two kinds of rationality. Let us take them up in order.

(1) Dupuy's discussion of Calvinism misleadingly suggests that what the believer does (or what the one-boxer does in Newcomb's problem) is to try to change the past. But this either presupposes the questionable causalist model of choice or it misdescribes what the agent is trying to do. Calvinists and one-boxers no more try to change the past than ordinary agents try to change the future. When you perform an action, the world is different from how it otherwise would have been. However, this does not mean that you have *changed* the future; you do not change how it *will* be but make it different from how it otherwise *would* have been. Compare the case of a time-traveler. Even if one could go back in time, one could not change the past but only act so as to make it different from how it otherwise would have been (Lewis 1976). It is a mistake to think, as science fiction stories sometimes pretend, that what the time-traveler does is to make the past different from how it was in the first place. Neither does the Calvinist.

(2) Dupuy asserts that the Calvinists must be compatibilists. But their reasoning does not assume the compatibility of free will with determinism, for that issue is irrelevant to their reasoning. What it does assume is

178

divine predestination. God's determination of who receives grace and who does not, is based on His anticipations of how people will live their lives (if it was random or otherwise arbitrary, then one's unwillingness to work would not be a sign of lack of grace). Nor does the Calvinists' predicament depend on their having free will. They could believe that what they will do has been fixed since before God's choices were made and still they would be faced with the question of what to do, of how to live their lives. They would deliberate just as if the course of events had not been fixed, and it would be up to them to decide what to do. This is possible only because they do not know how events have been fixed. To appreciate this point recall Scriven's superpredictor but this time assume that the agent, far from being counterpredictive, wants to do whatever he is predicted to do, say because he is rewarded for making the predictions come true. However, he has no idea what the predictor has predicted—he has not read his Book of Life. Knowing that the predictor (or the Book of Life) is highly reliable, should he try to anticipate the predictions and act accordingly? That would be pointless. He does not need any strategy to fulfill those predictions, whatever they are. He can just act normally and not worry about what he is predicted to do. This does not mean that he should somehow try to do whatever he would have done anyway, for he has no independent way of knowing what that is. Rather, it means that he can count on the fact that what he does, whatever it is, will have been predicted.

Dupuy describes the Calvinist as seeking to "invalidate the determinism" of the common cause C (of the Calvinist's action and his destiny). However, until he acts, the Calvinist is in no position to believe that C does or does not obtain, much less that it must obtain. So there is no way he can "invalidate the determinism." He can know that if C had occurred he would act one way and that if C had not occurred he would act the other way. But this tells him nothing about what he will do, since he does not know whether or not C actually did occur. He can find out whether or not it occurred only by doing one thing or the other—he cannot act on that information.

In any case, determinism is not the issue. The general question of determinism is not what the Calvinist is concerned about. His concern is quite specific. For what the Calvinist (or the one-boxer) believes is that his action is determined by the same thing, whatever it is, that determines his destiny. He does not know what that thing is and he does not know

179

what his destiny is—except by how he acts. Thus he can act in such a way as to provide himself with evidence both for what determined his destiny (and his act) and for what his destiny is, but he is shielded from knowing what this is before he acts. Thus, it can appear that his action determines his destiny when in fact both share a common cause.

(3) Dupuy's two kinds of temporality, "occurring" and "projected," by which I assume he means not two kinds of time but two ways of experiencing time, is a phenomenologically provocative way of explaining the appeal of the two conflicting principles of rational decision, causalist and evidentialist. However, temporality appears to be inessential to the issue, at least as it arises in the problem of mutually beneficial exchange, which Dupuy uses to illustrate the "backwards induction paradox." This is a genuine problem, but it can arise even without a temporal gap. Essentially the same problem can arise in a situation where the two players must act at the same time. Assume that both players act simultaneously but that one and only one has independent information about what the other will do (assume also that they mutually know this). For example, suppose one player offers the other a bottle of Chateau Lafite for $200. Since the other player does not wish to open it (he would want it for later use), he has no way of telling that, in fact, it is not a bottle of that $4 California wine, Chateau LaFeet (suppose that the seller has labeled the two bottles identically). The situation is essentially the same as Dupuy's but without a temporal gap—the asymmetry remains, for there is still an information gap. It still presents a problem of mutually beneficial exchange. Then there is the symmetrical version of this problem (suppose the buyer has both real and counterfeit money in his wallet). In the symmetrical case, neither player can ascertain that the other is cooperating until after the fact, as in the notorious Prisoner's Dilemma. Whatever the details, in all these cases the problem is essentially one of how to achieve the benefits of a mutually conditional commitment. The problem of mutually beneficial exchange is to find a sufficient reason for cooperation, so that each party can credibly say, "I'll cooperate if you do." Temporal gaps or not, the problem seems insoluble if, as is given, the agents are rationally self-interested and the situation is such that commitments are unenforceable and reputations and future exchanges are not at stake. But the impossibility of mutually beneficial exchange is a paradox only if it is assumed that circumstances must always allow a pair of rationally self-interested agents to arrange a scheme that maximizes their mutual interest. Perhaps this assumption is

simply false. Perhaps the Prisoner's Dilemma, for example, is just that, a dilemma, not a paradox.

(4) Finally, there are Dupuy's "two rationalities." Granted, there are two competing principles of rationality, which underlie causal and evidential decision theory respectively, but it is questionable whether they are both right. Some (e.g. Eells 1982, and Jeffrey 1981) have suggested that there is no real conflict between the two principles, once they are properly formulated, but Horwich (1987) has shown that they are not equivalent (179–89) and proceeds to give four arguments against the causalist principle (189–96). But suppose these arguments are inconclusive. The fact that there is a stalemate on Newcomb's problem (Horgan 1985) and that individual persons can find both principles compelling does not mean that both principles should be accepted and that, where their dictates conflict, both should be given weight. This is what Dupuy needs to show. Nozick (1993) actually does propose this, even suggesting a scheme for adjusting their respective weights to the circumstances of different variants of Newcomb problems, but he completely ignores Horwich's arguments.

2.5 Sunk Costs and the Passage of Time

The topics of the last section are not unrelated. Take the example of the disappointed new club member, which Dupuy uses to motivate his idea of projected time. He suggests that it is not totally irrational for the new club member to regard his having incurred costs as evidence that being in the club is desirable. Others' liking the club had provided evidence that membership is desirable, thereby providing a reason for incurring the costs. Of course, incurring the costs did not provide an additional, independent reason for liking the club but, still, because of the self-sustaining character of belief, a kind of rational bootstrapping is at work here. The question is whether this bootstrapping takes the form that Dupuy suggests.

First, consider Nozick's observation (1993, 26ff) that taking sunk costs into account can have not only symbolic but strategic significance. For example, believing that one will later value them can increase one's motivation to make the most of one's investment (in time, money, marriage, or whatever) before it becomes totally sunk. In counting on the fact that one will later place a value on sunk costs one is in effect making a mutually beneficial exchange with oneself: one increases one's future prospects by making an investment one might otherwise not make by psychologically committing oneself to take into account later the fact one made the investment. Neither commitment to oneself nor trust in someone else, as in mutually beneficial exchange, can be rationalized with respect to particular points in time. Anticipating possible future feelings of regret or guilt (as the case may be) can affect one's current motivation even though these feelings cannot be rationalized later. Emotional commitment, like strategic commitment, presupposes a diachronic rationale (see Frank 1988, on the strategic role of the emotions). Indeed, a coherent sense of self is impossible without such a perspective.

Now consider rational bootstrapping. I believe it is tied to a certain implicit assumption built into the default reasoning that characterizes people's deliberations on what to think and do (Bach 1984). In default reasoning one does not take something into account unless one deems it worth considering, and one does not need to consider something in order to deem it not worth considering—not considering it is tantamount to deeming it not worth considering. Of course, the quality of one's default reasoning depends (in part) on how good one is knowing what is and what is not worth considering. One relies on one's reliability in this regard. Also, there is a certain epistemic conservatism built into default reasoning: the very fact that one holds a given belief gives it a certain credence (Harman 1986, chaps. 4 and 5). This does not really involve what Dupuy calls "Davidsonian partitioning of the mind" but is simply a consequence of various constraints on our cognitive capacities. Rational bootstrapping is not a matter of treating one's own beliefs as if they were someone else's (in that case they could provide evidence for their truth, depending on the reliability of the believer). Rather, one acts on the implicit assumption that one had good reason for acquiring them. So the fact that one believes something is a fact in its favor, but it can be overridden by new considerations.

Dupuy describes the new club member as "choosing the past," by "copying what would be the causal consequences of a different, better past." This happens not in "occurring time" but in "projected time," from which one can only infer that it does not happen at all but only seems to happen. One acts so as to produce a reliable sign that what one wants to be the case is the case. What Dupuy calls (following Plantinga) "counterfactual power over the past" is not causal. It is noncausal probabilistic dependence between an action and some prior or otherwise causally independent event (Horwich 1987). Dupuy calls it a power because one really does choose the past, albeit at a symbolic level (see Nozick 1993, 26ff.):

one is "mistaking the sign for the thing." As we saw earlier, however, in the smoking and ice water cases this is irrational not because one is not really choosing the past, as the causal decision theory requires, but because the sign is phony. Given its source it lacks any evidential value.

This is less clear with the Calvinists, since the evidential value of their actions is not screened off. Their situation is thus quite unlike that of Quattrone and Tversky's experimental subjects, who do not appreciate the character of their manufactured evidence. The Calvinists' choice is essentially like the one-box choice in the Newcomb problem—in fact, it is a Newcomb problem. There is no essential difference that I can see between the Newcomb problem itself and what Dupuy calls "common cause Newcomb problems," because the Newcomb problem itself can be formulated as a common cause problem without any relevant difference. Just assume that the cause of the prediction is the same as the cause of the choice.

What Dupuy describes as a counterfactual power over the past is a subjective illusion. Not only is this power, as Dupuy says, not a causal power, it is not any other kind of power either. One has the illusion that one's choice makes a difference, not just about what will happen but about what did happen, because it is only through one's action that one's gains knowledge of what did happen. What did happen is cognitively inaccessible until one acts, whereupon it becomes accessible. But all one has is what Velleman (1989) calls "epistemic freedom": until one acts, one is "free from the evidence," and this epistemic freedom gives one the illusion, assuming determinism, that what will happen is open. But this is no more true in normal cases with respect to the future than in Newcomb-like situations with respect to the past. Given determinism and an initial state of the universe, whatever does happen must happen and nothing else could happen. But since one is ignorant of the details, one has the illusion that performing an action does not lead to what was bound to happen but somehow realizes one possibility and forecloses others. For as long as one is ignorant of what is bound to happen or of its causes, one is free—epistemically free—to provide evidence for facts that are otherwise inaccessible. One is not metaphysically free to do this because what one does (assuming determinism) is itself part of what was bound to happen. Newcomb-like cases are special only insofar as part of what is in question is something in the past. And they are distinguished from smoking cases and the like because the evidential value of one's action is not screened off. So far as I can tell, Dupuy's projected time, to the extent that it differs from occurring time, is the illusion of the openness of the past in Newcomb-like cases.

2.6 The Artificiality of Decision Theory

In the first part of this essay we examined the irrationality that is self-deception. In this part we have examined the irrationality, real or apparent, that arises in certain decision problems. In concluding this part, I will enumerate certain irrationalities in decision theory itself, at least in its orthodox practice, though its practitioners would be more apt to describe these as theoretical idealizations.

People generally do not spend their time sitting on their behinds contemplating their options. As Herbert Simon has long reminded us, people generally seek adequate rather than optimal solutions to their problems. The reason is not merely that they are satisfied with less than the best, or that the best is too hard to find or not worth the extra bother. It goes deeper than that. One way to see how deep it goes is to appreciate the difference between real-life problems and what moral philosophers, decision theorists, economists, and who knows who else take decision problems to be. Theorists typically make a number of highly unrealistic assumptions:

1. It is assumed that a given problem is explicitly posed to a person. However, in the real world decision problems often do not present themselves as such. Almost anything can pose a problem, and almost any problem can be avoided, or at least be replaced by some other problem.
2. It is assumed that a set of possible choices and outcomes is provided, complete with their expected utilities. However, in the real world alternatives are generally not identified in advance. Indeed, they may not be well defined, either in detail or in number.
3. It is assumed that the relevant information is available to the person, and presented as relevant. However, in the real world relevant information must be distinguished from irrelevant. This means that one must know what is worth considering and what is not, and it is not clear how that information gets into the picture.
4. It is assumed that there is no time limit on the decision. It is true that in everyday life many decision problems are temporally open-ended and can be put off indefinitely. On the other hand, many others must be

made immediately or not at all, because they are occasioned by passing opportunities or dangers or because they are involved in the implementation of ongoing activities, such as in speaking, dancing, or driving.

5. It is assumed that the decision cost is negligible. In the real world, the cost of making a decision may be too high relative to the importance of the problem. Sometimes it is better not to deal with the problem, but such a decision hardly constitutes a solution to that problem. (Notice that the extensiveness of a decision process, including the range of alternatives to be considered, the range of information to be gathered [including whether further inquiry is necessary, and if so what sorts], how carefully the information and the options should be evaluated, and how much time and cost should be expended in arriving at a decision, are themselves matters of decision.)

All five of these assumptions are unrealistic, not just collectively but even individually. In decision theory, sometimes one or two of these assumptions is relaxed, as in the study of decision making under uncertainty, but by and large these assumptions are implicit in various theoretical conceptions of rationality in thought and action. The underlying trouble with them and with the theorizing that depends on them is the pretense that problems come one at a time and can be dealt with in isolation. A problem situation is described and various ways of approaching it are then considered. But that is not the way things are in the real world.

The artificiality of these five assumptions aside, there is a more fundamental reason why they do not reflect the way things are in the real world. My eleven-year-old daughter appreciated this when I asked her, "what problem is everyone faced with at every waking moment?" She immediately answered, "the problem of what to do next." She was right: if mental action, like directing one's attention, is included along with physical action, we *are* continuously faced with the problem of what to do next. And that is a big problem or, rather, a bounteous multitude of little problems. In everyday life we tend not to notice these little problems, much less the big problem they exemplify, noticing instead only those problems on which we deliberate. Similarly, philosophers, psychologists, decision theorists, and cognitive scientists tend to focus on deliberate thought and action. They may speak of practical reasoning and of theoretical or factual reasoning, of beliefs and desires or of subjective probabilities and preferences, but their concern is with deliberate thought and action. A person is assumed to be faced with alternatives and to make a decision based on some evaluation of those alternatives. Needless to say, all this takes time. In contrast, at any given moment the problem of what to do next must be settled immediately, for another such problem will arise in the next moment. Fortunately, we usually come up with an adequate solution without much trouble. This is a fact for any serious account of human reasoning to reckon with.

With the problem of what to do next in mind, we can see the deeper significance of the fact that people are satisficers rather than maximizers. We satisfice not so much because we are content with less than the best, and not merely because we operate under obvious cognitive and temporal constraints. The real reason is that we have to do something at every moment. What satisficing amounts to is not that the thought of doing something leads to doing if it seems good enough (even if not the best) but that the thought of doing something leads to doing it if it does not seem not good enough. That is, we do what it occurs to us to do unless it immediately occurs to us not to. This often results not from the thought not to do it but from the thought of an alternative or of a reason against it. In other words, the psychological path from thinking of it to doing it is broken by some intervening thought. I am suggesting, then, that at every moment we next do the first thing that occurs to us, provided this thought is not immediately overridden by a further thought. Thus, something's seeming good enough to do at a given moment consists, practically speaking, simply in the unoverridden thought to do it, then and there.

Both self-deception and certain well-known decision problems are puzzling but not inherently paradoxical. Self-deception appears paradoxical only if it is mistakenly thought to involve the intentional cultivation of contradictory beliefs. I suggested that self-deception can be realistically described in a nonparadoxical way, namely, as the purposeful and motivated but not intentional avoidance of the sustained and recurrent thought that what one believes is so. As for decision problems, the reason for the semblance of paradox depends on the problem. In some cases there is no conflict between intuition and principle because the choices in question are clearly irrational—and conflict with the dictates of both causal and evidential decision theory. In special cases like Newcomb's problem, evidential decision theory is correct, but there is nothing magical, mysterious, or self-deceptive about taking noncausal considerations into account. As for the paradoxes of deterrence, sunk costs, and mutually beneficial exchange, I believe (I have not argued for this in any detail) that the semblance of paradox depends on the requirement of ratifiability. A decision is ratifiable only if the fact that one has made it does not change the rationality of making it. Unratifiable decisions result in intentions that are rational to form but apparently irrational to carry out (a prime example, which I have not discussed at all, is the intention in the Toxin Puzzle). This characterization assumes that (ir-) rationality is a property that applies only on a moment-to-moment basis. Accordingly, avoidance of paradox is possible only if there is a kind of rationality that applies on a diachronic basis. I believe that is the sort of rationality that Dupuy is trying to get at in his essay. It requires transcendence of the current moment. In the one-person case this is commitment to one's future and identification with one's past. In the two-person case this is commitment to another, "tying one's hands," be it a matter of willingness to carry out a costly threat or of agreement and trust, as in exchanges. It is clear that the rationality of commitment is paradoxical from the standpoint of a particular point in time, but paradox is not removed by invoking the notion of commitment, for commitment raises (apparent) paradoxes in its own right. What is most striking about the sources of the semblance of paradox both in self-deception and in the various decision problems is that they all involve some sort of gap between what one is at a moment and what one is over time.

187

References

Ainslie, G. 1992. *Picoeconomics: The Strategic Interaction of Successive Motivational States Within the Person.* Cambridge: Cambridge University Press.

Audi, R. 1988. "Self-Deception, Rationalization, and Reasons for Acting." In McLaughlin and Rorty, eds. (1988).

Bach, K. 1981. "An Analysis of Self-deception." *Philosophy and Phenomenological Research* 41:351–70.

———. 1984. "Default Reasoning." *Pacific Philosophical Quarterly* 65:37–58.

———. 1987. "Newcomb's Problem: The $1,000,000 Solution." *Canadian Journal of Philosophy* 17:409–26.

———.1992. Review of McLaughlin and Rorty, eds. (1988). *Nous* 26:495–504.

————.1994. "Emotional Disorder and Attention." In G. Graham and L. Stephens, eds., *Philosophical Psychopathology.* Cambridge, Mass.: MIT Press.

Carroll, L. 1895. "What the Tortoise Said to Achilles." *Mind* 4:279–80.

Davidson, D. 1997. "Who Is Fooled?" Paper presented at the Symposium on Self-Deception, Stanford, California, February 1993. In J. P. Dupuy, ed., *Self-Deception and Paradoxes of Rationality.* Stanford: CSLI Publications (this volume).

Eells, E. 1982. *Rational Decision and Causality.* Cambridge: Cambridge University Press.

Ellsberg, D. 1968. "The Theory and Practice of Blackmail." Rand Corporation working paper.

Frank, R. 1988. *Passions within Reason: The Strategic Role of the Emotions.* New York: Norton.

Goldman, A. 1970. *A Theory of Human Action.* Princeton: Princeton University Press.

Harman, G. 1986. *Change in View.* Cambridge, Mass.: MIT Press.

Horgan, T. 1985. "Newcomb's Problem: A Stalemate." In R. Campbell and L. Sowden, eds., *Paradoxes and Rationality and Cooperation: Prisoner's Dilemma and Newcomb's Problem.* Vancouver: University of British Columbia Press.

Horwich, P. 1987. *Asymmetries in Time.* Cambridge, Mass.: MIT Press.

Jeffrey, R. 1981. "The Logic of Decision Defended." *Synthese* 48:473–92.

Johnston, M. 1988. "Self-Deception and the Nature of Mind." In McLaughlin and Rorty, eds. (1988).

Lewis, D. 1976. "Paradoxes of Time Travel." *American Philosophical Quarterly* 13:145–52.

McLaughlin, B. P. 1988. "Exploring the Possibility of Self-deception in Belief." In McLaughlin and Rorty, eds. (1988).

McLaughlin, B. P. and A. O. Rorty, eds. 1988. *Perspectives on Self-Deception.* Berkeley: University of California Press.

Mele, A. R. "Two Paradoxes of Self-Deception." Paper presented at the Symposium on Self-Deception, Stanford, California, February 1993. In J. P. Dupuy, ed., *Self-Deception. and Paradoxes of Rationality.* Stanford: CSLI Publications (this volume).

Nozick, R. 1993. *The Nature of Rationality.* Princeton: Princeton University Press.

Osherson, D. N. 1990. "Judgment." In D. N. Osherson and E. E. Smith, eds., *Thinking: An Invitation to Cognitive Science.* Vol. 3. Cambridge, Mass.: MIT Press.

Quattrone, G. A. and A. Tversky. 1986. "Self-Deception and the Voter's Illusion." In J. Elster, ed. *The Multiple Self.* Cambridge: Cambridge University Press.

Rey. G. 1988. "Towards a Computational Account of Akrasia and Self-Deception." In McLaughlin and Rorty, eds. (1988).

Ruddick, W. 1988. "Social Self-Deception." In McLaughlin and Rorty, eds. (1988).

Scriven, M. 1964. "An Essential Unpredictability in Human Behavior." In B. B. Wolman and E. Nagel, eds., *Scientific Psychology: Principles and Approaches.* Dordrecht, Holland: Reidel.

Velleman, D. 1989. "Epistemic Freedom." *Pacific Philosophical Quarterly* 70:73–97.

Wood, A. 1988. "Self-Deception and Bad Faith." In McLaughlin and Rorty, eds. (1988).

189

Index